History of Palo Alto
The Early Years

Merry Christmas Mr. Woltz
May this day be bright
for you.
December 25, 1989
Michael Lussier

Michael Lussier - Broker
Coldwell Banker Carl Conelly Realtor

Overleaf frontispiece: Channing School, 1897. This handsome building in Queen Anne Victorian style, with six rooms, was built in 1894 to replace a temporary two-room school built one year earlier. Miss Powell and Miss Hudson stand at the rear. Paul Gibson, alias Kid Curly the Pirate, sits atop the right newel post. Courtesy Palo Alto Historical Association

History of Palo Alto
The Early Years

Pamela Gullard and Nancy Lund

Scottwall Associates
San Francisco, California
1989

Cover: Channing School, 1897. Courtesy Palo Alto Historical Association.
Endsheet Illustration: Courtesy Stanford University Archives

Book Design: James Heig, Scottwall Associates
Typography: Cathy Sinclair, Dynatype, San Francisco
Photo Halftones: American Printing, Palo Alto

First Edition

Publisher: Scottwall Associates
95 Scott Street
San Francisco, California 94117

Printed by Braun-Brumfield, Inc., Ann Arbor, Michigan

ISBN 0-942087-03-8 (Clothbound)
ISBN 0-942087-04-6 (Paperback)

A Dedication

This book is dedicated to the memory of Birge Clark, 1893-1989. More than any other resident, he symbolizes Palo Alto's first century.

Birge Clark's parents came to Palo Alto in 1892 when his father became a professor of architecture and art at the fledgling Stanford University. Birge was born in San Francisco (Palo Alto had no hospital) on April 16, 1893, just one year to the day before the town was incorporated. Except for a tour of duty in World War I, during which he won a Silver Star after being shot down in an Army Air Corps observation balloon, and time out for a graduate degree from Columbia, he lived in Palo Alto until his death on April 30, 1989.

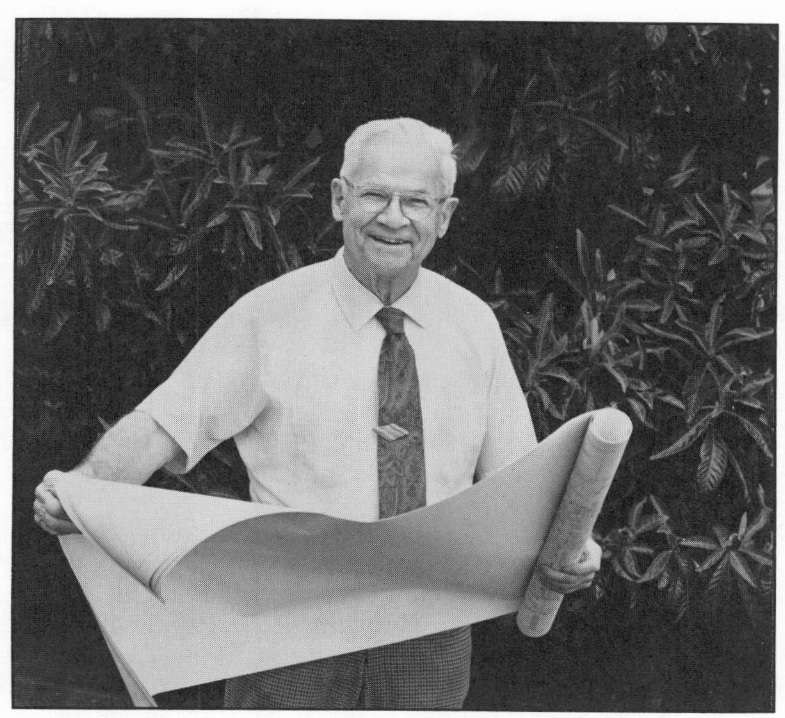

Birge Clark, 1975
Photo by Carolyn Caddes

He was Palo Alto's first architect, and in large measure he both shaped and reflected the character of the town. He was personable, gentle, and remarkable for the sharpness of his memory in his later years. One of Palo Alto's most revered citizens, he received the Distinguished Citizen Award (along with his sister Esther) from the Palo Alto Chamber of Commerce in 1981. In June, 1984, Palo Alto celebrated "Birge Clark Day."

He has been called "The Architect of Palo Alto," and Palo Alto has been called "The City that Birge Built." He designed 450 buildings in Palo Alto and on the Stanford campus, among them 98 in Palo Alto, and 39 at Stanford, including the Lou Henry Hoover house, home to university presidents. Other notable Clark designs are the Lucie Stern Community Center on Middlefield, the President Apartments on University, the Senior Center on Bryant, the Palo Alto Medical Clinic, the Peninsula Times Tribune Building at Lytton and Ramona, and the first Hewlett Packard Building on Page Mill Road. Thirty of his buildings are on the Palo Alto Inventory of Historic Buildings, and three, including the post office at 380 Hamilton, are on the National Register of Historic Places.

Throughout his buildings he used the characteristic features—thick stucco walls, red tile roofs, arches and arcades—that he called the Early California style. "His earlier work really tugs at my heartstrings," said architect Richard Elmore in a 1989 *Times Tribune* interview.

Clark reminisces about his career and the early days of the town in his memoirs, *An Architect Grows up in Palo Alto*, written for family and friends in 1982. "Birge Clark was Palo Alto's architect, not only in terms of the substance of buildings, but also in terms of our spirit," said Mayor Larry Klein in 1989. Birge Clark's legacy to Palo Altans is beyond measure.

Acknowledgements

Many people assisted us in completing this book.

We are indebted to Ruth Wilson, longtime Palo Alto historian, for encouraging us to begin this project in the summer of 1983, and for reading our final manuscript six years later. Steven Staiger, her successor, opened the Palo Alto Historical Association files for us and provided guidance through them.

Our gratitude goes to Gail Woolley, City of Palo Alto council member, for encouragement, advice, and support. We also thank the members of the Publications Subcommittee of her Centennial Advance Planning Committee who read the manuscript, including Meghan McCaslin, Bruce Cumming, and John Bracken.

At the Stanford University Archives, we were ably assisted by Roxanne Nilan, Robin Chandler, and Linda Long. We thank Julia O'Keefe, Santa Clara University Archivist, without whose understanding of original mission documents we could not have proceeded. Ernest Miramontes and Helen Collins of Los Californianos were competent guides through early California genealogy.

Special thanks to Betty Rogaway, who is engaged in an interesting oral history project, Marion Holmes, archivist of the San Mateo County Historical Association, Dr. Jeffrey Burns of the San Francisco Archdiocese Archives, Jeanne Thivierge of the History Room of the Redwood City Library, Mary Lou Taylor, Ohlone expert par excellence, and the reference staff at the Palo Alto Library, who always provided any strange thing we asked for quickly and with a smile.

We most especially appreciate the support of Mary Jo Levy, Warren Kallenbach and the Friends of the Palo Alto Library for believing in the book.

Our appreciation goes to our editor, Jim Heig, whose thin black pen is miraculous, and to Dorothy Regnery whose meticulous, wide-ranging research is an inspiration.

Nancy would like to thank Dr. Walter Warren of Foothill College and the California History Center at De Anza for introducing her to the fascination of historical research back in 1974.

Finally, thanks to Mike, Erik and Ben Gullard and to Tor Lund, who understood.

Foreword

Palo Alto is often lauded for its trees, schools, parks, cultural facilities, and active citizens. Not infrequently we read about our city in a national or international newspaper because we're forging new ground or are concerned about an issue considered trivial by the rest of the world. For many the decision to move here meant a significant sacrifice: in another town one could buy a much bigger house for the same price.

Palo Alto is indeed special. To me, the town's appeal lies in the sense of place it conveys. Although I couldn't tell you exactly why, I always know exactly where I am, where Palo Alto begins and ends. Downtown is focused, definite. People's views on basic issues like education or environment are predictable. Learning about this special place and its history has given me a strong sense of belonging.

My first encounter with Palo Alto's roots was in the deed to the house that my husband and I bought in 1965. The description divided our lot into two parcels, one located in Palo Alto and the other in Mayfield. "What is Mayfield?" I wondered. My curiosity was piqued, and my research into Palo Alto's history began.

With a little effort, I discovered that the Palo Alto parcel, in what is now Southgate, was purchased by Leland Stanford from Henry Seale. Apparently it was inherited by Jane Stanford, who deeded it to the university as a gift which did not have to be held in perpetuity, like other campus lands; it was later sold by the trustees. When the Stanfords decided to build the University, they bought the other parcel, probably from Alexander Peers, an early settler in Mayfield for whom Peers Park is named, so that a siding could be separated off from the main Southern Pacific track 68 feet further south. The Bonair siding, later dismantled, delivered sandstone from a quarry in south San Jose to build the Stanford quadrangle; today the name Bonair exists only as a short street in the campus Arboretum. As we planted 42 trees in our big back yard and dug up innumerable railroad spikes, I felt more and more pleased about having also dug into the history of our land.

History of Palo Alto: The Early Years vividly chronicles the tremendous changes which occurred in Palo Alto during its birth and adolescence. From six families in 1890 to today's 23,000 households, from a town founded to serve a university to a regional financial center at the head of Silicon Valley, from plank sidewalks and scattered oaks to a complex, computerized sidewalk-and-street-tree-replacement program, the town has undergone amazing transformations. Yet history reveals that Palo Alto has maintained a comforting, solid sameness. Those early organizers of the city's government, the schools, the municipal utility system, the libraries, and the hospital started us off at a high standard. Fortunately, succeeding generations have continued that rare level of citizen involvement, preserving and adding to our exceptional city services.

My own favorite illustration of Palo Alto's running start is Joseph Hutchinson, a lawyer and early commuter to San Francisco. His large house, built in 1891, was one of the earliest; it occupied the entire block bounded by Waverley, Cowper, Lincoln and Kingsley Streets. Hutchinson Avenue was named for him because he served as the first president of the Board of Trustees, from 1894 to 1902. Two years before incorporation, in 1892, when Palo Alto had a population of only 150, this forward-looking gentleman helped to found the Palo Alto Improvement Club. We've all been members in spirit ever since.

As we celebrate our 100th birthday, it is appropriate and fortunate that the residents of Palo Alto should be presented with this history. The scholarly research and lively style of Pamela Gullard and Nancy Lund bring Palo Alto's early years much closer than the century which separates them from us. The reader will surely find delight in discovering the roots of the modern city. I personally hope that delight will result in wider support for preserving historic structures, so that our children's children will be able to see Palo Alto's past as they celebrate the city's bicentennial a hundred years from now.

—Gail Woolley
City Council Member
Former Mayor
Past President, Palo Alto Historical Association
First Chairperson, Palo Alto Historic Resources Board

Historian's Note

Local history is the best history, the history with more of ourselves in it than other kinds. It is immediate, intimate, personally apprehended, and least in America it is by definition recent. —*Wallace Stegner*

For Palo Alto, Wallace Stegner's statement is especially accurate. Palo Alto's history has been lived by many who are still alive today. Friends, relatives or neighbors have played a significant part in that history, unlike national or world history, where our individual actions or contributions are relatively minute.

When we read local history we can begin to comprehend how a community has developed. The presence of two business districts in a city the size of Palo Alto is mystifying until one realizes that one of then is a remnant of the town of Mayfield. An understanding of history reveals why Embarcadero Road seems misdirected, or explains the origin of names such as Rinconada Park or Military Way.

Local history yields pleasure because it reminds us of a past that is close to each of us, either because we have experienced it personally, or because its outcome directly affects our daily lives. Its rewards are both immediate and permanent.

—Steven Staiger, Historian
Palo Alto Historical Association

Table of Contents

List of Illustrations

History of Palo Alto
The Early Years

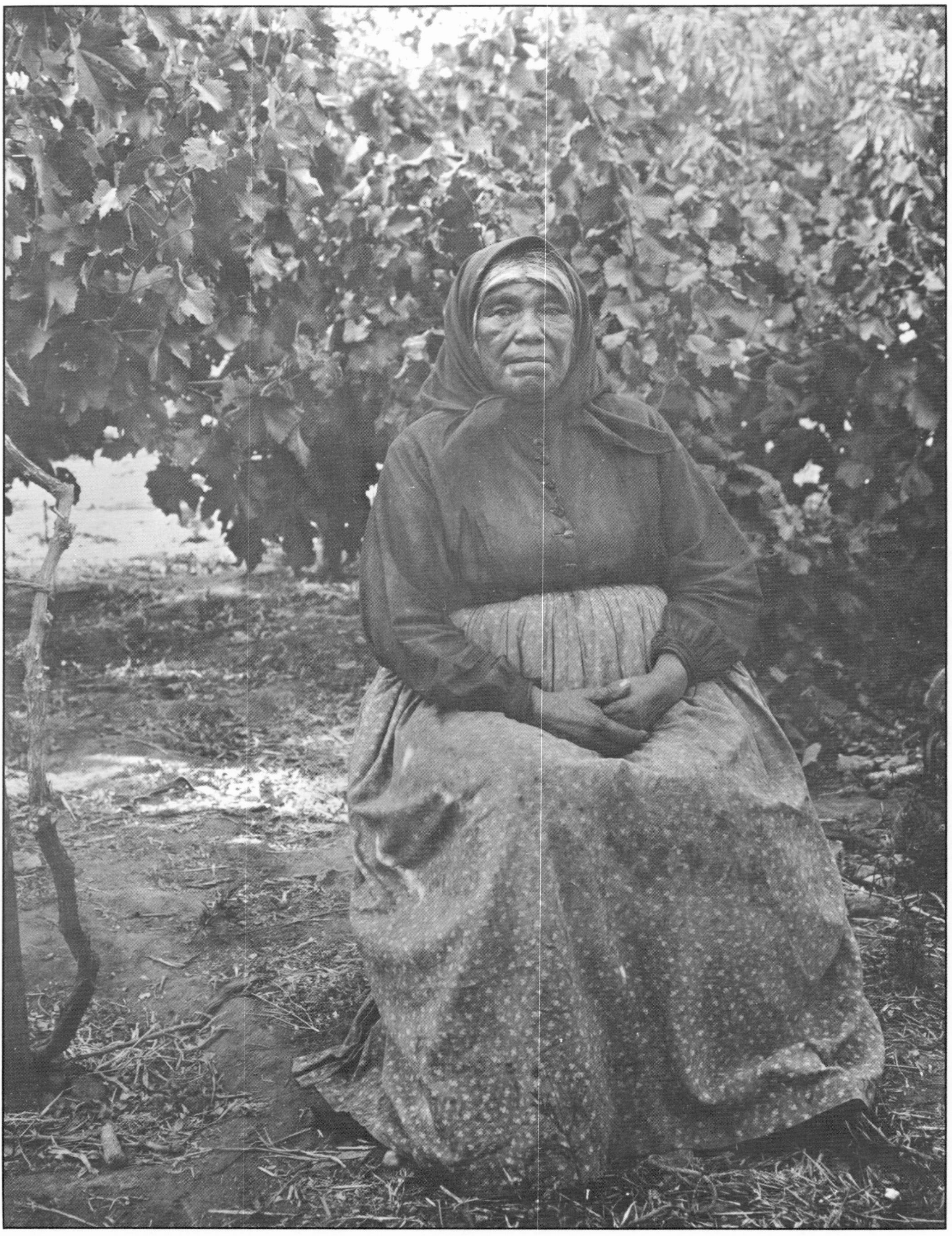

CHAPTER ONE

The Ohlones, First Palo Altans

The tale of the Ohlones, the first Palo Altans, begins with the trek of their ancestors 20,000 years ago from what is now the U.S.S.R. over the Aleutian land bridge caused by the Ice Age and down into Alaska. Gradually, the tribes marched south, and about 5,000 years ago, entered California and established villages in the region now known as Palo Alto. They found here a beautiful country that may be hard for today's residents to imagine.

In your mind, conjure a scene in which El Camino, Highway 101, and all the other roads and freeways have vanished. The office buildings, boutiques, stop signs and telephone poles, eateries, and computer stores are all gone. Even wipe from the scene the palms of Stanford University, its Quad, and Hoover Tower.

Now, cover the land with what one early explorer described as "copses of various forms and magnitude, verdant open spaces, ... enriched with stately forest trees." Fill the landscape with "the holy-leaved oak, maple-chestnut, and willow ... increased from dwarf shrubs to trees of tolerable size." Spread toyon, manzanita, the coyote bush, poison oak, and ceanothus across the plain, and, here and there, include stands of buckeye. The stately oaks dominate the forests, their twisted branches reaching to the sky.

Now add black-tailed deer, quail, rabbits, foxes, pronghorned antelope, gray foxes, grizzly bears, and hundreds of other forest animals roaming through the highland woods. Drop in a few bobcats, pumas, spotted jaguars, and wolves. Fill the air with the squawking and twittering of birds and scent the wind with wildflowers. Don't forget lines of quail families, their topknots bobbing as they walk, so numerous the first Anglo explorers claimed that a single shot could hit twenty birds. In fact, under almost every bush, paint in a creature so that the profusion of animal life is just as it was long ago.

Spread the marshland much farther inland than it is now, almost to present-day Middlefield Road, and cover it with tules ten feet tall in places. Add cordgrass and pickleweed along the shore and in the mud, bury the bent-nosed clam and the bay mussel. Where the Dumbarton Bridge ends now, place a few small tule elk standing in the *sausals*, or willow groves, and send a graceful California condor soaring over the cluster of sea otters and the sparkling leap of bay fish. This was the original Palo Alto, the land of "luxuriant fertility" where the Ohlone tribelets settled.

And what were the Indians like? The Ohlones lived simply, but their religion was a complex interweaving of the animal and human spirit. They valued graciousness and obeisance to elders, and yet they admired Coyote, who was known as the Trickster. They practiced chastity, and strict self-discipline to attain the purity of spirit required to hunt deer, yet they loved to gamble, dance, and gossip.

Long before the first small band of Spaniards poked into this area scouting sites for missions, the Ohlone Indians hunted and gathered seeds in what is now the Palo Alto hills, fished for salmon in what we call San Francisquito Creek, and gathered shellfish from San Francisco Bay. Anthropologists tell us that not for decades or even for centuries, but for over *five thousand* years (certainly longer than any European golden age), the Ohlones made peace with their gods, with nature, and with each other.

According to shell mound evidence unearthed by Dr. Bert A. Gerow, a Stanford anthropologist, and other scientists, a typical village was located at the mouth of one of the numerous freshwater creeks that bubbled across Palo Alto to the bay. One village,

Opposite: Barbara Salosano, photographed by C. Hart Merriam in 1902. The last surviving Ohlone at Mission San Juan Bautista, she was discovered by the Smithsonian Institution in 1930 (see sidebar, bottom p. 6). Courtesy Bancroft Library

settled by the Puichan tribelet, was located along the San Francisquito Creek. Malcolm Margolin, author of The Ohlone Way, describes the Indian life:

> An immense, sprawling pile of shells, earth, and ashes elevates the site above the surrounding marshland. On top of this mound stand some fifteen dome-shaped tule houses arranged around a plaza-like clearing. Scattered among them are smaller structures that look like huge baskets on stilts—granaries in which the year's supply of acorns are kept...Steam rising from underground pit ovens where mussels, clams, rabbit meat, fish, and various roots are being roasted.

The Indians were sturdy and robust, with rounded features. According to Margolin, the women dressed in skirts of tule reeds and deer skins. Sometimes they wore strings of shells from their waists that rustled pleasantly, and their necklaces were made of abalone and olivella shells and feathers. Father Vicente Santa Maria, one of the first Spaniards to see the San Francisco Bay, described the Indians here—Ohlones and the closely-related Miwoks—in great detail. He says the men wore little except a waistband skirt of reeds. "Besides comely elegance of figure and quite faultless countenance there was also—as their chief adornment—the way they did up their long hair; after smoothing it well they stuck in it a four-toothed wooden comb and bound up the end in a net of cord and very small feathers that were dyed a deep red ..." In the winter, both sexes covered themselves with woven rabbit or otter skins. For religious ceremonies, they fashioned ingenious decorations of feathers and shells, and daubed themselves with regular bands of pigment.

In addition to black and white body dyes, the Indians prized the sticky red mud, cinnabar, which they got from Devil Cave, southwest of San Jose. Ironically, this dye contained mercury which was somewhat toxic, so it is lucky that it was usually reserved for special occasions. Years later, the cinnabar cave was developed into the valuable New Almaden quicksilver mine, which financed a large land purchase in Palo Alto's rancho days.

At different seasons of the year, the tribelets would leave their villages and trek into the mountains and plains for hunting and seed-gathering. At intervals of one to five years, the Ohlones set controlled fires to burn the underbrush and produce a healthier seed crop for the future. In every way possible, the Ohlones fashioned methods for living off the land and the bay without depleting the environment.

For goods that were insufficiently available locally, such as salt, certain beads, and obsidian, Ohlone chieftains bartered with itinerant members of neighboring tribelets. Etiquette required constant

Georg Heinrich von Langsdorff, member of a Russian expedition commanded by Count Nikolai Rezanov, made this picture of Indians dancing at Mission San Jose in 1806. The meticulously painted designs, striking headdresses suggest an occasion of high ceremony, rather like opening night of the opera in modern times. The curious diaper-like garments are probably the artist's invention. Courtesy Bancroft Library

generosity during the delicate negotiations, which were conducted in whichever of the numerous Indian languages was known best by both parties.

For each of the forty different Ohlone tribelets had its distinctive language and customs. In fact, as Malcolm Margolin points out, the Ohlone name is really a fiction of unknown origin—maybe the name of a prominent village along the San Mateo coast—now used to cover about ten thousand people living between Point Sur and the Golden Gate. The tribelets of about 250 people each were linked by trade and marriage, but separated, each with its own territory, name, chiefs, and strong tribal loyalty. Valuing conformity and generosity, the Ohlone groups used diplomacy to avoid open warfare between tribelets and to maintain their astonishing civilized stability.

That is, the Ohlone culture remained stable until the Spaniards came in 1769. Within about seventy years after that date, the Ohlone people were destroyed.

Overleaf: Aerial photograph, 1947, shows the Castro Shell Mound being leveled and carted away for use as topsoil in gardens. The mound was on San Antonio Road, where Hewlett Packard stands today. As large as 600 feet long and 30 feet high, such mounds were created over centuries by tribes who deposited shells, bones, and human remains in them; 300 to 400 burials were disturbed in this site. Stanford Archeologist Barbara Bocek says there were many, many Indian sites in Palo Alto. Courtesy Palo Alto Historical Association

World News

Although anthropologists argue about exactly when the Ohlones arrived in the Palo Alto area, shell mound evidence indicates it was about 3000 B.C. World population was 100 million. As the Ohlones fished for salmon in San Francisquito Creek and gathered acorns in the area that is now Palo Alto, other civilizations rose and fell.

The Ohlones' ancestors first strode down the San Francisco Bay peninsula as the Egyptian civilization was beginning to flourish. Legend has it that the 1st Dynasty of the Egyptian pharoahs was established about 3200 B.C. when the king of Upper Egypt, Menes (or Narmer), conquered the Lower Kingdom of the Nile delta and began to rule the entire region.

The hallmarks of ancient Egyptian civilization—the great pyramids—were not yet begun when the Ohlones came to Palo Alto, but Egyptian artists already were developing their characteristic flat style: the human head shown in profile, eye and shoulders in front view, and legs and feet in profile. A surviving masterpiece from this era, called the palette of Namer, shows battle scenes with silhouetted human and animal forms.

For thousands of years, the Ohlones pursued their quiet ways; "Golden Ages" of other cultures came and went. The Greek Age of Pericles, begun about 495 B.C., produced such masterpieces as the philosophy of Plato and Sophocles' dramas, including *Oedipus Rex*. But nothing lasts forever (or, "all is flux," as the Greek scientist Heraclitus phrased it) and Pericles died of plague in 429. The Republic of Rome, founded in 500 B.C., subdued Egypt (making that country a granary) during Cleopatra's era at the close of the last millenium before Christ was born. Roman expansion eventually brought much of Europe under its control, but as every school child knows, even the Roman Empire was vulnerable. It finally disintegrated about 476 A.D. under repeated attacks by such invaders as Attila the Hun.

Skipping forward about 1000 years, we find another Golden Age in Spain, the country so important to California's early history. The Austrian Hapsburgs intermarried and formed alliances with Spanish kings, who ruled half the world (in the 1492 Treaty of Tordesillas, Spain and Portugal divided the globe into two spheres of influence). Expansionist Spain eventually took over much of South America and Mexico, but even this powerful empire began to falter, perhaps beginning as early as 1588 with the Spanish Armada's utter defeat during its attempt to conquer England.

As nations warred, the Renaissance was reaching its height in humanistic fields. In Spain itself, the masterpiece *Don Quixote* was written by Miguel de Cervantes (published 1605), leaving an indelible mark on all subsequent novels. In England, Shakespeare wrote *Julius Caesar* and *Hamlet* at the end of the 16th century. The earliest form of the scientific method was conceived by Sir Francis Bacon at about this time, and other advances catapulted civilization forward.

But people in power did not always learn from the past; governments continued to form and be destroyed. In Spain, the Hapsburg-related dynasty finally gave way to the French-connected Bourbon kings in 1700, and although Spain kept its autonomy, its former glory was lost. Sapped by domestic inflation and impoverished by the costly wars brought about trying to maintain its vast colonial empire, the Spain of 1769—the year Spanish military commandantes and padres first poked their way into Ohlone territory—was a weakened giant.

Ascension Solorno, the Last of Her Tribe

Ascension had been a "doctora" for many years for Indians and Mexicans. She treated them with herbs and prayers. She never turned anyone away without a meal. Many who were ill she kept for weeks or even months—her back yard was her hospital.

At age 83, Ascencion was discovered by the Smithsonian Institution. She started telling her story in September when she was very ill. She had had herself dressed in her burial clothes. She seemed to develop a great will to live in order to tell her story. She talked on and on each day about the life of the San Juan Indians. When she had finished she quietly passed away on January 5, 1930. She is buried at the Indian burial ground at San Juan Bautista. At her death she was surrounded by her relatives, friends and the people she had cured. She was the last of her tribe.

San Francisco Chronicle
July 13, 1930

The above news article describes the woman shown in the portrait at the beginning of this chapter, facing page 1. C. Hart Merriam, who took the photograph, recorded her name as "Barbara Salosano, Last of the Ohlones." Her Indian name was Hoo Mon Twash, according to Earthwatch, a publication of the Coyote Point Museum. A brochure published by Mission San Juan Bautista calls her "Ascension Solarsano, last pureblood Mission Indian."

Documents of the Senate of the United States during the special session called March 4, 1853.

Senate Document 4, p. 45. Adam Johnston from San Francisco. Sept. 16, 1850.

Almost the entire tribes of Costanoes, or coast Indians, have passed away. Of the numerous tribes which but a few years ago inhabited the country bordering on the bay of San Francisco, scarcely an individual is left. The pale-faces have taken possession of the country and trample upon the graves of their forefathers. In an interview with a very aged Indian near the Mission of Dolores, he said, "I am very old; my people were once around me like the sands of the shore—many, many. They have all passed away. They have died like the grass. They have gone to the mountains. I do not complain; the antelope falls with the arrow. I had a son—I loved him. When the pale-faces came, he went away; I know not where he is. I am a Christian Indian; I am all that is left of my people. I am alone." His age, his earnestness, and decrepit condition, gave full force to his language, and I left him under the deepest sense of sympathy.

Chapter Notes

The 1987 Ph.D. thesis by David W. Mayfield, "Ecology of the Pre-Spanish San Francisco Bay Area," which describes the flora and fauna before the Spaniards arrived, is available at the San Francisco State University library.

Malcolm Margolin's classic *Ohlone Way* reads like a novel and should be required for any modern-day person entering Ohlone territory. Margolin details every aspect of the Ohlone way of life.

The memoirs of English map-maker George Vancouver, written during 1792-1794 and published as *Vancouver in California* provide firsthand impressions of the land as seen through European eyes. Merchant Alfred Robinson travelled through this area in the 1830s, and his fascinating diary is published as *Life in California.* Possibly the most interesting account of the first contacts between Spaniards and California Indians is the diary of Padre Vicente Santa Maria, who sailed into the San Francisco Bay aboard the supply ship *San Carlos*, published in John Galvin's beautifully-produced book, *First Spanish Entry into the San Francisco Bay, 1775.*

Mary Lou Taylor, a Menlo Park resident, gives absorbing lectures to school children on Ohlones, illustrated with her personal collection of authentic artifacts.

The People's Chronology by James Trager is an astounding single-volume compilation of world events from prehistory through 1973. It is the most important source for information included in the World News sections throughout the book.

A. L. Bancroft & Co. Lith.

Father Junipero Serra, O.S.F.

Apostle of Upper California

CHAPTER TWO

The Missionary Period: A Clash of Cultures

As we look at the history of the missionary period, we find that the Ohlone and the Spanish Catholic cultures were almost exact opposites. The Ohlones valued subtle negotiation and extreme politeness. They went to great lengths to settle disputes without warfare, and, although each tribelet had a chief, his power actually derived from obtaining a consensus among the adults in the village.

The Spaniards, on the other hand, were expansionists willing to use force to secure territory and even to save souls. Their society was organized along strict lines of hierarchy from God down through governmental authorities to paternal families.

The Spaniards valued the stability of agriculture; the Ohlones were gatherers who needed to be able to move as the seasons changed. The Spaniards worshiped a single god; the Ohlones believed that all living things were animated by spirits. The mission fathers valued a life of sacrifice and deprivation in hopes of a richer life in heaven; the Ohlones believed that every day should be spent trying to stay in harmony with other living things.

Perhaps it's no wonder that the Spaniards quickly concluded that the Ohlones were stupid, lazy, and undisciplined. But what looked like disorganization to the Spaniards was actually a complex interweaving of cultural pressures within each village that balanced the needs of individuals against the needs of the others. The stone tools of the Ohlone seemed crude to the Spaniards, who valued fine porcelain, but in fact the Ohlones had little need for breakable bowls that were hard to transport—they spent their time on elegant basket-weaving instead.

The Spaniards sneered at the Indians' refusal to wear clothes, misinterpreting it as a sign of sexual promiscuity. Little did the Spaniards realize that the Indians' sex lives were strictly regulated by ritual and by the custom of celibacy during the two years Indian mothers nursed their children. The Ohlones, for their part, found Spanish food difficult to eat at first, little understanding how precious these recipes from a country far away were to the homesick missionaries.

Opposite: Father Junipero Serra in an undated but early portrait published by A.L. Bancroft, the only picture showing Serra with facial hair. The artist anticipated the possibility of Serra's sainthood by supplying a halo. Courtesy Bancroft Library

Perhaps the blindness to each other's cultures was inevitable, but the devastation of the Indians that followed is a sad episode in the history of California. Those Indians who weren't murdered by soldiers or settlers were captured and enslaved by the missions, and succumbed to smallpox, syphilis, and other diseases in the twenty-one missions that were established by Spanish Franciscan padres from San Diego to Sonoma. Says Alfred Kroeber, an expert on California Indians, "The brute upshot of missionization, in spite of its kindly flavor and humanitarian roots, was only one thing, death."

The Ohlone point of view has been largely lost to us through the death of the culture. But it is not hard to imagine how the Ohlones felt as they listened politely to sermons given by the fervent Spanish padres, men who must have seemed strangely possessed, and certainly incomprehensible.

The First Spanish Explorers

In 1767, Spanish Inspector General of Mexico Joseph de Galvez hatched a plan to block other countries from colonizing Alta California. The Russians were already well established on the Alaskan coast and threatening to advance south. Great Britain had won Canada from France, and the English navy had become far superior to Spain's once formidable sea power. Galvez's idea was ingenious. He dispatched Father Junipero Serra, a zealous Franciscan priest, with a twofold purpose: to convert the Indians to Catholicism through a string of missions up the center of California, and to establish Spain's military presence. Bands of friars were therefore paired with military commandants, some of whom later became the *majordomos* who controlled and disciplined the Indians working the mission fields.

Some scholars have faulted Father Serra for allowing his religious endeavor to be exploited for militaristic purposes. Indeed, the presidios associated with many of the missions, such as Mission Dolores in San Francisco, housed the military, who meted out some of the worst abuses of the Indians. Although Catholic historians depict the Franciscan fathers as loving and gentle, and bent only on reaping the "ripe harvest" of heathen souls, the clash of cultures resulted in an almost complete decimation of the Indian population.

On November 6, 1769, a Spanish officer, Don Gaspar de Portola (pronounced with the accent on the last syllable), brought a tiny band of exhausted scouts and padres into Palo Alto territory looking for Monterey harbor, where they planned to meet two supply ships—the *San Antonio* and the *San Carlos*—and establish the first northern California mission. Starting in Baja, Mexico, the overland explorers had briefly camped in San Diego, then set out again July 14 on horseback and on foot and trekked over 500 miles seeking the great Monterey Bay that sea captain Sebastian Vizcaino had glowingly described in 1602.

According to the Palo Alto Historical Association pamphlet, "Portola Discovers San Francisco Bay," Portola rode at the head of the column of six red-vested Catalonia volunteer soldiers and two priests. "Next came the (fifteen) Indian sappers and miners, with spades, mattocks, crowbars, axes, and other implements used by pioneers. These were followed by the pack animals, with (seven) muleteers and (over twenty) soldiers." Sergeant Jose Francisco de Ortega scouted ahead, and Captain Fernando de Rivera brought up the rear.

Portola and his men did not realize that they had already over-shot Monterey Bay. He sent Ortega north to look for it. Food was running so low that the soldiers had begun to eat their mules, and most of the men had flu-like symptoms. Fleas crawled under their leather vests. They had been miserable for weeks, but their spirits were lifted by the beautiful countryside and the friendly Indians, who brought them black tamales and *atole*.

Exhausted but cheered, they slumped down to camp for five days under a tall redwood near San Francisquito Creek, which now defines the northern border of Palo Alto. The friars carefully recorded the magnificence of the stately tree that was eventually called El Palo Alto, the symbol of the city.

After exploring the San Francisco Bay area and, unwittingly, the Monterey area, Portola and his men returned in December 1769 to San Diego and reported that they had not seen the bay. However, the captains of the supply ships, which returned to San Diego a month later, convinced Portola that indeed he and his band had stood on the shores of the very harbor he sought. Buoyed by the news, Portola set out again in April, recognized Monterey Bay, and on June 3, founded a presidio while diarist Padre Juan Crespi established a mission.

Five years later, in 1774, Don Fernando Rivera, a Spanish commandante, with Padre Francisco Palou and a small party, found El Palo Alto again and Father Palou preached a sermon to a few Ohlones who bashfully approached the strange-looking men on mules. The Spaniards were so taken with the location, they erected a cross for an expected mission.

But it was not to be. Juan Bautista de Anza, a Spanish explorer, visited the spot in the spring of 1776 and found the creek dried up and thus unsuitable to support a colony. The closest to Palo Alto of the twenty-one California missions was Mission Santa Clara, located (after several moves) at the current college site of the same name.

Palo Alto land was critical to the mission—and so to colonization of the entire southern peninsula—for it provided the fertile pasture that eventually made Mission Santa Clara prosper.

Mission Santa Clara Prospers on Palo Alto Pastures

Because of its location near fertile Palo Alto land, Mission Santa Clara quickly became one of the leading missions. At its founding in 1777, the outlook for the mission did not seem so auspicious.

Father Jose Antonio Murguia, who had nineteen years' experience in the missions of Mexico, originally shared the religious leadership of Mission Santa Clara with Father Tomas de la Pena. They baptized seven hard-working local Indians who, along with six Indian converts brought from Baja California, built the first Mission Santa Clara palisade, a primitive building made entirely of poles set in the ground close together and plastered with mud. The flat roof was covered with tules and earth. By the end of the first year, the good padres reported in their *Informe*, an annual report required of each mission, Santa Clara had produced 2 1/4 *fanegas* (about 100 pounds) of wheat. The Indian neophytes used such crude tools as plows made from the large crooked branch of a tree, weed hooks and digging sticks, called *coas*.

The astonishingly accurate map at right, drawn by Pedro Font in 1777, shows the tall tree at the point where the Mission road crosses San Francisquito Creek. Font had borrowed a graphometer from Mission Carmel to measure the tree, which Palou had described in his diary of a 1774 expedition.

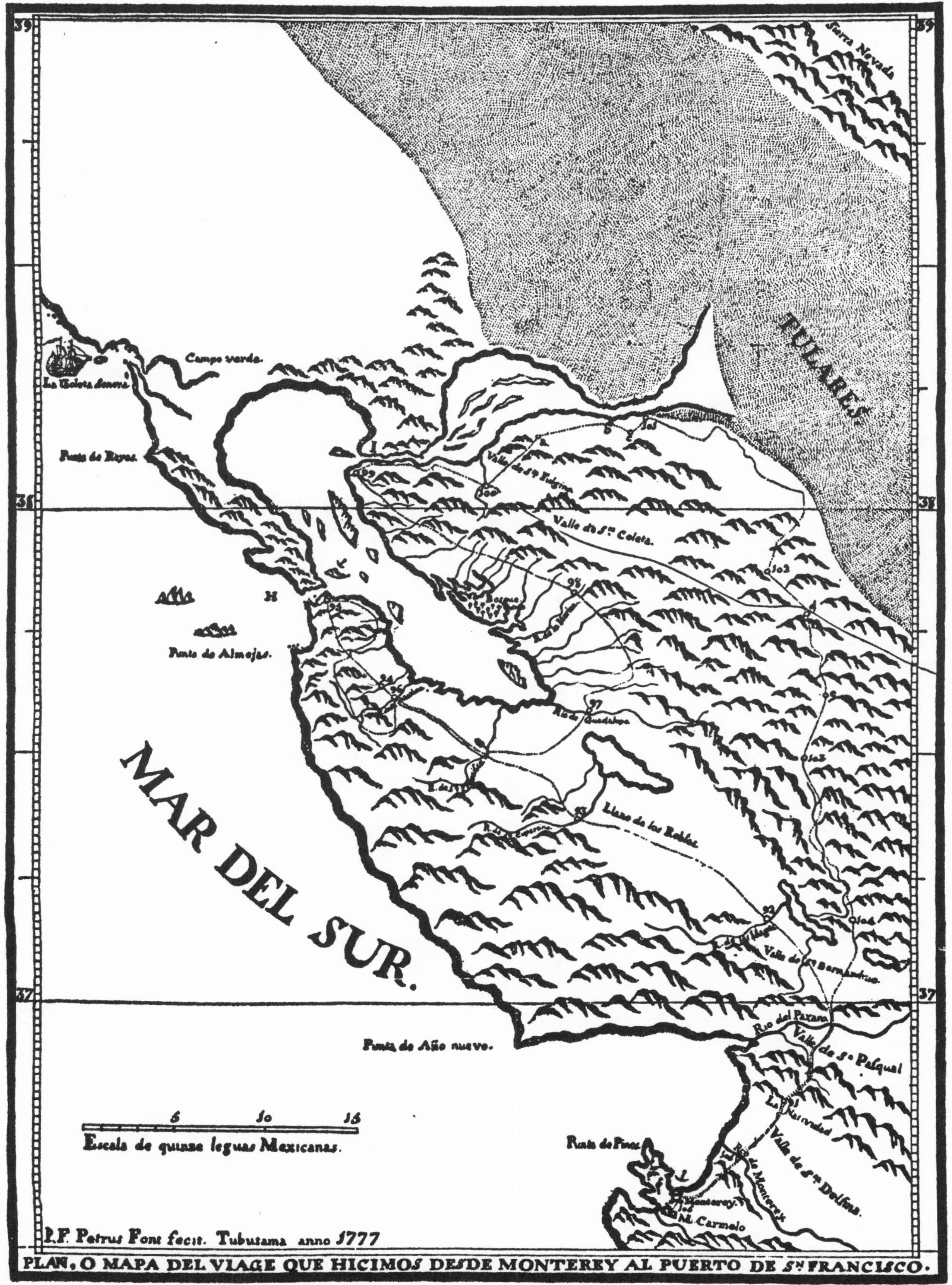
Sierra Nevada
TULARES.
Campo verde.
Punta de Reyes.
Valle de Sta. Coleta.
Punta de Almejas.
Rio de Guadalupe
MAR DEL SUR.
Llano de los Robles.
Valle de Sn. Bernardino.
Rio del Paxaro
Valle de Sn. Pasqual
La Natividad
Punta de Año nuevo.
Punta de Pinos
Monterey
M. Carmelo
5 10 15
Escala de quinze leguas Mexicanas.
P.F. Petrus Font fecit. Tubutama anno 1777
PLAN, O MAPA DEL VIAGE QUE HICIMOS DESDE MONTEREY AL PUERTO DE Sn. FRANCISCO.

Mission Santa Clara was originally situated on the banks of the Guadalupe River, but on January 23, 1779, the river flooded, sending a wall of water through the church, the corrals, the clerics' quarters and the neophytes' dormitories. The padres decided to rebuild on higher ground, a few hundred yards northeast of what is now the University of Santa Clara. Excavations made in 1911 at Campbell and Franklin streets uncovered the cornerstone of the new permanent, adobe church, which was dedicated May 15, 1784. This cornerstone contained coins, medals and a cross Father Serra himself had wrapped in an oiled hide. These artifacts can now be viewed at the de Saissett Museum at the university.

Until 1818 when the church was damaged by an earthquake and rebuilt along narrower lines, it was the largest and most imposing of the missions. Senor Augustin Davila, a noted Mexican painter, decorated the adobe church walls with the aid of Indian journeymen. He worked in the *trompe l'oeil* style, making flower garlands and figures of the saints appear three-dimensional. The green, black, and yellow color scheme may have been gaudy, but it appealed to both Indians and the Spaniards who had come to live in brightly-colored California.

Two bells, which were rung joyously morning and night, had been brought by the ship *San Antonio* from Spain to Monterey, then loaded on oxcarts for the overland trip to Santa Clara.

Palo Alto's rich pastureland quickly brought Mission Santa Clara to the forefront of the mission system. Sheep and the rather scrawny long-horned cattle brought from Mexico roamed through what is now Palo Alto by the thousands. Alfred Robinson, an early English trader, estimated that by 1829, the five missions around the San Francisco Bay—Dolores, Santa Clara, San Jose, San Francisco Solano and San Rafael—raised over 40,000 head of cattle. Mission Santa Clara had by far the largest herd. Robinson describes the excitement of the annual *matanza*, the slaughtering of the cattle in May:

> Numbers of the poor animals lay stretched upon the ground, already slaughtered; others just suffering under the knife of the butcher, whilst, in a spacious enclosure, hundreds were crowded for selection. The vaqueros, mounted on splendid horses, and stationed at its entrance, performed by far the most important part of the labor. When the majordomo [a soldier appointed to control the Indians] pointed out the animal to be seized, instantly a lasso whirled through the air, and fell with dextrous precision upon the horns of the ill-fated beast...

According to Edith Buckland Webb in *Indian Life at the Old Missions*, cattle raising was the missions' chief industry. The padres obtained life's necessities—from shovels to thimbles—by trading hides and tallow (animal fat used for soap and candles) with merchants on English, Yankee, Russian, and French vessels. Spanish commercial regulations strictly forbade selling to foreigners but, as Hubert Howe Bancroft explains in *History of California*, by 1816 the padres were allowed to winked freely at the regulations. Spanish authorities came to realize that the missions could not carry on their growing enterprise without a large influx of goods, more than the Spanish ships alone could supply.

Webb explains that once a deal had been struck between a padre and a merchant, the hides were taken from the mission storehouse and carried to the *embarcadero* (landing place) on oxcarts called *carretas*, by pack mules, or on the heads of Indians. The hides from Mission Santa Clara were taken to ships waiting in San Francisco Bay. Webb cites Guadalupe Vallejo, who wrote *Ranch and Mission Days*, to describe a typical scene:

> But often in winter, there being no roads across the valley, each separate hide was doubled across the middle and placed on the head of an Indian. Long files of Indians, each carrying a hide in this manner, could be seen trotting over the unfenced level land through the wild mustard to the embarcadero, and in a few weeks the whole cargo would thus be delivered...

In addition to raising cattle, Mission Santa Clara also farmed Palo Alto land with success. Farming methods were prescribed in tattered copies of "Secrets of Agriculture, Fields and Pastures," written by a Catholic Father in 1617 and lovingly packed by the missionaries on mules coming all the way from the early missions in Mexico itself. Seeds also were brought from Mexico. Maize, peas, and beans did well, and also hemp and linseed.

Sir James Douglas of the Hudson's Bay Company reports in 1841 how the Indians toiled to produce a large harvest using the crude tools supplied by the padres:

> I saw near the Mission of Santa Clara ten of these ploughs at work, drawn by 60 oxen with 10 Indian drivers, all following each other in the same direction, but so irregularly that scarcely two furrows were in parallel line as they met, crossed and receded according to the vagaries of the cattle.

Mission Santa Clara also grew a beautiful fruit orchard with peaches, apricots, apples, pears, and figs providing luscious fruits after several years. Vineyards did not thrive, however, and visitors who saw the withered plants ascribed the problem to lack of proper cultivation techniques.

What the padres lacked in cultivating skill, they made up for in labor. But if the fathers worked hard, the Indians worked even harder. Webb exclaims, "One can well imagine the stir and excitement that ran high throughout those months of harvest. From the gathering of the grain, the picking of the grapes; the round-up, branding, and slaughtering of the cattle; the shearing of the sheep; with all the tasks attending those operations ... the missions were indeed beehives of activity."

Partly because of this forced labor, it was not always easy for the padres to keep the Indian neophytes convinced that mission life was in their best interests. Many tried to escape and were brought back for punishment, whippings and the stockade. Indeed, soon after the founding of Mission Santa Clara, Indians killed some of the Spaniards' mules and were found roasting mule steaks that afternoon. Although the Indians did nothing to conceal their meal (obviously believing that the "game" was free), soldiers killed three Ohlones and took the leaders back to the mission for flogging.

The missionary fathers told the Ohlones that once a person had accepted baptism, he could no longer return to his native village or his tribal ways. How much this communication or any other was understood is problematic. The Ohlone tribes had developed a remarkably diverse number of languages and, according to Margolin, this multiplicity of tongues created complete chaos at the missions. At Mission Santa Clara, the number of Indian languages was probably about twenty—the Indians even had trouble talking among themselves! Though, to his credit, Father Serra urged the padres to become linguistically competent in the Indian languages, the Franciscans were only dimly aware of the diversity of the Indian languages. The problem was compounded by the padres' insistence on offering Mass in Latin.

Nevertheless, through the years the padres and some of the neophytes found ways to join together to celebrate Catholic festivals. Many travelers, including a French visitor, Duflot de Mofras, remarked that the Santa Clara Mission Indians were adept musicians. De Mofras writes:

> Music was also taught with marked success, and their neophyte orchestra was known throughout the land. One of the Fathers purchased from a French whaler thirty complete uniforms and organized a band of musicians. Our party was privileged to attend some of their performances when at Santa Cruz on September 14, 1841, the fete day consecrated to the exaltation of the Holy Cross, and it was not without keen surprise that we heard musicians brought over from Santa Clara, singing the Marseillaise, as the congregation rose, and escort the procession singing Vive Henri IV. After the Mass, upon asking one of the Fathers how

> these Indians happened to know these airs, I was informed that one of his predecessors had bought a small organ from the French and that the Indians, after hearing the airs, had instinctively arranged the songs for use by the various instruments.

Feast days were a time of rejoicing for all, and some of the strict mission rules were relaxed a little. Unbaptized Indians as well as neophytes attended the celebrations. At the beginning of each feast, the padre's carriage would be brought to the door of the church and his attendants would help him out, followed by a number of Indian leaders. Red and blue ribbons fluttered in the wind from their hats. Bells pealed joyously. Indian girls in scarlet petticoats and white bodices would watch modestly. After Mass, the priests would retire to their apartments under a shower of rockets.

Then the dancing would begin. Indians dressed in feathers and painted in their traditional red and black, "looking like so many demons," according to Robinson, formed a circle and began dancing. Other performers appeared through the evening as much hilarity and good feeling arose between participants and audience. At sundown, the bells would be rung again, more rockets shot and guns fired, but the carousing continued long into the night.

Neighbors

The Spanish government encouraged colonists to settle in California and thereby help secure the land for Spain, but at first only those with the fewest prospects at home could be induced to come. According to some reports, convicts from Mexican jails were even forced to settle in the lands to the north. The missionary fathers were dismayed to have to cope with soldiers and civilians who were "drunkards, assorted criminals and deserters from the regular army," according to J. S. Holliday.

Just after the first year's harvest, on November 7, 1777, Mission Santa Clara acquired Spanish neighbors. Lt. Jose Joaquin Moraga, who had escorted the missionaries and soldiers to Santa Clara, returned from a trip to San Francisco with nine soldiers and five colonists and their families. Thus, the pueblo of San Jose, the first Spanish town in Alta California, was begun.

The goals of the soldiers were not always compatible with those of the mission fathers, and the history of Mission Santa Clara shows a sometimes uneasy truce between the town and its spiritual center.

The value of the mission's fertile pasturage was quickly recognized by settlers in the pueblo San Jose. As the town grew, the townspeople became ever more envious of the rich mission land. Sometimes they squatted on acreage controlled by the Franciscans.

By the time Father Catala, a charismatic leader called *El Profeta* (the prophet), took over the mission in the 1820s, relations with settlers encroaching on Santa Clara mission land had reached a tense pitch. Father Catala wisely asked for a legal survey, which called for acreage seized by the civilians to be returned. The disgruntled settlers retaliated by harrassing the Indian neophytes as they tried to go about their work. Father Catala, perhaps one of the first public relations geniuses in the area, decided to soothe the populace by planting three beautiful rows of trees, forming a wide avenue lined with black willows—currently The Alameda—between the mission chapel and the town. Legend has it that two hundred Indians set to this task, and the townspeople were pleased with this mission gift, which gave them a promenade to parade in their best clothes each Sunday.

Says Robinson, describing the day of rest in about 1830:

> [The Alameda] is frequented generally on the Sabbath or feast days when all the town repair to the church at Santa Clara. On a Sunday may be seen hundreds of persons, of both sexes, gaily attired in silks and satins, mounted on their finest horses, and proceeding leisurely up the road. No carriages are used, and of course, the scene is divested of all the pomp and splendour which accompanies church-going in the larger places of the republic....

Secularization

The story of the downfall and secularization of the missions in general—and Mission Santa Clara in particular—is confused by the shifting relationship between Mexico and Spain until Mexican independence in 1822, and by the succession of governments in Mexico during the first decade after the revolution. The one fact that stands out from the blur of history is that through the years, various governmental officials and citizens, such as San Jose residents, eyed the growing mission wealth and schemed to take control of it.

As early as 1767, property possessed by the Jesuits was seized by the Spanish government to form what became known as the Pious Fund. This was supposed to be used as a kind of endowment for all the missions, including those run by the Franciscans in California. According to J. P. Munro-Fraser in his 1881 *History of Santa Clara County, California,* in 1806, the Mexican financial officer waylaid $200,000 (a huge sum at the time) and did not send it on to aid the California missions. His reasons for doing this are unclear. What is clear is that the struggling padres, trying to make a living in the wilds of California, felt

Mission Santa Clara as it might have looked in 1849, as painted by artist Andrew P. Hill in 1882. Original in Mission Archives. Courtesy Palo Alto Historical Association

deprived of vital assistance. Letters from the padres begging for supplies showed how deeply they were mired in poverty, and how they had to scrimp to establish even a toehold in California.

This and other injustices left deep resentment against the Spanish colonial government in Mexico among the padres. The act for secularization of the missions passed by the Spanish Congress on September 13, 1813 further alienated them. Ostensibly, the wealth of the missions was to go to the Indians and colonists, but in fact half of the mission land was to be sold. Exactly what would happen to the proceeds is unclear. This decree was not immediately carried out, but one can imagine how the threat of confiscation affected the padres. As one reads the *Informes*, one senses the padres' increasing frustration with the Indians and with the insufficient government support.

Munro-Fraser says that after 1813:

> The internal state of the missions was becoming more and more complex and disordered. The desertions [of the Indians] were more frequent and numerous, the hostility of the unconverted more daring, and the general disposition of the people inclined to revolt. American traders and freebooters had entered the country, spread themselves all over the province, and sowed the seeds of discord and revolt among the inhabitants.

And the newcomers took an increasing interest in the growing mission wealth. This wealth was astonishing. Munro-Fraser states that in 1823:

> The Mission of Santa Clara branded twenty-two thousand four hundred calves as the increase of that year; while in 1825 the mission is reported to have owned seventy-four thousand two hundred and eighty head of cattle, four hundred and seven yoke of working oxen, eighty-two thousand five hundred and forty sheep, one thousand eight hundred and ninety horses broken to the saddle, four thousand two hundred and thirty-five breeding mares, seven hundred and twenty-five mules, and one thousand hogs.

Mission Santa Clara prospered; the Indians performing the labor did not. They continued to die in alarming numbers from syphilis, measles and smallpox. From 1802 to 1822, 7,324 Indians were baptised at Mission Santa Clara—far more than at any other mission—and 6,556 died.

This combination of disease and wealth seems to have been lethal to the missions. Corrupt administrators saw that the Indians—who were supposed to inherit the land—were too weak to resist plundering of all they had built.

Overleaf: Alan K. Brown drew this map in 1963 after meticulous research into old survey records, maps, and other documents. The Soto, Mesa, and Pena (later Robles) Ranchos are shown, as well as the roads which later became Middlefield, Embarcadero and El Camino, and the arroyos or creeks: San Francisquito, Matadero, and las Yeguas (Adobe creek). Alternate roads for winter and summer allowed carts to cross creeks at high or low water. Courtesy of Alan K. Brown and Palo Alto Historical Association.

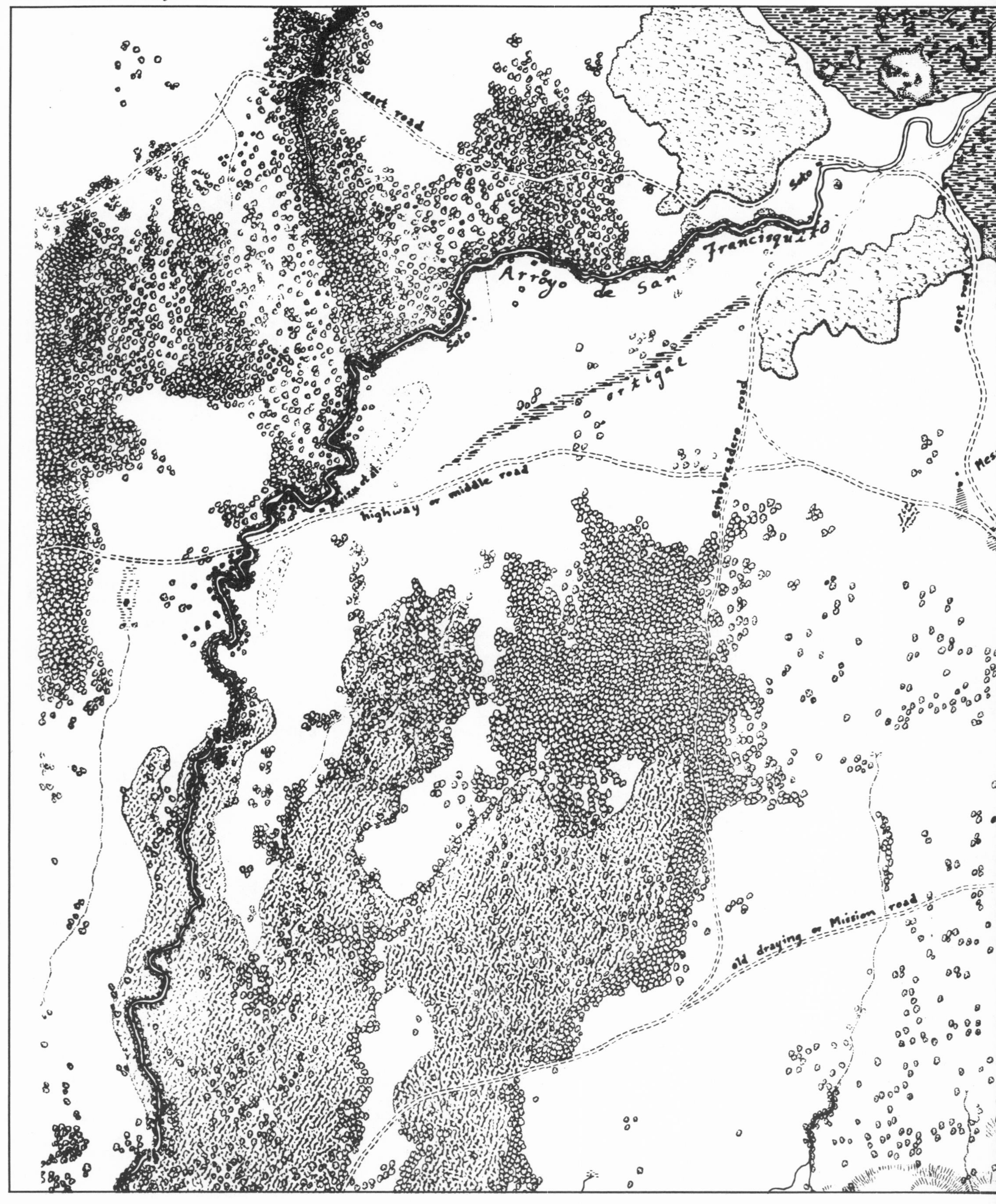
cart road
Soto
Arroyo de San Francisquito
Soto
ortigal
highway or middle road
embarcadero road
Mesa
cart road
old draying or Mission road

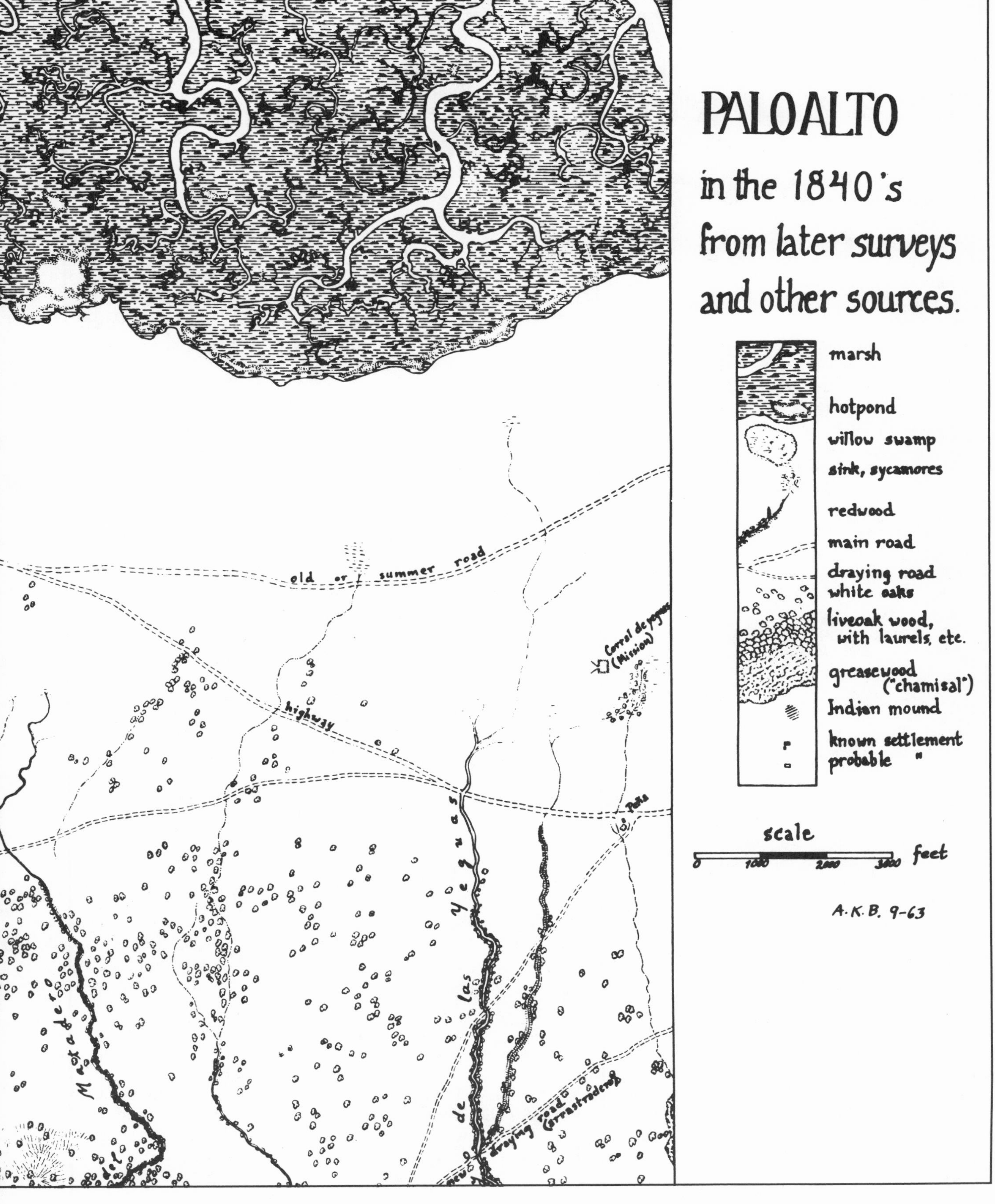
PALO ALTO
in the 1840's
from later surveys
and other sources.
marsh
hotpond
willow swamp
sink, sycamores
redwood
main road
draying road
white oaks
liveoak wood,
with laurels, etc.
greasewood
("chamisal")
Indian mound
known settlement
probable "
scale
0 1000 2000 3000 feet
A.K.B. 9-63
old or summer road
highway
Corral de yeguas
(Mission)
Posta
de las Yeguas
del Matadero
new draying road

The Circus of Sainthood

On September 25, 1988, Pope John Paul II beatified Father Junipero Serra, founder of the Franciscan mission system that transformed California and set the stage for the beginning of Palo Alto. Beatification is the second of three steps—venerable, blessed, and canonized—in making Serra a full-fledged saint. Serra's first Vatican-approved miracle involved a Franciscan nun, Sister Boniface Dyrda, who claimed to have been cured of lupus in 1960 after praying to the padre. Serra's backers need to document another holy intercession to promote him finally to irrevocable sainthood. That he is being seriously considered at all is thought to be miracle enough by Serra's detractors.

As Rupert Costa, president of San Francisco's American Indian Historical Society, told a reporter from the *Wall Street Journal*, "The Spanish beat and raped us [Indians]. As far as we're concerned, this would be akin to canonizing Hitler."

Costa and other critics contend that although Catholic representatives think that the early padres saved Ohlone souls, in fact the Indians were abducted into mission slavery. Opponents of Serra's sainthood detail the abuses of the "converts" at the 21 missions built along the length of California. Indians who tried to run away were publicly whipped and put in stocks. James J. Rawls points out in a *San Jose Mercury News* article that even Serra's contemporaries were sometimes appalled by the goings-on at the missions. French explorer Jean Francois Galaup de La Perouse recorded a 1786 scene at the Carmel mission: "We mention it with pain. The resemblance [to a slave plantation] is so perfect, that we saw men and women loaded with irons, others in the stocks; and at length the noise of the strokes of a whip struck our ears."

Father Noel Francis Moholy, Serra's vice postulator and a monk who has devoted most of his adult life to bringing the padre recognition as one who dwells "truly in heaven," staunchly defends his man. He says that the motives of the mission padres must not be judged by twentieth century standards. Flogging of innocents was common in those dark days. Moreover, Moholy points out, the worst abuses of the Indians occurred *after* Serra's death in 1784. According to Moholy, Serra, who beat himself with a leather thong to increase his holiness, was personally humble yet charismatic, and eventually heartbroken that so many Indians died at the nine missions he founded.

Moholy's colleague, Bishop Thaddeus Shubsda of the Diocese of Monterey, puts it succinctly: "The church recognizes the extraordinary holiness of this Father Serra, founder of civilization in California. Before Father Serra there was no agriculture, no buildings, no music, no animal husbandry and no written language."

Detractors, however, are not convinced that the Europeans brought a more enlightened culture to California. CheQuweesh Auh-Ho-Oh, a longtime Indian opponent of Serra, emphasizes the political, not cultural, motives behind the Spanish incursion into this area. "Serra came here with the military to conquer souls," she points out in a 1988 *San Francisco Chronicle* article. "Serra is the symbol of the conquest of California. His beatification is an insult to our people. What message is the church giving the world by sanctifying this man?"

One message is that sainthood does not come easy, even to those with backers in high places. Moholy, who seems as tireless as his hero, has raised more than $1 million for Serra's cause. With the sly skills of a public relations expert, Moholy has guided a successful effort to put Serra's likeness on an airmail stamp, raised outright contributions from religious and lay individuals, promoted the sale of Serra medallions struck by the U.S. mint, and helped to record an album of "Songs of the California Missions."

For Serra's beatification at the Vatican in 1988, Moholy led pilgrims on a tour that culminated at the padre's birthplace on the beautiful Mediterranean island of Majorca. The cost was only $1,588. Not to be outdone, Shubsda provided a one-week package that included a private papal audience to those willing to lay out $1,650. Moholy was clearly miffed at the holy competition. "Serra belongs to us," he told a *San Francisco Chronicle* reporter. "All of a sudden the bishop (Shubsda) is on the bandwagon."

Political in-fighting aside, scholars of the Catholic Church will analyze over 10,000 pages of testimony regarding Serra's life before they rule officially on whether the dedicated Franciscan was, as Rawls says, a saint or a sadist. When the padre's men explored the San Francisco Bay Area with Lt. Col. Juan Bautista de Anza in a search for mission sites, did they bring with them a higher civilization, or destruction of a sophisticated and delicately-balanced culture?

Eustaquio Valencia, an early colonist and nephew of the *alcalde* of San Francisco, notes in his diary that before the arrival of the Spaniards, the Ohlones met regularly beneath the huge redwood tree later called El Palo Alto to settle arguments by peaceful council. The Indians felt they were in the presence of the Great Spirit that reached out through the branches. Regardless of the church's ruling on Serra's sainthood, some critics will undoubtedly remain convinced that the padre and his followers desecrated this holy ground.

Final Downfall

After Mexican Independence on September 16, 1822, the destruction of the missions began in earnest. The new Inspector, Jose Padres, appointed Jose Maria Echeandia governor of the Californias with the expectation he would carry out the decree of 1813. Instead of an orderly transition, however, orders for secularization were given, then rescinded, so often that life at the missions became ever more chaotic. Shouting "Soy Libre!," Indians at some of the missions rebelled and ran away. The padres became increasingly disheartened.

The secularization plan seesawed back and forth for several years. It is practically impossible now to detect Echeandia's own motives in his final decree of January 6, 1831, ostensibly leaving the missions to Christianized Indians. Did he himself plot to steal mission wealth and lands? No matter who was the original culprit, within a few years, everything the Franciscan fathers and the neophytes had built was either lying in neglect, or had been taken over by ranchers spreading out into the vast, fertile holdings. As Robinson says, "Many [Spanish and Mexican-Californians] that were poor soon became wealthy, and possessors of farms, which they stocked with cattle." After the first euphoria of liberation, the few remaining Indians realized that they were to be dispossessed again.

Mission Santa Clara was one of the last to be secularized, with a civil administrator taking over in 1836. By 1843 when the mission system was finally, officially closed, Father Mercado desperately tried to get General Mariano Vallejo to return 4,000 sheep taken "for services to the government," but even Father Mercado probably realized all along that this final gesture was futile. His successor, Father Jose Real, supported himself by renting rooms.

Long a center of education, the mission was turned over to the Jesuits in 1851 for the college that later became Santa Clara University.

In the next era, Mexicans, Spaniards and Anglos secured the land that is now Palo Alto, including tracts garnered from declining Mission Santa Clara, by gift, stealth or imagination. They were ambitious, brave people who were able to envision a prosperous future. But the Ohlones were here first. Perhaps Malcolm Margolin has provided the best epitaph for the original culture:

> The Ohlones, then, lived in a world perhaps somewhat like a Van Gogh painting—shimmering, and alive with movement and energy and ever-changing patterns. It was a world in which thousands of living, feeling, magical things, all operating on dream-logic, carried out their individual actions. It was a basically anarchistic world of great poetry, often great humor, and especially great complexity.

Chapter Notes

Margolin's *The Ohlone Way* provided understanding of the clash of cultures between the Ohlones and the Spaniards.

Through the years, the Palo Alto Historical Association has published a series of pamphlets, "Tall Trees," which can be seen at the association's desk at the Palo Alto Main Library on Newell Road. "Portola Discovers San Francisco Bay" (vol. III, no. 1, July 1967) is especially good.

H. E. Bolton's *Historical Memoirs of New California* (1925) includes Padre Francisco Palou's diary of the trek, a significant document.

Innumerable books and articles have been written about the missions of California; probably the best of these is Edith Buckland Webb's *Indian Life at the Old Missions* (1930). Webb writes with simple eloquence and her enthusiasm for understanding the mission system is contagious.

The story of the secularization of the missions can be pieced together from J. P. Munro-Fraser's *History of Santa Clara Valley* (1881), Alfred Robinson's asides in his diary about the unfolding of mission events, and Webb's short but comprehensive chapter on the complex and gradual destruction of the mission system.

The *San Francisco Chronicle* has provided news stories on the progress of Father Serra's canonization through the years, including Kevin Leary's May 3, 1988 article "Pope Will Beatify Father Serra," and his feature of September 19, 1988, "Beatification of Serra Opens Old Wounds." The *San Francisco Examiner* has also followed the story, including Don Lattin's July 10, 1988 article, "Serra Mass Stirs Holy War on Tours."

Other publications that ran occasional stories on Father Serra include the *Wall Street Journal* ("Sainthood Candidate has Tireless Backer in California Priest" by Michael Cieply, October 1985 issue) and *California Magazine* ("The Million-Dollar Canonization" by Greg Critser in the August 1985 issue). One of the most complete accounts of Serra's life and work was written by Diablo Valley College history professor James J. Rawls ("Serra's Mission: Saint or Sadist?" *San Jose Mercury News*, July 5, 1987).

Below: The double trunk tree, looking south, before January 1886, when the left trunk fell after 24 inches of rain fell in 3 months. The fallen giant was 960 years old. Right: The single tree, today's Palo Alto, in a north-looking view taken in 1891.
Courtesy Palo Alto Historical Association

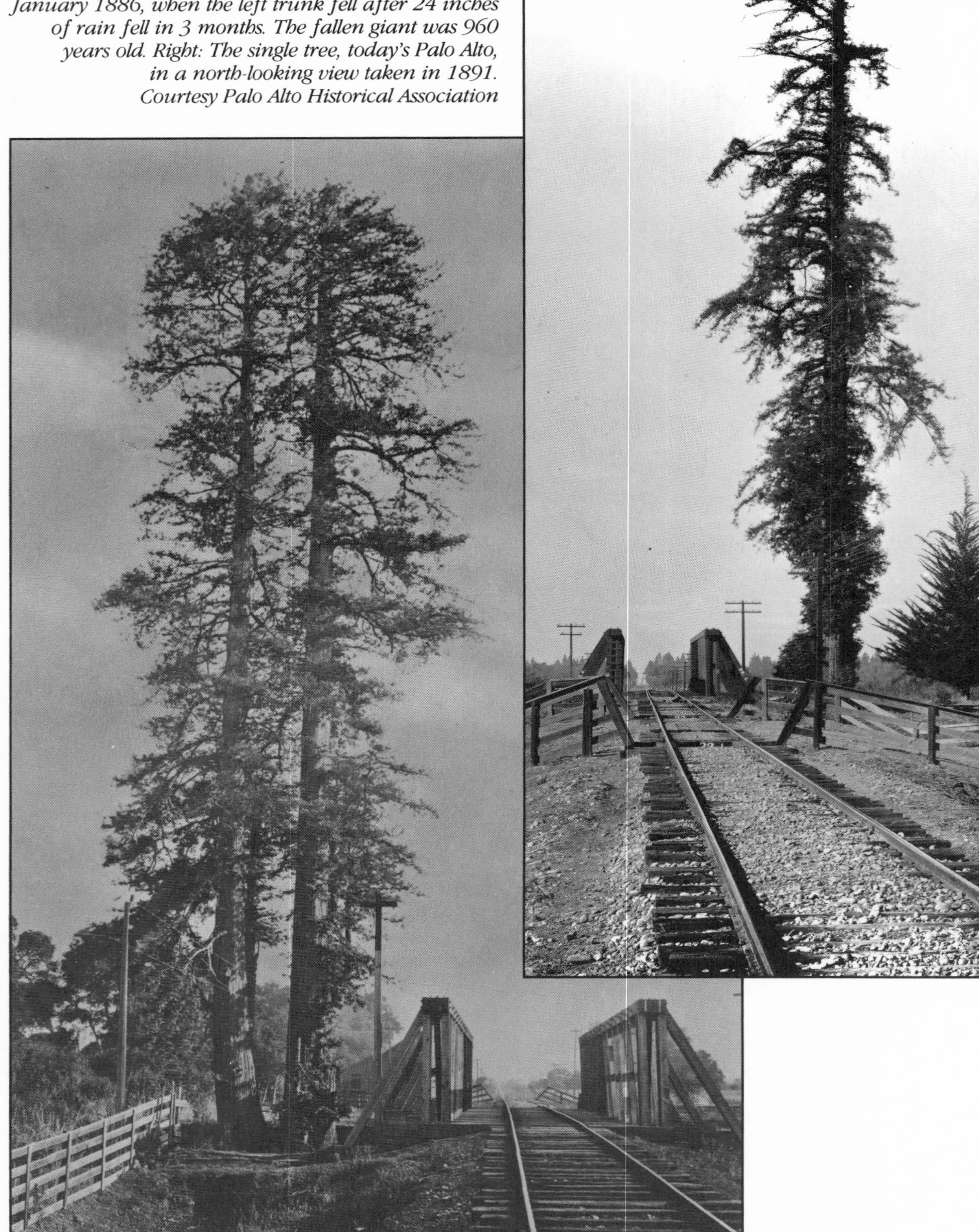

CHAPTER THREE

El Palo Alto, Mythic Tree

It stands in lonely, scraggly splendor, just off Alma Street, hard by the Southern Pacific tracks and San Francisquito Creek—El Palo Alto. Beloved symbol of a town and a university, called the oldest living California landmark and the most famous site along El Camino Real between San Diego and San Francisco, the coast redwood is considered to be 1063 years old in 1989 at the beginning of Palo Alto's centennial.

However, even this living legend may turn out to be a myth. Strong evidence suggests that the tree currently revered is not the same landmark that guided the early Spanish explorers.

The controversy revolves around the fact that, although the Spaniards referred to only one tree, El Palo Alto used to have twin trunks. Newspaper accounts, an old photograph and an old drawing show El Palo Alto with two trunks. A 19th century map calls the Palo Alto train station, "Twin Tree Station". Visible from both San Francisco and San Jose, the twins were called Saint Paul and Saint Peter or San Pablo and San Pedro.

Guy Miller, former Palo Alto historian, spent years trying to determine exactly when the twin fell. No absolute proof has ever emerged, but his best guess is that it occurred in the winter of 1886, probably in January, after 24 inches of rain fell in a three month period. The tree was 960 years old.

Concepcion Fuller Ramirez reminisced to Henry Peterson, a Palo Altan who was curator of Stanford Museum and later of Sutter's Fort in Sacramento, about a visit her family made to the twins in 1837. They traveled by carreta from San Francisco.

> It was a clear day and as we topped the summit of the hill, I saw the two noble trees intertwined like brothers towering high above the oaks and buckeyes. In those days the twin redwoods, growing from a common stump, were indeed beautiful trees, green and stately, and not the scraggly and grizzled old trunk it is today.

Actually there is some evidence that El Palo Alto was once a triplet. Emory E. Smith, a professor of horticulture at Stanford, was assured of this by several pioneers of 1849. Eduard Vischer, in *Pictorial of San Francisco* in 1870, also refers to the then twins as formerly a trio.

Popular history and legend tell us that Gaspar de Portola and his Spanish expedition camped under El Palo Alto in 1769 as did several succeeding exploratory parties. A mission was planned for the site until one group found San Francisquito Creek dry and therefore not a satisfactory water source. Local historians have researched and argued for the better part of a century over these facts. The problem: Is El Palo Alto the actual tree the Spanish expeditionary parties used as a landmark and campsite?

Despite the fondest wishes of many historians and most Palo Altans, the preponderance of evidence seems to suggest that it is not. No researcher has ever been able to find mention of a tree called El Palo Alto in any document before 1853. Although the historic record is often either unclear or non-existent, the Spanish diarists who accompanied the explorers and kept detailed records of their travels write of only one tree, not of a tree with two major trunks.

Padre Pedro Font actually measured their landmark tree in 1776 using a chronometer borrowed from the mission in Carmel. He recorded one height and one circumference: 50 varas (one vara was 33 inches) high and 5 1/2 varas in circumference.

In 1922 Nellie Vande Grift Sanchez wrote in *Spanish and Indian Place Names of California:*

> It seems rather strange that no mention was made in the diaries of the fact that the tree was a twin ... This description of Font's gives rise to a strong suspicion that the tree now so highly venerated is not the original Palo Alto from which the place took its name.

In 1949 in *Place Names of California,* Erwin Gudde states unequivocally that the El Palo Alto of today isn't the same tree the Spanish noted in the late 1700s. Dorothy Huggins, assistant editor of the University of California Press, wrote to Guy Miller to refute his criticism of Gudde's statements:

> I do not agree with your conclusions that the twin trees were the Palo Alto mentioned in the diaries of Palou and the Anza expedition. I feel certain that had the early Palo Alto been twin trees some of the Spanish diaries would have mentioned that fact ... The Spanish Californians were quick to note "twinship" of anything. (They even called Mount Shasta and Lassen Peak "the twins" in Spanish.)

She continues with various complicated evidences from diaries and old maps to substantiate Gudde's allegation that the El Palo Alto of today is not that of the Spanish era. Finally she politely challenges Miller to produce authoritative and positive proof from a land grant case or a personal recollection of an inhabitant from Spanish days that today's El Palo Alto is the historic tree, something no one has ever been able to do. Two later editions of Gudde's book maintain his contention.

Alan Brown, noted local historian, stated his view in a letter to Lucy Evans in 1969 on the occasion of Palo Alto's Diamond Jubilee when an attempt was made to have state historic landmark status conferred on El Palo Alto:

> I can't see any way a *single* tree as described (and drawn by Font on his map) in 1774-76 could possibly have become a double tree by the 1850s. So it must have been another ... I would say the weight of the evidence points to the Palo Alto not having become a notable landmark until the year 1850, or more especially 1852, when travelers on the County Road (El Camino) could begin marking their journey by it ... This fact would account for the name (in Spanish and English) not being recorded until 1853 but being so well known then and since.

The 1969 documentation for historic landmark status for El Palo Alto concluded that research could not prove it was the tree of the Spanish diaries and

The famous Vischer view of a train at Big Tree Station, from Vischer's Pictorial of California, April 1870. Courtesy Palo Alto Historical Association

drawing but because of its age of 1044, it merited consideration as one of the ancient historic redwoods from the time when Portola and his men camped along the banks of San Francisquito Creek. On March 20, 1974 El Palo Alto was assigned number SCI-026 and registered with the state of California as a Point of Historical Interest, an honor but not as significant as a registered state historic landmark.

There are two other candidates for the honor of having sheltered Portola and his colleagues. One was the large Pope Street redwood, which fell around 1852. The other likely prospect was a very large tree located somewhere around Hale and Forest which was carried away by high water in 1911.

At the very least, El Palo Alto deserves one's admiration for surviving. It has endured crumbling creek banks, insufficient water, termites, several grade changes and all the various hazards of encroaching civilization. In the 1920s, for example, 72 trains per day roared by, all belching smoke.

Perhaps not the least of these hazards were the climbers. Around the turn of the century it was rather trendy for Stanford students to scale to its heights to fly a banner or flag. In 1894 25 freshmen climbed up in the dead of night to take down the sophomore flag and win the battle of the classes. Arthur Zschokke, class of 1902, climbed it four times. The last known climber was Vincent Levesque who went up on the eve of Admission Day, 1909. He was marooned there for hours until, by the light of a bonfire, fellow classmates got a rope to him.

Lest readers conclude that these ascents were merely the pranks of callous students insensitive to the historical significance of the aged tree, let the record show that at least three of the flags carried up by the students belonged to such august Palo Alto citizens as J. F. Parkinson, a mayor; Jasper Paulsen, one of the first businessmen; and Charles Lathrop, Jane Lathrop Stanford's brother.

Overall, however, residents have held El Palo Alto in such esteem that prodigious efforts have been made over the years to preserve it in good health. Jane Lathrop Stanford had cement buttresses installed to protect against crumbling banks. Pipes sunk eight feet into the ground have provided irrigation. Water pipes reaching to the top of the tree have offered the cool spray of artificial fog. Pressure jet ground feedings have supplied additional nutrients. Experts perform regular inspections to catch any incipient problems.

Yet the day will inevitably come when El Palo Alto will be gone. Then people interested in history will have to travel about town to visit its offspring. As early as 1917 seedlings which had sprung up around its roots were transplanted to the front of Stanford's old Physics Building. The Holiday Inn on El Camino has a grove of such seedlings. The students at the old Loma Vista School (now Juana Briones) planted its seedlings in 1968. There are still others in the oval in front of Stanford's business school. In 1976 the Stanford Mothers' Club offered seeds from its cones.

Perhaps it is comforting to those who love El Palo Alto to know that people have been worrying about its imminent demise for decades. Headlines in the 1920s warned that it was in immediate jeopardy. Still, old and wizened, not much to look at today, it endures.

Chapter Notes

Almost all of the information on El Palo Alto comes from three thick PAHA folders of newspaper clippings, correspondence, programs from ceremonies, and applications for official historic status. Especially interesting are letters to and from Guy Miller, former Palo Alto historian, and an assortment of letters from Palo Alto's Diamond Jubliee in 1969. Most important are the October 14, 1948 letter from Dorothy Huggins to Guy Miller and the February 13, 1969 letter from Alan K. Brown to Lucy Evans.

Erwin Gudde's 1949, 1960, and 1969 editions of *California Place Names* explain the confusion about the tree's significance. The *Sequoia* of January 6, 1892 contains E. E. Smith's research. *The Palo Alto Tree* by Alice Jenkins Weymouth, 1930, recapitulates in seven pages the Spanish explorers' visits.

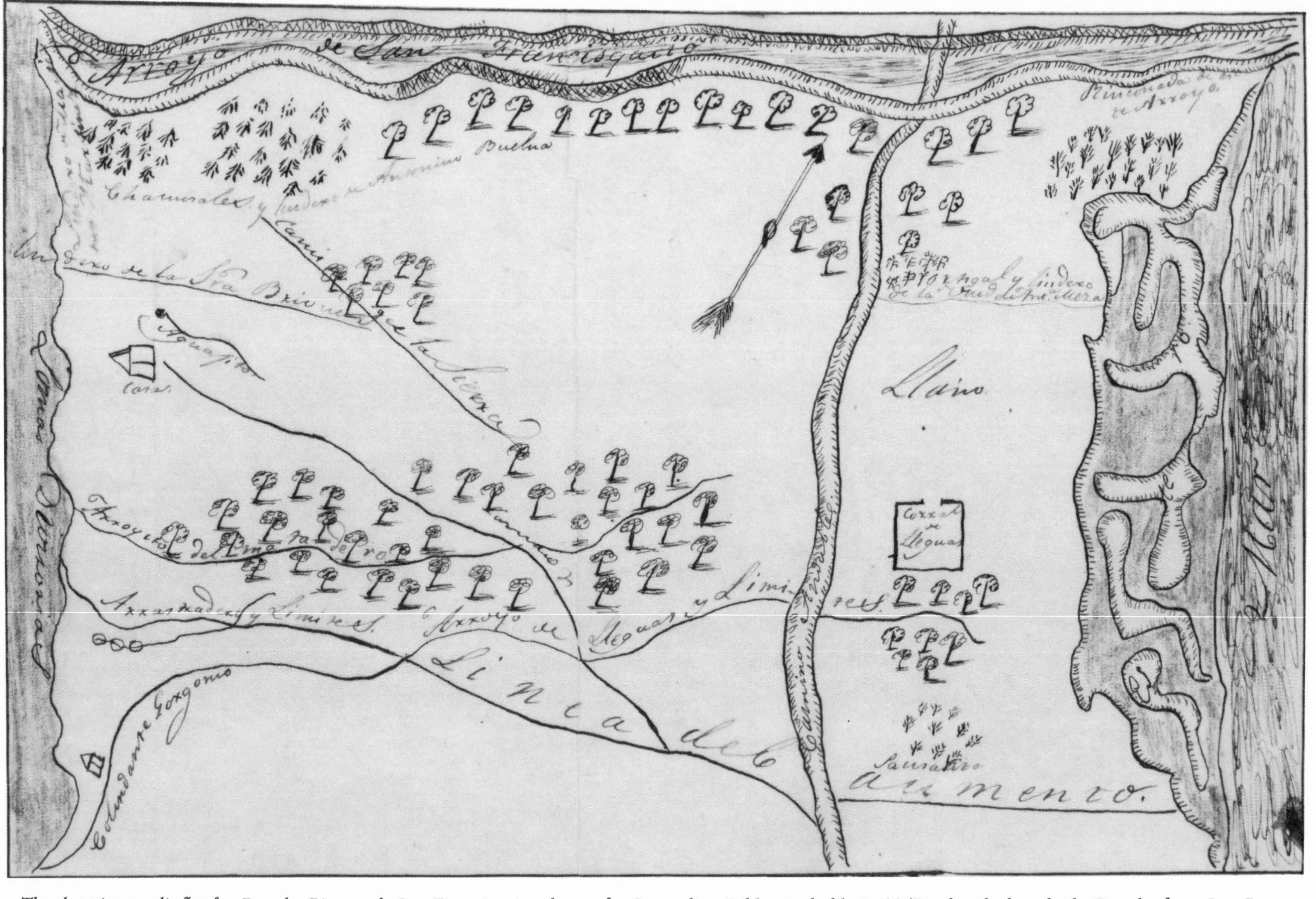

The drawing or diseño for Rancho Rincon de San Francisquito, drawn for Secundino Robles, probably in 1847, when he bought the Rancho from Jose Pena. San Francisquito Creek runs along the top; the fat vertical roadway is apparently El Camino. Llano is a plain or field; sausalito is little willows. At top right is the boundary of Antonio Mesa; at top left, the lands of Martinez, Buelnas and Senora Briones, and a road to the mountains (camino a la Sierra). Aguajito is a little spring, close by a house. Lower left are the arroyos of Matadero (slaughtering grounds) and Lleguas (mares) now Adobe creek, leading to a corral de Lleguas, which once belonged to Mission Santa Clara. Along the bottom is Arastradero Limites (border), extending to Linea del Aumento, the southern border of Rancho Rincon de San Francisquito. This diseno is more detailed than most, showing different kinds of trees and the marshes and esteros (far right). Yet as a basis for a claim before an American land commission it is hardly convincing. Courtesy San Jose Historical Museum.

CHAPTER FOUR

The Robles Family— Rancho Rincon de San Francisquito

When it became fashionable to own land instead of merely live on it, the area that was to become Palo Alto was divided among only three families: The Robles, the Buelnas and the Sotos. These families presided over three large ranchos named for the stream that forms the border between San Mateo and Santa Clara Counties, San Francisquito Creek. Thus the rancho names were confusingly similar: Rancho San Francisquito, Rancho Rincon de San Francisquito and Rancho Rinconada del Arroyo de San Francisquito.

In addition to these three, a small portion of Juana Briones' holdings, La Purisima Concepcion, was located along the Palo Alto-Los Altos Hills border. Another, El Corte de Madera, spilled slightly over the boundaries of San Mateo County into today's Palo Alto hills.

These were the vast ranchos of the Mexican era, the days of the dons. Although it is typical to say Spanish land grants, Mexico actually owned California after 1821; all of Palo Alto's grants came after that date.

It is almost impossible to imagine today how large they were. San Francisquito encompassed the main part of today's Stanford campus, Rinconada del Arroyo de San Francisquito extended from the Menlo Park border of Palo Alto to the Midtown region, and Rincon de San Francisquito, the largest, occupied all of today's south Palo Alto, from the bay to the foothills. Vast indeed!

Initially these ranchos were gifts from the government of Mexico to people who had performed special favors, who had friends in high places and/or who were willing to settle the Alta California wilderness to help hold the land for Mexico against possibly aggressive foreign governments.

The owners of the land that became Palo Alto obtained their property in the 1840s, the decade after the closing of the missions and before the gold rush. They rode their beautiful horses, herded their cattle, traded hides to Yankee ships in exchange for manufactured goods, and little knew that the era of their beautiful ranchos was to be short-lived, thanks to the little yellow nuggets that brought foreigners into California by the tens of thousands.

Only glimmers of the stories of the ranchos remain, and much of the record that does exist is unclear. Many of the early rancheros couldn't read or write, and they considered careful record-keeping of land ownership unimportant. After all, in those days acquiring land was almost as easy as stopping your horse out on a California plain and declaring to the sky that all you surveyed was yours. The land was covered with oaks, the nearby hills were still inhabited by grizzly bears, and California was a lonely outpost of Mexico.

The Robles Family

Secundino Robles, owner of the rancho that occupied all of today's south Palo Alto, must have been a nearly perfect specimen of what history and legend report the dons of old California to have been. He was tall, well over 6′3″, and a handsome, blue-eyed native Californian, born in Santa Cruz in 1811. In an era when excellent horsemanship was the main delight in life, he was said to be the finest rider in the Santa Clara Valley. Early settlers reported seeing him pick up a row of silver dollars placed six feet apart on the ground while riding at a full gallop.

One can conjure up an image of him, arising at dawn, dressing in a satin jacket and velvet breeches, pulling on knee high buckskin boots, arraying his fine horse with silver studded tack and galloping for miles toward the foothills on his own land.

The story of Don Secundino and Rancho Rincon de San Francisquito can begin with cinnabar, quicksilver, the same substance that the Indians prized for decoration and that the miners would later use in gold processing. As young men, boys really, in the 1820s, Secundino Robles and his brother

Teodoro rode through the Santa Clara Valley and along steep hillsides at its western edge to a cave containing large quantities of cinnabar. They may have been led to it by Indians, or they may have discovered it while hunting grizzlies. At any rate, they were probably the first Europeans to know about the New Almaden Mine, which became one of the richest sources of mercury in the world.

The site contained thousands of tons of pure cinnabar and hundreds of thousands of tons of less rich ore. By the 1860s there were miles of tunnels underground, the main one as large as a railroad tunnel. William Brewer, a geologist of the time, estimated the mines were worth one or two million dollars. But the value of the find was not apparent to the Robles brothers. When they discovered that the mine did not contain silver, as they had hoped, they abandoned work.

Meanwhile, in 1822, the year Mexico took possession of California from Spain, one Jose Pena, a soldier from the San Francisco presidio, received permission from Mission Santa Clara to occupy 4400 acres of its grazing land. An intelligent and shrewd man, he applied for seven grants in all. He called this one Rancho Rincon de San Francisquito, a corner or bend of the little St. Francis. It included virtually all of today's south Palo Alto. The southern border was approximately where Arastradero Road and Adobe Creek (formerly known as both Yeguas and San Antonio Creek) are today. San Francisquito Creek on the northwest, today's Colorado Avenue on the northeast, the western foothills and the bay were its other approximate boundaries.

Apparently the land was little used by Pena. He built a wood house on the south side of today's Lagunita Drive on the Stanford campus, and there was a herdsman's hut at what is now the corner of Alma and San Antonio Road. Nevertheless, on March 29, 1841 he was formally granted the rancho by Mexican-appointed Governor Juan Bautista Alvarado. Pena was teaching at Santa Clara by then and was 64 years old.

H. H. Bancroft lists Secundino Robles, then 30 years old and married, as the majordomo of the Santa Clara Mission in 1841. Robles was about to play a small role in Santa Clara County's only incident in the events surrounding the American conquest of California.

The California of the 1840s was a confusing and complicated place. The United States and Mexico were engaged in a war that would change the ownership (and the language) of California. Several feuding factions of the Mexican government clashed with each other and with their military and civil representatives in California. The Californios separately presumed that they ought to rule the land they lived on. American settlers became an ever increasing threat to the Mexican government in California, staging in 1846, without U.S. government authority, the Bear Flag Revolt in an attempt to make California a separate nation.

The American Conquest

Although a peace treaty between the United States and Mexico wasn't signed until February of 1848, the Americans officially raised the stars and stripes over California on July 7, 1846 and declared California a U. S. possession. Even then, the U. S. Navy and Army disagreed over which had higher authority. The rancheros expected to live in peace with the new government, but it didn't quite work out that way.

Unfortunately, the American soldiers stationed in San Francisco and San Jose during this era of instability in the late 1840s had the habit of requisitioning supplies from the rancheros without permission or payment. Proud vaqueros were left without horses; serapes, boots, spurs and blankets were taken; rancho families were turned out of their houses so soldiers could use their beds. The rancheros' indignation rose.

In December of 1846, the *alcalde* of San Francisco, Washington Bartlett, and an armed scouting party approached the rancho of Francisco Sanchez, near today's Millbrae, seeking cattle. Francisco Sanchez's brother Manuel had just been arrested, and perhaps that insult compounded Francisco's anger over the repeated raids. He organized a plan that led to the capture of the scouting party. With the mayor a hostage, the Americans should listen to reason.

The anger over the Americans' arrogant raids was so widespread on the peninsula that a group of about 100 Californios had gathered, Secundino Robles among them, to protest and seek guarantees that the outrage would stop. They had been ordered to surrender their arms earlier; now they mustered 38 guns, one pistol, 19 lances (knives tied to willow poles) and 10 swords. The rancheros were ready to negotiate.

The seven hostages were moved to various locations about the peninsula, and finally a camp was set up near the Santa Clara Mission.

Meanwhile, about a hundred Americans with a cannon were hurrying down from San Francisco to rescue their mayor. The confrontation between these two groups did not amount to much. Three shots were fired from the American cannon, which became mired in mud. The Californios retreated. The Americans retired to the mission.

Although no rancheros had even been wounded, Carlos Weber, one of the American leaders, executed a neat bit of psychological warfare. He send word for

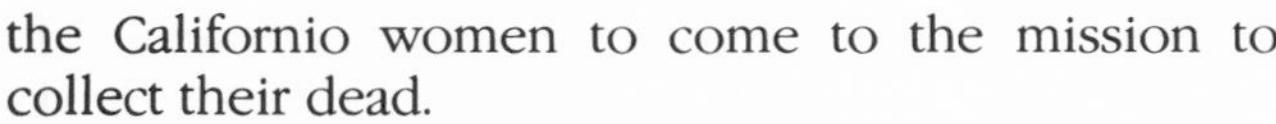

Maria Antonia Garcia Robles

Secundino Robles

the Californio women to come to the mission to collect their dead.

One of those notified was Maria Antonia Robles, Secundino's wife. Barely over five feet tall, about 26 years old, she harnessed the oxen and yoked them to the rough cart called a *carreta* for the drive to the mission, fervently hoping her husband was still alive. But she did not flinch. She had proved her courage earlier by not losing faith when several of her children died, and once, in refusing to give up blankets to an American intruder. Reports say this tiny woman struck the intruder and pushed him out of her house. Fortunately her bravery wasn't to be tested again this day. Secundino was alive and well.

On January 3, the two sides sat down to talk, which was the rancheros' original goal. The treaty was simple: the hostages would be released, the Californios would surrender their arms and return home, the Californios would not be molested by the American military, and horses and other supplies wouldn't be taken from the ranchos without receipts.

Treaty ceremonies took place on January 7, 1847. Upon the promise that there would be no more raids, the rancheros laid down their arms. One of Palo Alto's enduring legends is that Secundino Robles broke his sword in half before he surrendered it. However, in her book on the Battle of Santa Clara, local historian Dorothy Regnery, a meticulous researcher, says that no Californio made any dramatic gesture at the ceremonies. Perhaps it says something of the character of the man that this legend exists.

Nine months later, in September 1847, Secundino Robles and his brother Teodoro bought Rancho Rincon de San Francisquito from Jose Pena. The purchase price for a large part of present day Palo Alto was around $3500 and was financed through that cave of cinnabar.

A few years earlier, the Robles brothers had taken Andres Castillero, a Mexican mining expert, to their cave. He immediately recognized the cinnabar and its value, filed a claim with the Mexican government and organized a company to work the mine. Secundino and Teodoro received a one-sixth interest in that company. The Robles brothers used this share to purchase the rancho.

Local historians disagree as to whether the Robles brothers sold the one-sixth interest and then bought the rancho or whether they traded the mine shares for it. Since Jose Pena doesn't seem to appear in the considerable litigation over New Almaden Mine ownership, the former seems most likely.

Theirs is not the only real estate transaction in the

Robles Brothers

The story of Secundino Robles' many brothers offers an interesting insight into Secundino's character. In the 1820s or 1830s, the four eldest Robles brothers joined the army and developed into steady, responsible men. Four of the five youngest brothers, Teodoro, Avelino, Nicolas and Fulgencio, continued to live with their parents in Branciforte, herding cattle and living the high lives of rancho caballeros. Leon Rowland, a Santa Cruz journalist and historian, told their story in 1941 in his book *Villa de Branciforte.*

The four young Robles brothers raced around on horseback, visiting cantinas and gambling houses from San Jose to Monterey, not always careful of whose horses they used, catching the girls' eyes in their velveteen breeches with silver filigree trimming, satin jackets, earrings and silk sashes. They had a fondness for drinking *aguardiente,* a powerful alcoholic beverage. Often in trouble with the *alcalde* (mayor) and *regidors* (councilmen), they were treated leniently out of respect for their father.

Nicolas had a long record of horse theft, from at least 1834, but influential friends of his father arranged for light punishments when he was apprehended. In 1838, however, his luck ran out. He was found guilty of horse theft, fined and exiled to Santa Barbara or beyond until invited back.

Exiles were brief in those days and by early 1839 Nicolas was back, ardently pursuing a young lady named Lucia Soria. Lucia welcomed his attentions, but her father disapproved of a match between his daughter and this wild young man. Nicolas, not to be deterred, cut through a woven rawhide window covering at Lucia's house and escaped with his beloved.

When representatives of the alcalde found the pair and attempted to arrest Nicolas, he pointed a loaded flintlock at his would-be captors. They left; he and Lucia remained together a short while longer. By the time the officials returned, Nicolas' brothers were prepared to defend him.

The Robles Brothers were overpowered by the authorities and ordered to walk to San Juan Bautista, fastened together with a rope around each man's neck. As horsemen, they were outraged by such humiliation and refused to comply. The soldiers opened fire and Avelino was killed. Nicolas was wounded. After another brief exile, Nicholas and Lucia married in 1841, but he died three years later.

Brother Fulgencio was no less reckless. Bancroft calls him "the terror of all the region." In 1842 he took exception to derogatory remarks made by an immigrant about the Californios. Mounting his horse, he rode it at full gallop directly into the foreigner's home, where he and friends were gambling. Fulgencio was fatally shot, and he flew off his horse, his body hitting the gambling table and spilling pesos in all directions.

At this point Teodoro decided to leave Branciforte for Mission Santa Clara to join his brother Secundino, who fit chronologically in with the younger group of Robles boys. For some reason, Secundino was not lured into the profligate ways of his immediate peers but chose instead to follow the responsible example of his elder brothers.

California of the late 1840s and 1850s that is difficult to trace. In 1848, California became a United States territory, and a new set of laws governing land ownership soon took effect. In 1849, gold seekers swarmed to the territory, often squatting on land that seemed empty. In fact, this acreage was often part of a California rancho that perhaps had never had a real deed, or whose owner had only a vague idea of his land's boundaries. Litigation over land ownership was constant, profuse and lengthy. Suits and countersuits, claims and counterclaims were filed. There were land commissions, surveyors general, district courts, and even Supreme Court rulings on the cases. Resolution sometimes took decades.

Whatever their method of payment, the Robles brothers took possession of the rancho in 1847. Although Teodoro disappears quickly from the story, for the next 40 years, into the era when Palo Alto was being established, Don Secundino Robles presided over his land, affectionately called "Rancho Santa Rita" in honor of a daughter.

The Robles family already had deep roots in California when they took over stewardship of half of Palo Alto. Secundino's parents, Jose Antonio and Gertrudis, had arrived in Monterey in 1797, part of a group of 80 families sent to settle Branciforte (now Santa Cruz). Plans for government support were cancelled, and living conditions were very primitive, but the Robles family stayed on, farmed, and produced 12 children, one of whom was Secundino.

When the Secundino Robles family took over Pena's rancho, they enlarged the adobe that stood on the northwest corner of Alma and San Antonio. A plaque at Alma and Ferne commemorates its location. This house, sheltered by an ancient black maple tree, stood until the 1906 earthquake. Even then the strong supporting posts and shingle roof remained. A barn was built under and around the remnants and was a visible reminder of rancho days until the late 1950s.

The two story adobe had walls 29 inches thick covered with plaster inside and out. The main floor was divided into 3 rooms, each with redwood ceilings. The main room was 17 feet square. The large kitchen, 15 by 33, was separate except for a connecting stairway. All evidence indicates that for many years the second story was a dancing floor open to the stars. Eventually the upstairs was enclosed and divided into three rooms. On each floor, doors opened to verandas which extended the full length of the house on two sides.

Here, during the 1850s, the Robles family extended their famous Spanish hospitality to everyone around. There were almost monthly feasts, fandangos, and barbecues. Guests would feast and dance from Sunday morning through Saturday night. The men would be up at dawn to ride Don Secundino's fine horses, inspect herds, hunt grizzlies and show their skill at galloping over the fields, not bothering to slow down for gopher holes, ditches, fences or gulches. The women would sew and talk. At night everyone would dance.

The Robles adobe became a stage stop on the route between San Francisco and San Jose. Don Secundino was renowned for his generous and friendly offering of liquid refreshments. He staged bear and bull fights in his arena which drew large crowds. Hunters enjoyed stopping to rendezvous with others before and after the hunt; bear, mountain lion, deer, quail, ducks and geese still thrived in profusion nearby.

Although the Robles hospitality was legend, Don Secundino and Dona Maria Antonia are best remembered for the size of their family. History records that they produced an astonishing 29 children in the decades between 1830 and 1860. Less well known is that only eight lived to adulthood. Ten died before they were named. Juan I and Jose lived for eight days, Juan II for twenty, Jesus Maria, Gertrudis and Ascencion lived only to see their first birthdays. Maria Leonidas was two when she died, Lourdes was three, Rosario six and Maria Angela eight. The record of another who died in childhood is lost.

Of the eight who survived, six were girls. Five of them had the first name of Maria. Jesusita and Guadalupe married Espinosa brothers, whose family owned the property in Monterey where the Hotel Del Monte was later built. They carried on family tradition, bearing 24 and 19 children.

Jesusita is said to have been a beauty, the belle of fandangos and bull fights. According to a report by historian Cora Older, who interviewed Jesusita, then an old lady, in 1918, Jesusita once rode in a bull fight at Mission Dolores with 5000 people in

The Robles adobe, where many of the Robles children were born. At left is a separate kitchen. The upper gallery was once a dance floor open to the sky. The adobe walls collapsed in the 1906 earthquake, and the building was then demolished. Courtesy Palo Alto Historical Association

Four Robles descendants: (left) Guadalupe Robles de Espinosa, Secundino's daughter; her daughters Jennie Tollner (1877-1947) top, and Mary Inez Rich (b. 1869), right; and baby Alfred.
Courtesy Palo Alto Historical Association

attendance. Unfortunately, Older gave no further details.

Andrea "Carolina" collapsed and died in 1922 at age 81 beside the casket of Guadalupe. Rita and Luisa survived into the 1930s. The record of Dormitia is lost except that she married a man named Smith, and died when she was 27. The sons, Nicolas and Secundino II, both died in 1930. Secundino and Maria's children gave them more than 100 grandchildren.

Life followed a pattern at Rancho Santa Rita: a new baby every year, the sorrow of losing a child repeated 21 times, generous hospitality to all neighbors near and far; and trips to Mission Santa Clara or to St. Denis Church, built in 1853 (on a site near the today's Stanford Linear Accelerator Center on Sand Hill Road), every Sunday for Mass.

And of course there were the cattle, a large herd that roamed freely over the valley. The Robles daughters helped as vaqueros in the early 1850s, becoming expert riders themselves in the process. During great roundups, called rodeos, Robles cattle were separated from those of neighboring ranchos—calves were branded, hides and tallow were prepared for shipment, and all this work was accompanied by great parties with barbecues, contests of skill on horseback, and dancing.

On March 9, 1854, the following article, which appeared in the *Santa Clara County Register,* indicates that the two cultures—Anglo and Hispanic—were not always blending without difficulty. The letter was signed at the bottom with the mark of Secundino Robles.

> **To the Public:**
>
> A few nights since while I was asleep in my house, one of the servants about 11 o'clock at night informed me that some thieves were driving a band of cattle along the road near my house. Having lost about one hundred head of cattle a short time before, I went out with some men that were in my house, to see if the cattle were mine. It wa so dark I could not see the marks or brands, but being satisfied that the cattle were stolen, I took them and drove them into my corral. Next morning, I saw that the cattle belonged to some of my neighbors. I notified them to come and get them, which was done. The next day a party of men (Americans) came to my house, and after insulting my family, told them that they came there to kill me—that I had stolen the cattle, etc. By the intervention of some good Americans, and the entreaties of my wife and children, I was not killed. This is not the first time that me and my family have been thus treated, and unless the good citizens and the law will afford protection to a citizen and his family, men will be compelled to defend themselves by force of arms. Being a law-abiding man, I give notice that I have been imposed upon long enough, until forbearance has ceased to be a virtue, and if not protected by the law, I must protect myself.
>
> X Secundino Robles

The vast acres of the rancho had been dwindling from the very beginning. Land was an inexpensive commodity in those days—a good horse could cost more than many acres. The record of exactly what happened is confused, with sales, gifts, trades, mortgages, foreclosures, deeds and counter deeds, squatters and lawsuits in profusion. There were 31 defendants in one suit.

Some facts, however, are clear. Teodoro and his wife divorced in 1855 over a mystery woman named Lola, and his ex-wife was granted one half of Teodoro's half of Rancho Santa Rita. Large portions were sold at various times to various people for low prices. Some land was sold to Jeremiah Clarke and to E. O. Crosby, early residents of the town of Mayfield. In a 1918 interview with Joe Greer, a rancho descendant, Cora Older learned that Secundino traded 500 acres of his rancho to Clarke for a span of horses and a buggy. Robles was happy with the deal until an axle broke on the first trip. More land was sold to pay for gambling debts, taxes, legal fees and for Secundino's generous hospitality.

Guadalupe Robles de Espinosa (1840-1922), born in an adobe, mother of 19 children; the cares and joys of 80 years show on her face in this superb photograph. She lived to see the age of the automobile.
Courtesy Palo Alto Historical Association

J. S. Mockbee offered this explanation in 1881: "It was their open handed generosity and abiding trust in all mankind that caused them to lose their vast holdings little by little. Eastern men took advantage of their hospitality and generosity." American and Californio ways of looking at land values were different.

The infamous circus story is a good example. By all accounts, Secundino was a happy man who loved life, laughter and good times. When the circus came to town, of course he wanted to take his family. Being short of cash, as the story goes, he borrowed $75 from a "Yankee" and pledged land as security. The reports do not say why it was such an expensive outing. Still short of cash when the repayment was due, Secundino deeded 50 acres of his rancho to the nameless Yankee. By 1876 the sprawling Rancho Santa Rita had shrunk from 8400 acres to 300 acres.

Gradually Secundino began to slow down. He gave up his beloved trips to San Francisco to see the sights. He was not seen so often riding along the roads of the peninsula astride a handsome horse. He loved to sit in the shade of his grape arbor and have a grandchild read the newspaper to him or visit with friends passing by. His land and therefore his access to money was largely gone, but he could still offer the modest hospitality of a glass of wine. It has been said that he had more friends than any other man in California. He died, a ward of the county, on January 10, 1890, a year after Palo Alto's first streets were laid out.

Maria Antonia survived him for several years, continuing the famous Robles hospitality by serving wine, milk and thin, sweet tortillas to bicyclists along El Camino. Mary S. Barnes interviewed her in 1894 for an article in *Sequoia*, a Stanford University publication.

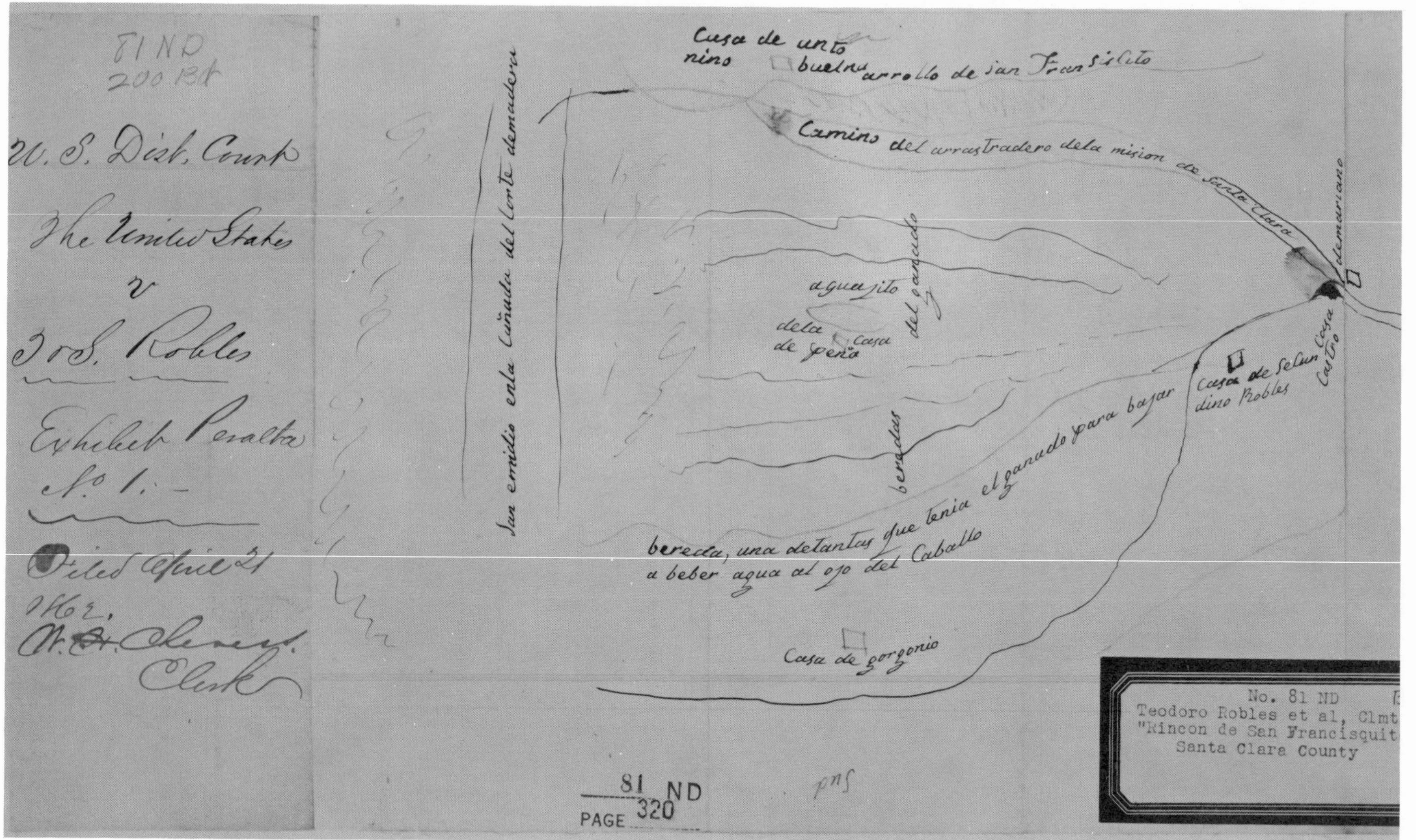

This map or diseño, filed at the U.S. District Court on April 21, 1862, apparently satisfied the court that Secundino and Teodoro Robles held legitimate title to Rancho Rincon de San Francisquito, although it is not much clearer than the earlier one (p.24). At far right is the house of Secundino Robles; casa Castro is adjacent. Casa de Antonino Buelna is at the top. The spring for the house of Pena is at center. Below, above the Casa de Gorgonio, is a place where cattle and horses can safely drink water. Courtesy Bancroft Library

> We found a charming old lady who, in spite of the seventy years which she laughingly counted by tens on her fingers, kept much of the grace and vivacity of youth, while her hair was still as black as a raven's wing ... Lights and flowers still adorn the shrines of "Our Lady" in her own room, and she will die as she had lived, true Californian, sweet Castilian her tongue, and "Our Lady of Guadaloupe" her patron saint.

Maria Antonia Garcia de Robles died on January 6, 1897.

Eldest daughter Jesusita spent her last years in Gilroy. She kept as beloved reminders of the old days two shawls, one tomato red and the other cream with flowers splashed on the background. She dreamed of one day going back to the old place and the old ways and of wearing them once again. When Cora Older asked her about them in 1918, she said, "I had to eat. They came for them again and again. They said it would be better to sell the shawls than to be hungry. I sold them."

In the 1940s, 100 years after Secundino and Teodoro acquired their 8400 acres, grandchildren were living in the family home on the remaining three and a half acres, near today's Dinah's Shack. This last remnant of Rancho Santa Rita was sold and passed out of the family in 1948.

Chapter Notes

All evidence suggests that the rancheros who owned the land that has become Palo Alto were illiterate. Thus, none of those treasures to historians—diaries and letters—has come to light. Daily life on the ranchos must be pieced together from the smallest tidbits of information.

Stanford graduate student Roy Ballard interviewed and researched the Robles family in the early 1890s. His notes and unfinished manuscript are on file in the Stanford University Archives. He wrote brief articles in the Stanford publication *Sequoia* in 1894 and 1895. Mary S. Barnes interviewed and wrote of Maria Antonia Robles in the September, 1984 *Sequoia.*

H. H. Bancroft took an oral history, a *relacion*, from Secundino Robles in 1877. The untranslated original is at the Bancroft Library of the University of California. A translation by F. M. Stanger is in the San Mateo County Historical Archives. Bancroft also mentions the Robles family in Volumes IV and V of his *History of California.*

In 1918, reporter Cora Baggerly Older interviewed the surviving Robles daughters for segments in her lengthy series "When San Jose was Young" in the *San Jose Evening News.*

Local historian Dorothy Regnery's important research on the Robles genealogy and on various land transfers is in the PAHA files. Her excellent book, *The Battle of Santa Clara*, 1978, briefly includes Secundino Robles.

Other recent historians offer brief accounts of the family. The most complete of these are entries in Hoover, Rensch and Rensch's *Historic Spots in California*, Miller's *Palo Alto Community Book* and Woods' *History of Palo Alto.*

Samuel Dickson, a spellbinding author, wrote of Secundino and Maria Antonia in *San Francisco Kaleidoscope*, 1949. Ralph Rambo includes Secundino in his 1970 *Adventure Valley.* Philip Tollner's manuscript, *History of the Robles Family in California*, 1957, is housed in the Palo Alto Historical Association [PAHA] Archives. Jeanne Holtzclaw, Mountain View historian, wrote a manuscript, *The Robles Family in California*, in 1979. A copy is in the Mission Santa Clara Archives.

Information on the New Almaden Mine comes from *Up and Down California in 1860-1864* by William Brewer, 1930. The story of the notorious Robles brothers is drawn largely from Leon Rowland's *Villa de Branciforte*, republished in 1980 as a segment of *Santa Cruz, The Early Years.*

Various old newspapers such as the *Palo Alto Live Oak*, the *Mountain View Register* and the *Santa Clara County Register* as well as the *Palo Alto Times* offer glimmers of the Robles story through brief articles and obituaries.

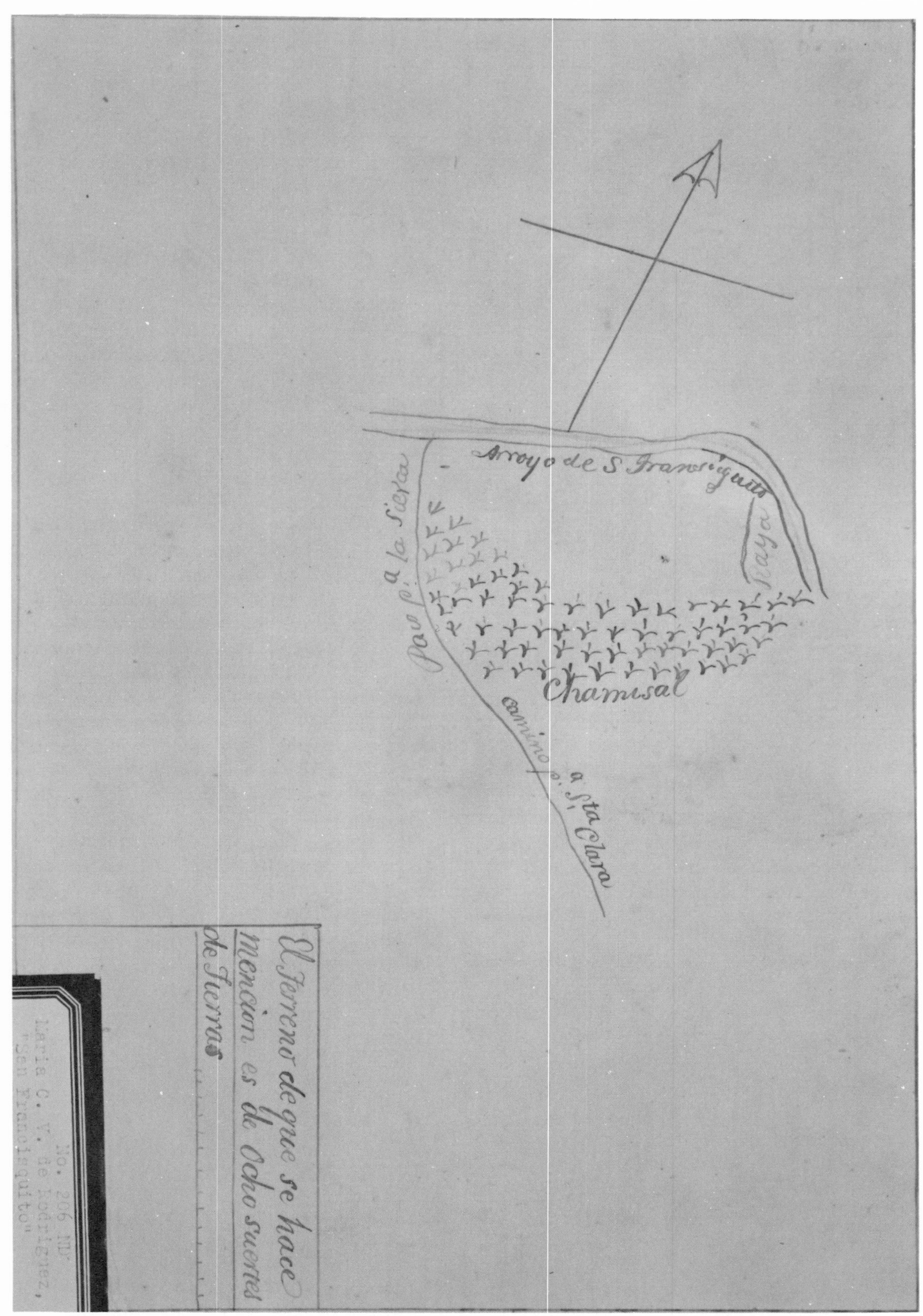

This map or diseño of Rancho de San Francisquito, granted to Antonio Buelna in 1839, is the simplest of the four. The Rancho was only 8 suertes (1471 acres), smaller than the others. The arrow points north; El Camino crosses the creek at a ford leading to la Sierra, the mountains. Chamisal *is a kind of tree or bush, possibly manzanita. Courtesy Bancroft Library*

CHAPTER FIVE

The Buelna Family—
Rancho de San Francisquito

Antonio (or Antonino) Buelna, the original grantee of the rancho where Stanford's main campus is today, has been variously identified as a soldier, Indian fighter, spy, the Patrick Henry of the Alvarado revolt and, in the words of H. H. Bancroft, premier chronicler of California history, "an ignorant and commonplace man."

The land Buelna owned was called Rancho de San Francisquito. The 1471 acre rancho, a rather small one, was granted to him in 1839 by Governor Juan Alvarado. Buelna died shortly thereafter, and the land passed to his widow who then remarried.

By the 1850s, squatters had begun to occupy various portions of the property, resulting in Rancho San Francisquito's being involved in more legal battles than many larger holdings. Between 1852 and 1862 at least 20 people reputedly owned or claimed portions of it. In 1863 the litigation ended because George Gordon, a wealthy San Franciscan, bought out the squatters and the Buelna heirs and proceeded to create a country estate for himself, which he subsequently sold to Leland and Jane Stanford.

Prior to owning his rancho, Buelna played an active role in California's history in the 1830s when there were a mere 2000 or 3000 Spanish/Mexican Californios in all of California. He was an officer in the army, charged with putting down revolts and leading expeditions against foreigners and Indians. He sat in the legislature for more than a decade, and he emerged as one of four leaders of an 1836 insurrection designed to throw Governor Nicolas Gutierrez out of office.

Feuding among various factions had become a way of life in California by the 1830s. Should power be in Mexico City or Monterey? Should military or civil authorities have more power? Buelna gave a speech reminiscent of the stirring words of Patrick Henry, stating that if Governor Nicolas Gutierrez wouldn't call regular sessions of the legislature and allow it power, then California should become a free and independent country.

Since Gutierrez wasn't responsive to these demands, Juan Alvarado, Buelna and their followers decided to take action. The revolt began. Off to Monterey went a supporting group with a cannon (and one cannonball) to lay seige to the governor's quarters and enforce their demands. They practiced with their ordnance all night, and next morning the cannonball found its mark on the porch of Gutierrez's military commandant's home. As Buelna and the others were planning a rifle attack to follow up the cannonball, Gutierrez surrendered.

The revolt had succeeded. Buelna's friend and co-leader Juan Bautista Alvarado became governor, and Buelna received title to Rancho San Francisquito as a token of appreciation from the governor. After Alvarado took charge of California in 1836, Californios had more power to govern themselves in the remaining years of Mexican rule.

Buelna probably camped on his land or occupied a rough shack at first. He then built a small, three-room adobe, 12 to 14 yards long, about 50 yards from the bank of San Francisquito Creek, near the most northerly point of today's Stanford Golf Course. There was a small garden between the house and the creek. It must have been a pleasant spot, ideal for a quiet retirement.

According to an article in the *California Historical Society Quarterly,* in 1840 Buelna was once again called into service by Governor Alvarado. The governor, having heard numerous rumors about the growing numbers of Yankees taking up residence in California and their plans to overthrow him, became involved in a plot to invite these unwelcome new residents to a feast and, in the midst of the festivities, shoot them down.

Fearing that the foreigners had learned of the plan, Alvarado sent Buelna on a spy mission to mingle with them and find out what they knew. Sure enough, they had heard of the planned massacre and promised return fire if assaulted. Buelna's best assurances to the Yankees that there were no grounds for fear went unheeded. They ordered him to leave. Realizing that his persuasions were useless, he and the others cancelled the massacre plans.

Buelna lived for only three years after receiving Rancho de San Francisquito. He served as *juez de paz* (justice of the peace) in San Jose from at least October of 1841 until his death in November of 1842. He kept a few hundred head of cattle that roamed through the thickets. He raised some melons and corn. He built a road between his other rancho, San Gregorio, near the coast, and San Francisquito, the first road in San Mateo County to cross the outer coast range. Across this road he brought half-ton rawhide bags of tallow to ships waiting in the bay.

Conflicting information obscures the truth about the Buelna children. Most historians report no natural children and two adopted ones. Marie Northrop, an expert on early Spanish/Mexican genealogy in California, reports in her book *Spanish-Mexican Families of Early California* three natural children: Antonio who died in 1816 immediately after birth, Juan Bautista who was born about 1817 and who died in 1844, and Maria Concepcion for whom Northrop found no vital statistics. (An Encarnacion Buelna is entered in the Mission Santa Clara baptismal book as being born on April 18, 1841 to Maria Josefa Briones and Antonio Buelna.) Perhaps she is the adopted daughter. It is probably Juan Bautista's son, also named Juan Bautista, (Antonio and Maria Concepcion's grandson), who has been considered the adopted son. The second Juan Bautista Buelna was baptized on December 13, 1844, just three months after his father's death. He spent his later years as a gardener in the new town of Palo Alto.

After her husband's death, Senora Buelna had about ten more years left on her land. She stayed on in the adobe and tended to affairs of the rancho. In 1844 she married a widower from Monterey, Francisco Rodriguez, father of seven children who opposed the marriage at first, but the new household settled down and appeared to live a quiet and happy life. Jesus, the eldest Rodriguez son, built his own house nearby and lived there for ten years.

Francisco Casanueva

In the mid 1850s the tranquil life at the rancho ended. The trouble began with the appearance of a cordial, high-spirited man who never came visiting with empty hands. He became a friend to several of the rancheros, charming them with liberal quantities of alcohol. His name was Francisco Casanueva. He was an ex-consul from Chile and a San Francisco lawyer.

Perhaps he found Rodriguez more naive and gullible than the others. During one visit, when Rodriguez and his son Jesus were "roaring drunk" on liquor generously supplied by their guest, Casanueva produced a document which he called a lease. He convinced Rodriguez to sign it. Actually it was a deed to the entire rancho. Despite various attempts by Rodriguez to retrieve his land, Casanueva owned it in the eyes of the law. It cost him about one dollar and a bottle of whiskey.

At about the same time another event occurred which ended the San Francisquito era even more decisively than Casanueva's deed. The Buelnas' adopted son Juan Buelna, (or grandson) who was perhaps 10 or 12 at the time, was a witness. In 1918, he recounted the facts as he remembered them to local historian and reporter Cora Baggerly Older.

For many years Rodriguez and a neighbor, Geronimo Mesa, hadn't liked one another. Mesa was the son-in-law of Rafael Soto and an uncle of the Greers, who had settled in Woodside. One dark night in September 1855, Mesa was coming down what is now Sand Hill Road on his way home from the Greer Ranch. When he reached the spot near today's 2400 San Hill Road he met Rodriguez and the boy, Juan.

The men began arguing, over what the boy couldn't hear. Their anger grew, and a vicious struggle followed. The frightened boy watched Rodriguez draw his sword, which he always carried, stab Mesa and throw his body into a nearby gully. Rodriguez rejoined the boy without a word of explanation or apology, and they returned home.

Next morning a neighbor reported Mesa dead. The Rodriguezes sold everything they could to raise money so that Don Francisco could escape to Mexico. According to Cora Older, the rancho lands were sold to greedy Americans for a song. Years later, when he felt the danger of prosecution was over, Rodriguez returned from Mexico, poor and old. He lived the remaining years of his life near Watsonville.

The Squatters Move In

All during these years squatters were occupying parts of the rancho, but they didn't seem to worry Francisco and Maria Concepcion Rodriguez. The Californios didn't consider the land as valuable as the Yankee foreigners did. Mostly the squatters seem to have been honest men who came to establish homes and trades. The land looked empty and it was tempting. By the 1850s California was part of the United States, and there was great uncertainty about land titles in the first half of the decade. Enter-

Juan Buelna (b.1844) on the site of the Buelna adobe. This Juan Buelna is probably the grandson of Antonio Buelna. In 1918 he described the murder of Geronimo Mesa to Cora Baggerly Older; he worked as a gardener in Palo Alto. Courtesy Palo Alto Historical Association

prising young men hoped the courts would declare the Mexican ranchos open for settlement. So they settled in.

Thomas Bevins, a printer from New York, claimed land where the cactus gardens and the mausoleum are today. He cleared about forty acres, planted wheat, then sold out and went to work for a San Francisco newspaper.

Jerry Eastin was a young married man who farmed and had a blacksmith shop made of wood with a shake roof on Eucalyptus Avenue near the Stanford Museum. There was a big demand for lumber wagons, which became his specialty. He did all of his work by hand and sold the wagons for $200 or $300 each.

William Little squatted near the very site where the Stanfords built their mansion, where the Children's Hospital at Stanford is located today.

Sandy Wilson, a blue-eyed, husky Virginia bachelor,

occupied a portion of the land until 1861 when he disposed of most of his property and enlisted in the California Volunteers. One story about him concerns the genial and flamboyant Francisco Casanueva.

After Casanueva gained title to the rancho from Rodriguez, he occasionally came down from San Francisco to ride the perimeter of his land and flaunt his ownership by dragging a chain behind him. The arrogance of this and the damage to his crops sufficiently angered Wilson that he gave Casanueva a beating during one of these visits.

Casanueva immediately reported the event to the sheriff who came calling on Wilson. The population must have been large enough so that everyone wasn't acquainted, because as the sheriff neared Wilson's adobe, he met him on the road. The conversation between Wilson and the sheriff went something like this:

Sheriff: "Is this the road to the Wilson adobe?"

Wilson: "It sure is."

Sheriff: "Do you know if Sandy Wilson is at home?"

Wilson: "He was there about 10 minutes ago."

Sheriff: "Thanks. I have some business with him."

The sheriff went on, found no one home (of course), and Sandy Wilson disappeared. That evening, he approached his house cautiously and even called out for himself to be sure no one was lying in wait to arrest him. After avoiding the sheriff for several days, he gave himself up and paid a fine.

In the late 1850s systematic clearing of the land began. Large groves of fine old oaks were cut and charcoal ovens appeared everywhere. The charcoal was shipped to rapidly growing San Francisco.

The events of this roughly twenty-five year history of Rancho San Francisquito, 1837-1863, perhaps show some of the chaos in all of California then. By the time Dona Maria Concepcion Buelna/Rodriguez was given the patent to her rancho by the United States government in 1868, the land was actually already lost to her. The document simply meant that the Buelna/Rodriguez family had had the legal authority to sell or give away the 1471 acres and that those who had gained title from them were entitled to keep it. During the years of the United States government's research into the grant's authenticity, the quiet life of the rancho had dissolved into squabbles, subdivisions and litigation. In fact, by 1868 George Gordon, a wealthy San Francisco entrepreneur, had effectively eliminated the confusion by buying everything from all possible owners and was already five years settled

World News

As the nineteenth century approached and passed its midpoint, the attention of the entire world focused on California. Captain John Sutter and James Marshall tried to keep secret Marshall's January 24, 1848 discovery of gold at Sutter's Mill on the American River, but on May 12 Sam Brannan brought gold to San Francisco, and the rush was on. On August 19, the *New York Herald* published news of the strike. By fall, hundreds from Mexico, Peru and Chile had arrived in California. By 1849, 77,000 Forty-Niners were at work. In the next seven years, California's population grew from 15,000 to 300,000; the gold fields yielded $450 million.

The area that was to become Palo Alto remained quiet, except for a few stragglers who gave up the search for gold or who, recognizing that the need for lumber in San Francisco could bring wealth, came to cut timber in the hills. In 1850, daily stage coach service between San Francisco and San Jose began. The fare was $32, and the trip took nine hours.

Meanwhile, Garibaldi's redshirts fought in Italy in support of the Roman republic. Louis Napoleon ended France's Third Republic. Great Britain annexed the Punjab, unrest and rebellion disrupted Hungary, and civil war in China killed twenty or thirty million souls. In 1853, the Crimean War began.

Even without military strife, life could be hard in the mid- 1800s. In 1850, only half the children born in the United States survived to age five. There was famine in Europe; several countries erased duties on food imports. Cholera epidemics in London killed thousands; in 1849, cholera carried by gold seekers heading for California wiped out the leadership of the Comanches in the Texas panhandle. In 1851, citizens of Ireland suffered widespread blindness resulting from malnutrition during the potato famine which began in 1846. In 1853, a yellow fever outbreak in New Orleans killed 7800, and the steamer *Jenny Lind* exploded in San Francisco Bay off today's Redwood City, killing and wounding 31 people.

In 1850, the year of a new fugitive slave act, there were 1.8 million slaves in the southern United States. Arguments over slavery were rampant; convictions for aiding escaping slaves continued as Harriet Tubman and countless others operated the Underground Railway.

Women were beginning to seek opportunities for themselves other than as wife and mother. In 1848, a women's rights convention in Seneca Falls, New York, introduced "bloomers," full-cut trousers for women. In 1849, Elizabeth Blackwell, the first U. S. woman M.D., graduated from medical school. In 1850, the first national women's rights convention met in Worcester, Massachusetts. In 1853, a Massachusetts constitutional convention received a petition to grant women's suffrage.

Stephen Foster's songs were on everyone's lips. *Lohengrin* and *Il Trovatore* were performed for the first time. Jenny Lind, the Swedish Nightingale, toured America, earning $1000 per night. Marx and Engels issued *The Communist Manifesto.* Elizabeth Barrett Browning wrote *Sonnets from the Portuguese;* Walt Whitman, *Leaves of Grass.* It was the time of *The Scarlet Letter, Moby Dick, Camille, Tanglewood Tales* and *Walden.* But it was Harriet Beecher Stowe's *Uncle Tom's Cabin* that electrified the nation.

Creativity and innovation brought technological advances. Telegraph lines were going up between New York and Chicago. In 1849, French physicist Armand Fizeau calculated the speed of light, and Joseph Monier patented reinforced concrete containing iron bars, paving the way for high rise buildings. In 1852, Elisha Otis invented the safety elevator. Railroads were expanding rapidly; in 1853, a survey began to establish the best transcontinental route. Forty clipper ships were built and began plying between the east coast and California. In 1854, the *Flying Cloud* sped from New York to San Francisco in 89 days, a record that stood for 135 years, until *Thursday's Child* sailed through the Golden Gate in February, 1989 after a voyage of eighty-one days. Inventions of the mid-1800s include the Bunsen burner, Singer sewing machines, the safety pin, the safety match, and the potato chip.

And in 1853, the year Commodore Matthew Perry opened ports in Japan to world trade and the year the first telegraph line between San Francisco and San Jose was completed, James Otterson opened his roadside inn in the midst of the ranchos on the land that became Palo Alto.

Chapter Notes

Roy Ballard provides the best information about the Buelnas, their rancho, and the squatters. His work is in the Stanford University Archives, and in the Stanford *Sequoia*, May 1895.

H. H. Bancroft includes the family in Volumes II, III, and IV of his *History of California.* It is in volume 2, page 735 that he calls Antonio Buelna ignorant and commonplace.

Marie Northrop has the Buelna genealogy in her excellent volumes *Spanish/Mexican Families in Early California.* Another genealogical reference of great importance is *Some Alta California Pioneers and Descendants,* commonly referred to as the "Mutnick Records." It was compiled at St. Mary's College by Brother Henry and Dorothy Mutnick. Many Buelna family milestones are recorded in the Santa Clara Mission records. Inconsistencies and missing data, however, obscure their story.

Cora Baggerly Older focused on the Buelnas in several "When San Jose Was Young" columns in February and March of 1918. The eyewitness account of Geronimo Mesa's murder is substantiated by Ballard's earlier research. Mesa's death register at Santa Clara Mission records he was "killed by an enemy."

The more modern histories briefly include the Buelnas. *Historic Spots in California* and Wood's *History of Palo Alto* are the most complete.

Interesting accounts of the Alvarado Revolt and the "Graham Affair," including Buelna's role, can be found in Bancroft's *History of California,* Volumes III and IV, and in the *California Historical Society Quarterly,* December, 1936. "The Journal of a Crazy Man" by Albert Morris (*California Historical Society Quarterly,* May and September 1936) recounts the Yankee assassination plan.

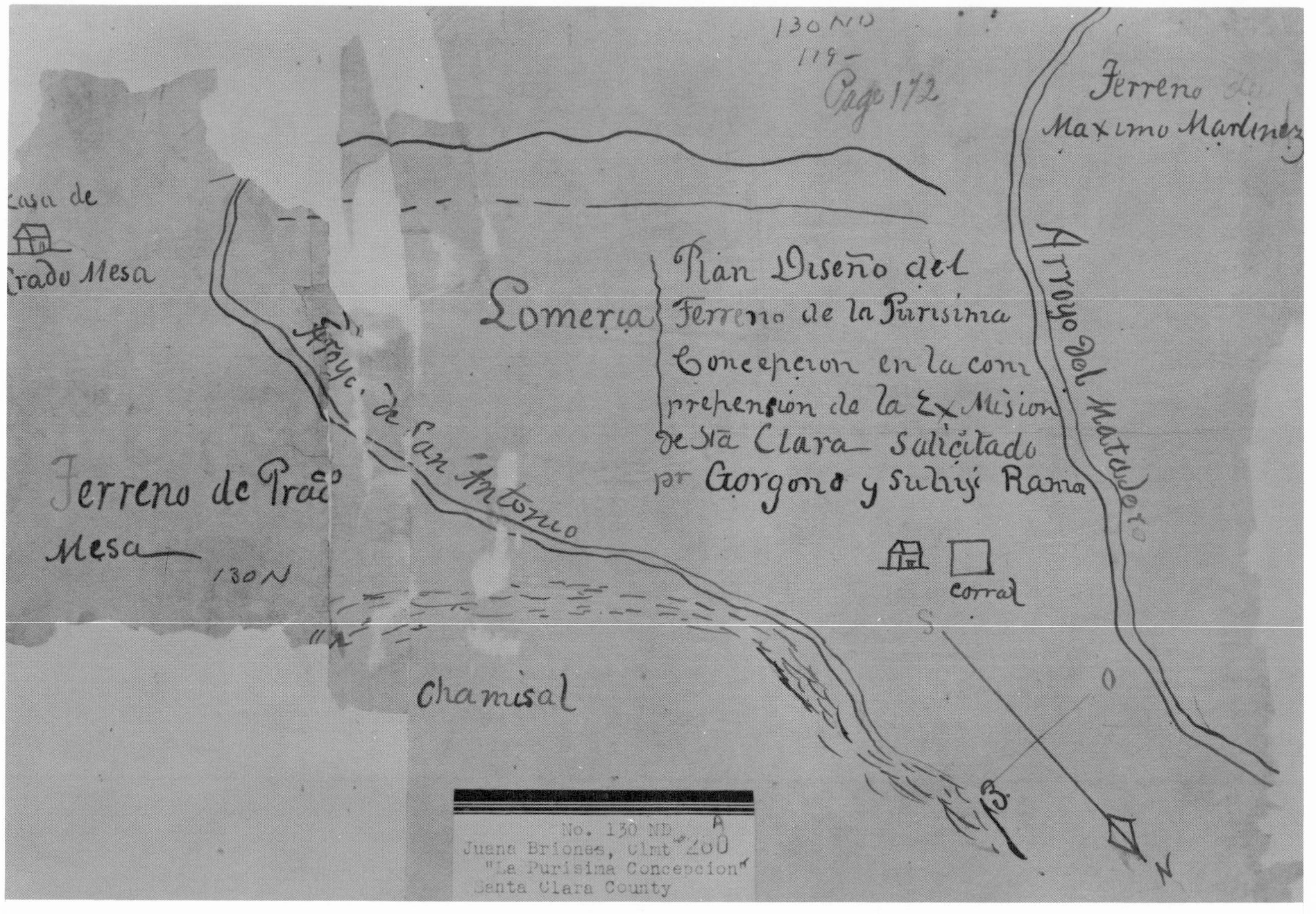

This tattered map is easier to decipher than those of the other ranchos, possibly because Juana Briones knew better what was needed. The house and lands of Prado Mesa are shown at left; across San Antonio Creek is Lomeria, or hills, today's Los Altos Hills. The legend at center reads "Plan Diseño of the Lands of La Purisima Concepcion in the understanding of the Mission Santa Clara, solicited [originally] by Gorgonio and his son Ramon." Across Matadero Creek is the property of Maximo Martinez (today's Portola Valley). Courtesy Bancroft Library

CHAPTER SIX

Juana Briones—Rancho La Purisima Concepcion

Juana Briones was perhaps the most famous California woman of her time. She was so well known that the original name of North Beach in San Francisco was "La Playa de Juana Briones"—Juana Briones Beach. Although her story really belongs to Los Altos Hills, she deserves a small place in the history of Palo Alto. There is a park named for her on Arastradero Road at Clemo Avenue, and a school at 4100 Orme in Barron Park. There are streets in Los Altos Hills—Purisima, Concepcion, Manuela, and Miranda—which take their names from her family and rancho. Still, her name is little known today, and fact and legend are so intertwined in her story that sorting out reality isn't easy.

She owned a 4400 acre rancho named La Purisima Concepcion—the Immaculate Conception—which today is the site of Los Altos and Los Altos Hills. The small portion of her land that falls within Palo Alto's boundaries contains reconstructions of her house, however, portions of which make it by far the oldest structure in the town and, in fact, on this part of the peninsula; it was built in the 1840s. A private residence, it is located off Arastradero Road on Old Adobe Road, and is open occasionally for tours.

The house is a State Registered Landmark. It has been so greatly changed and enlarged that Juana Briones probably would not recognize it today. Because of various controversies about authenticity, it has only recently been listed in the *Palo Alto Historical Buildings Inventory.*

By most accounts Juana was born a twin in 1796 in Carmel, the area's first Hispanic baby. (However, Marie Northrop's search of the Carmel Mission records indicates that the twin Juana born in 1796 died after only a week. Another Juana was born to the same family in 1802 or 1803. Northrop believes it is she who became the owner of La Purisima Concepcion.)

In 1820 she married a soldier, Apolinario Miranda, in Yerba Buena, the old name for San Francisco, and they obtained a land grant there. Their marriage wasn't a happy one; court records suggest that she was a battered wife.

In 1844 she sent a letter to the Bishop in Santa Barbara asking for a separation; she mentioned her husband's drunkenness, unsavory companions and failure to provide. She signed the letter not with her name, but with a cross, suggesting that she was probably illiterate. She left their home on the Ojo de Agua de Figueroa grant at the edge of the Presidio with her six or seven (or eight) children, built an adobe house of her own at what is now Powell and Filbert, in San Francisco, the first private home built between the Presidio and the Mission.

William H. Thomes, an American sailor who knew Juana, wrote about her in 1884 in his book *On Land and Sea.* Calling her a bright, vivacious senora whose voice could be heard from afar scolding her servants and exhorting them to do many things at the same time, he wrote:

> She always welcomed me with a polite good morning and a drink of fresh milk and then scolded her servants in a shrill voice as though she desired to infuse in them much of her own activity ... If the men had had some of the energy of that buxom, dark-faced lady, California would have been a prosperous state even before it was annexed to this country, and we would have had to fight harder than we did to get possession.

She was called the "Widow Briones" even before her ex-husband died in 1844. She sold milk and vegetables and offered a refuge to deserting sailors in the busy port, stowing them in her loft until they could be safely sent on. Her nursing skills, knowledge of medicinal herbs and good-hearted kindness made her famous among sailors from many countries.

In the mid-1840s she bought La Purisima Concepcion from Jose Gorgonio and his son Jose Ramon, Indians who had received the initial grant

A Day In the Life Of 1852

Let's imagine what a typical day was like on this land before it became Palo Alto. We can select a warm summer day in about 1852. The Mexican War was over, and California was in the hands of the United States. A little golden nugget had been discovered at Sutter's Mill, and people had rushed in from the world over. The western foothills were being logged so that San Francisco could be built, but the flatland at the western edge of the bay hadn't seen too much change. The rancho era which had so recently begun was already ending, but the main characters didn't yet realize it.

We can begin the day down at the Robles adobe near the intersection of today's Alma/San Antonio overpass. Don Secundino had built a log corral there to entertain family, friends and passersby with a very popular rancho entertainment—bear and bull fights. On this particular day he sent his vaqueros out before dawn to capture a grizzly. They killed a steer for bait and dragged it around a bit so its scent would permeate an area near Matadero Creek that bears were known to frequent. As a hapless grizzly approached, three or four vaqueros, expert with reatas (lassos), mounted their well-trained ponies and lassoed the bear with two reatas, one around the neck choking him and one around a hind leg, lifting him partially off the ground. Pulling in opposite directions, the vaqueros immobilized the bear and a little at a time dragged him back to a cage near the corral.

In the afternoon, Don Secundino called his guests together. The vaqueros tied the bear to a bull with a long chain. At first the two powerful animals looked warily at one another. Then the bear snarled, lunged forward with a roar, and the furious fight was on.

The crowd knew the victor could be either—the bear might be agile enough to elude the horns, sink his teeth into the bull's neck and hang on. Or the bull might plunge his horns into the bear's side, throw him into the air and finish him off with a second attack as he hit the ground, stunned. As always, this afternoon it was a fight to the death. The growls and roars from the enraged, suffering animals were horrendous. The dust flew, and the cheering crowd loved it. At last the bear collapsed at the feet of the exhausted bull, unable to rise, and the battle was over.

Laughing and talking excitedly, Don Secundino's family and guests returned to the house or sat under the shade of a huge maple tree, drinking and waiting for a steer to be barbecued on a bed of hot coals. They changed into their silks, satins, velvets and spangles and danced until the small hours of the morning in the second-story, open-air dance hall of the Robles ranch house.

Meanwhile, along San Francisquito Creek by today's Oak Creek Apartments at the northern end of the land that became Palo Alto, another characteristic rancho event was taking place, one of quite a different tempo. The Rodriguez family of Rancho de San Francisquito were washing clothes. Early in the morning Dona Maria Concepcion had instructed their Indian servants to load the family laundry onto the rough, two-wheeled carts called *carretas* and drive to a ford on the creek. The clothes were washed and hung on bushes to dry. Between chores, the women sat under the oaks and visited with their friends from the Martinez rancho which occupied today's Portola Valley.

Around sundown stringy beef that had been roasting all afternoon was ready to eat, and Senor Rodriguez joined the crowd for an evening's entertainment. Since the whole washday process took more than a full day, everyone enjoyed the opportunity to dance in the moonlight to the don's violin. When the clothes were dry, the carretas were loaded again, and everyone returned home to the ranch house, which sat near where Willow Road crosses San Francisquito Creek.

So on a warm summer night in 1852, fandango music drifted toward the stars from two different places on the land that has become Palo Alto. Although there were faint lights shining from a few squatters' cabins and from the Soto house along the Embarcadero, the land was mostly dark. But this wasn't Alta California, a lonely outpost of Mexico, any longer. This was California, a two-year-old state of the United States, and the evening's breezes were bringing changes faster than any of the dancers could have guessed.

from Governor Alvarado in 1840. Her purchase price for the 4400 acres was $300. She loaded her children and her heavy furniture onto *carretas* and started a new life.

For the next fifty years she lived a quiet life in her house on Old Adobe Road and in her daughter's house, which stood at Page Mill Road and Birch Street, where a condominium complex is now located. She either enlarged the existing house on the rancho or built a new one of her own, added several outbuildings, ministered to the sick, and was sought as a midwife. It is said that she believed in the curative powers of mudbaths. Her most famous patient was allegedly the bandit Joaquin Murietta. Supposedly, during the few days he remained at the rancho for treatment he buried treasure somewhere nearby, but it has never been found.

Despite probably not being literate, Juana Briones was a shrewd and careful businesswoman. In addition to independently petitioning for her own property in San Francisco and buying La Purisima Concepcion, she bought three rooms in a long adobe in Santa Clara and a lot in Mayfield near her daughters' houses. In each case authorizations and paperwork were so meticulous that Juana wasn't subject to the prolonged litigation that plagued so many Californios once the United States took over. Ownership of her rancho was confirmed to her by the United States government in 1856. There is only one record of her involvement in a land dispute.

There are no known pictures of Juana Briones; this is an artist's conception, drawn by Robert Gebing, based on a description and a picture of a niece. From Los Altos Hills, *by Florence Fava (1976). Courtesy Gilbert Richards*

Juana Briones was a woman alone in a day when that was unusual. She enjoyed her family. She raised cattle, farmed her land, and made regular trips to San Francisco to deliver hides in her carreta, three days up and three days back.

A surveyor, one Chester Lyman, included Juana in his diary in 1848.

> We find our quarters at Madam Briones quite comfortable. The family is composed of the widow Briones, three daughters (two grown), two or three boys, half a dozen Indians, two little pet pigs in the cook house and fifteen or twenty dogs ... there are two sick persons in the house, an Indian girl, of fever, and a man, a sailor, apparently a Portuguese, who has a very bad cough.

In her later years, wizened and stooped by age and arthritis, she walked with the aid of a cane. Yet, according to an account left by a grandson, when she became angry, she could rise to her full height, flash her dark eyes and resume her youthful power. By the time she died on December 3, 1889, the buildings of Stanford University were rising and Professorville was opened for development.

Chapter Notes

The various details of Juana Briones' life have been pieced together from a variety of sources. Often, the facts conflict or vital information is missing, weaving an intriguing mystery.

Northrop and Mutnick include Briones genealogical records. Wood's *History of Palo Alto* and Rensch's *Historic Spots in California* offer interesting accounts. Phyllis Butler mentions her in *The Valley of Santa Clara, Historic Buildings, 1792-1920.* Older includes Juana Briones in her 1918 series. Florence Fava gives a thorough rendition of the Briones story in her 1976 book, *Los Altos Hills.*

The accounts of the people who knew her and included her in their books, Chester Lyman and William H. Thomes, are tantalizingly brief. Lyman's diary is included in his book, *Around the Horn to the Sandwich Islands and California 1845-1850,* 1924.

The September, 1957 J. N. Bowman article in the *Historical Society of Southern California Quarterly* has been considered the most definitive biography, yet some of its facts are being called into question by contemporary research.

Most exciting is the recent interest in discovering the real Juana Briones, spearheaded by Jeanne McDonnell, executive director of the Women's Heritage Museum, headquartered in Palo Alto.

Maria Luisa Soto Copinger Greer with her sons Robert (b.1851), left, and John Lucas (b.1852), right, in a picture taken about 1864. She is a link between the Mexican Rancheros and the European settlers, two of whom she married. Courtesy Gilbert Richards.

CHAPTER SEVEN

The Soto Family—
Rancho Rinconada del Arroyo de San Francisquito

Most of early Palo Alto was carved from the fourth grant, Rancho Rinconada del Arroyo de San Francisquito, the "little corner of the San Francisquito Creek." It consisted of 2229 acres of oaks and scrubby brush and today is bisected by Embarcadero Road.

The ranchero, Don Rafael Soto, had a reputation as an excellent Indian fighter, horseman and bear hunter. Supposedly he could identify a bear's path through the underbrush. He'd dig a large hole, cover it with brush and bait, climb in and wait with great patience for an unfortunate creature to come ambling along. When a victim appeared, he would fire from below and add another pelt to his reputation.

Rafael and his wife Maria Antonia Mesa provide a link between the days of the Spanish explorers and those of the modern era. Rafael's parents and Maria Antonia's grandparents were members of the Anza expedition sent in 1775 to establish a permanent settlement in Alta California. They actually passed under El Palo Alto, and by some accounts, camped under its shelter.

Rafael's brother, Francisco, born August 10, 1776, was the first Spanish child born in San Francisco. His baptism was entered into the Mission Dolores records in Father Palou's own hand. Maria Antonia's parents were both confirmed by Father Serra himself, she at Mission San Antonio de Padua in 1778 and he at Mission Santa Clara in 1779.

Don Rafael's connection with the modern era is provided by his daughter Maria Luisa, who married an Irish sea captain named John Greer. Greer became a leading citizen in the early years of California statehood.

Don Rafael Soto's land was granted in 1835, when Rafael was 46 years old. There was difficulty, as usual, gaining U.S. title to the land. The dispute continued for more than two decades, but the Soto heirs received the official U.S. patent in 1872.

Soto apparently lived on part of the Corte Madera rancho along Alpine Road in about 1827 and was later allowed to use a portion of Mission Santa Clara's land after its secularization. It was in a bend in the creek and had been the headquarters of the mission's sheep ranch. Soto then moved north across the creek and hoped to acquire land there. Unluckily that land was part of the huge Pulgas rancho owned by the powerful Arguello family and not available.

So he settled on the 2200 acres that were bounded on the north by San Francisquito Creek from El Palo Alto to the bay, on the east by the bay itself, on the south by present-day Colorado Avenue and on the west by Buelna's Rancho San Francisquito and present-day El Camino Real.

Not much is known today about Rafael and his wife Maria Antonia. According to Mission Santa Clara records, Rafael was born on April 17, 1789, the next to youngest of thirteen children. He married Maria Antonia in 1819, when she was seventeen.

The records of their children are unclear, but there were several, at least seven, and two adopted orphans. Bancroft lists three whose names do not appear in other early accounts. Rafael's will, written in 1839, lists nine and one yet unborn, so there probably were ten children, all told.

In those days the creek was navigable by small boats to where Newell Road is today, and it was here that Rafael built a small wharf. Lumber was brought to the wharf over rough trails which eventually settled into Embarcadero Road, and supplies from San Francisco were deposited there.

The Sotos had a large house on Middlefield just north of Oregon Avenue. Almost no records chronicle their life there. In 1918 a Mrs. Juan Romero reminisced to reporter Cora Baggerly Older about attending balls at the Sotos. There is another report of a three-day party after Maria Luisa's 1839 wedding. One record has the house being demolished about 1889, just before the houses of the new town of Palo Alto began to appear. This same account reports the Soto barn

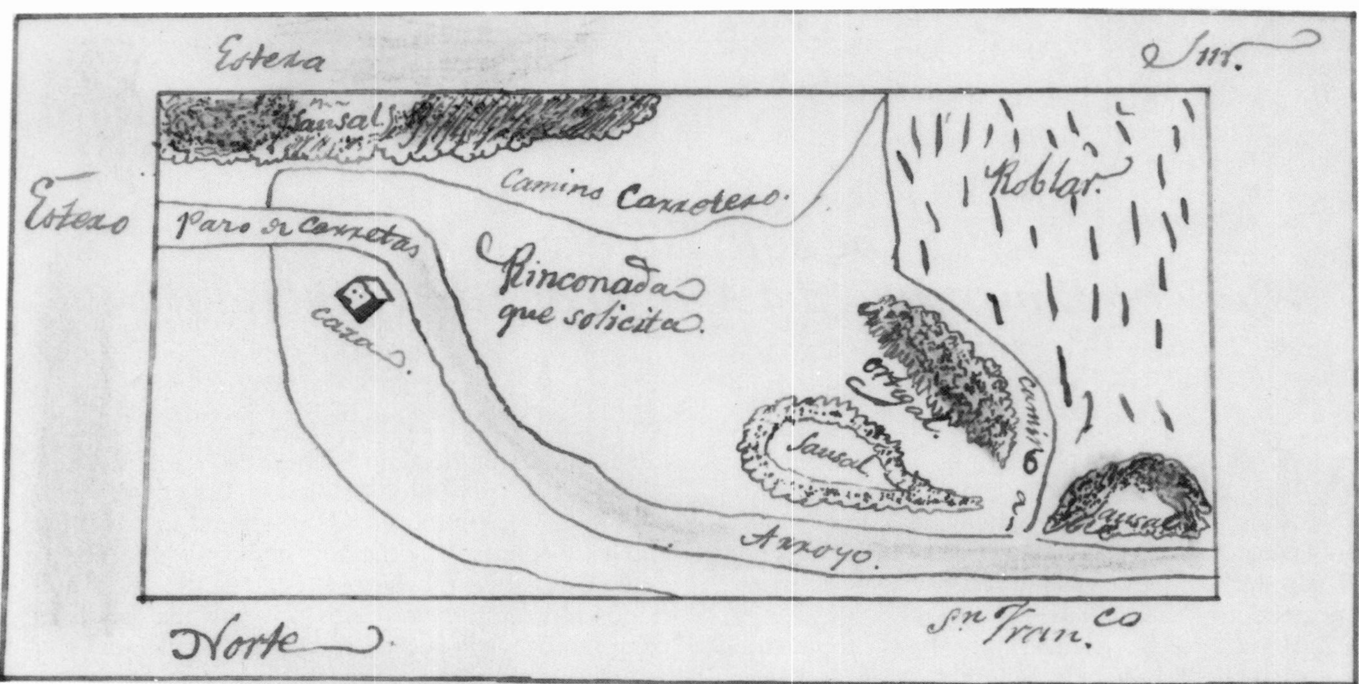

The Soto diseño, with north at bottom and south at top, shows San Francisquito Creek (Arroyo) with a house on the north side, near a ford (paso de carretas). Sausal (willows), Roblar (oaks), and Ortigal (probably poison oak) are shown on the Rinconada being requested. San Francisco (lower right) is the destination of the road (Camino Carretero) crossing the creek. Courtesy San Jose City Museum

Final Portion of Expediente for Rinconada del Arroyo de San Francisquito grant

Whereas Dona Maria Antonia Mesa has solicited for her personal benefit and that of her family the place known by the name of Rinconada del Arroyo de San Francisquito bounded by the lands of Las Pulgas and with the lands of the establishment of Santa Clara, the primary proceedings and investigations having been made according to the requirements of the laws and regulations exercising the powers conferred upon me in the name of the Mexican Nation I have granted to her the land mentioned declaring it to be her property by these presents, subjecting it to the approval of the Most Excellent Departmental Asssembly and the following conditions.

1st: She may fence it without prejudice to the crossings, roads and easements and enjoy it freely and exclusively destining it to such use or cultivation as she may desire but within one year she shall build a house which shall be inhabited.

2nd: She shall solicit the proper Judge to give her juridical possession in virtue of this dispatch, by whom shall be marked the lines, at the limits of which she shall put besides the monuments some fruit or forest trees of some utility.

3rd: The land referred to is one half a square league (of one half a sitio of large cattle) as is shown by the map accompanying the Expediente. The Judge who gives the possession shall cause it to be measured in conformity to the ordinances, the surplus remaining to the nation for its convenient uses.

4th: If she contravenes these conditions she shall lose her right to the land and it shall be denounceable by another.

Wherefore I order that holding this title to be firm and valid a record be made of it in the proper book and that it be delivered to the petitioner for her security and other uses.

Given at Monterey February 16, 1841.

Juan Bautista Alvarado
Constitutional Governor of the
Department of the Californias.

being moved to High Street where it became Paulsen's stable, one of the first businesses of the fledgling town.

Rafael Soto died in February 1839, just four years after acquiring his rancho. His widow Maria Antonia rode to Monterey to register the claim, and she was granted title to the land in 1841 by Governor Alvarado.

Thus Rafael did not live to see his daughter Maria Luisa marry a British naval officer named John Copinger (Coppinger) on February 23, 1839. Their wedding took place at Mission Santa Clara and was the first in the area involving an English-speaking person. Reportedly the bridal pair rode to the church on a single horse and returned to the Palo Alto rancho for a wonderful party which lasted three days and included the roasting of a whole steer.

John Copinger was the recipient of a San Mateo county grant, Rancho Canada de Raimundo, where the newlyweds set up housekeeping. Copinger's exact arrival in California has been a mystery historians have tried to solve. It is known that he was with Jose Pena and Antonio Buelna in the 1836 Alvarado revolt, thus earning the governor's gratitude and his rancho of 12,545 acres.

The Copingers built an adobe which stood at the northwest corner of Kings Mountain and Woodside Roads until 1906. They raised crops and cattle, built a dam and put up fences. Copinger became a justice of the peace for about half of present-day San Mateo County, allegedly closing his eyes to at least one still in his jurisdiction. (Making moonshine was against Mexican law too.) Just eight years, to the day, after their marriage, on February 23, 1847, John Copinger died, at the age of 37, leaving Maria Luisa, age 30, with a large rancho and a child on the way. Maria Luisa returned to her mother's rancho and lived there quietly, until her life changed once again in January 1850.

Captain John Greer

Captain John Greer was an Irish sea captain who, after sailing the world and learning Spanish in South America, arrived in San Francisco Bay aboard the *Wild Duck* in 1849. While men from his ship joined countless others rushing off in search of gold, he decided instead to board a small boat and explore the southern part of the bay.

By chance, he followed San Francisquito Creek inland and happened to meet the widow and heiress to two ranchos, Maria Luisa Soto Copinger, who lived nearby. He decided to stay on in the area, quite charmed by the land and its inhabitants. Greer rented land from Maria Luisa and started raising vegetables.

The two soon fell in love, married at the Santa Clara Mission in 1850, and returned to the adobe at Rancho Canada de Raimundo to live. In a sentimental gesture, Maria Luisa brought with her to the rancho cuttings from rose bushes at the mission. The padres had brought them from Spain and planted them 75 years earlier. One was a pink Rose of Castile, strongly fragrant and favored by the Spaniards for its special beauty. The roses thrived in the new setting and reminded Maria Luisa of her Spanish heritage as she entered an increasingly English-speaking world.

Captain John Greer, 1808-1883

The Greers remained at Canada De Raimundo for about fifteen years and had five children. In the early years of their residency they supposedly traded 1000 or 1200 acres of their rancho to a salesman named Dennis Martin (famous himself in San Mateo County history) for locks, latches, doorknobs and other such household hardware, probably worth about $10.

While the Greers were having trouble proving title to this rancho, Manuela Copinger, Maria Luisa's daughter, married, sold her share of the land to maintain a high lifestyle and built a large house at 3333 Woodside Road whose mortgage could not be maintained. Arguments over the rancho's borders lasted eighty years.

Meanwhile Cap'n John Greer became a leading citizen of Greersburg, now called Woodside. He became a justice of the peace, was involved with

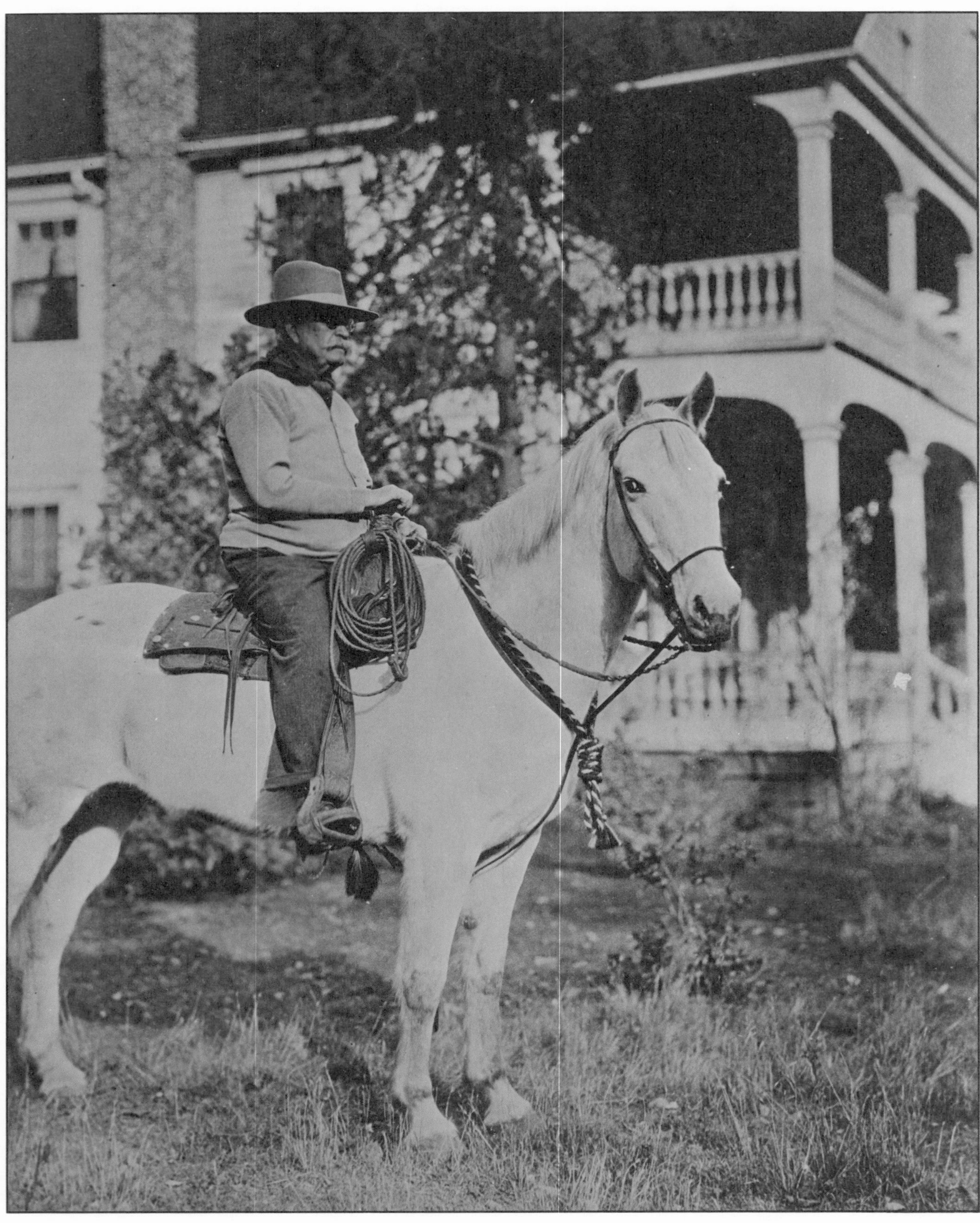

schools and the library and was considered a community benefactor. The family moved back to the Soto rancho in the 1860s and built a twenty-two room house on the northeast corner of Churchill and Alma.

In 1867, because of another of the constant land disputes of the era, the Greers decided to move the house onto property that was definitely theirs. This meant transporting it across the newly-built railroad tracks between the morning and evening trains, the only two there were. They cut a wide path through the dense chaparral on the site of the present Palo Alto High campus and, using horses to turn a giant winch, rolled the house to a site near the intersection of El Camino Real and Embarcadero, where it remained for nearly a century. (It was razed in 1952 to allow the building of the Town and Country Village shopping center.) Maria Luisa brought cuttings from the Rose of Castile at Canada de Raimundo to her new home in Palo Alto.

The house became a social center of the area. There were week-long parties with friends from San Francisco, and two cooks often prepared dinner for twenty-five guests. Their huge, Spanish-style barbecues were famous. In the evenings, the furniture would be pushed back, Cap'n John would recline in a comfortable chair at one end of the room, and the young people would dance.

One son of Cap'n John and Maria Luisa, Lucas Greer, survived well into the modern era. A shaggy-haired man in a black sombrero, he delighted in riding a white horse around the area. Even at an advanced age, he sat tall in his saddle through long hours. He was often a central figure in parades and rodeos. Although he never married, he was reportedly a ladies' man who loved to dance and won trophies in waltzing contests. He sat on the porch of the tall, faded yellow house through his declining years into the 1940s, watching Stanford football fans walk by on Saturday afternoons.

And what was Palo Alto like in the late 1860s? Lucas recalled about six houses, thick underbrush everywhere except along the creek, horses costing $15 to $40, and land offered for $10 an acre. A French Canadian named Charley was thought to be a horse rustler. And Lucas said there was a vigilance committee that would hang horse rustlers if they caught them.

Rafael Soto's rancho was finally patented to his heirs on July 26, 1872. By this time California had been a state for twenty-two years. At one point his widow's claim to the rancho was rejected by the U.S. authorities because they said she had no proper description of her land. The size and shape were unclear, and only the creek was deemed a clear indication of rancho's location. The maps of the grants were indeed vague by U. S. standards. Arguments raged over ownership until the Greers and other heirs despaired of ever gaining clear title.

Sometime in the 1850s, John Greer had met the Seale brothers, Thomas and Henry, contractors in San Francisco who were looking for pasture down the peninsula. One thing led to another, and the Seale brothers offered to try to secure title for the Soto heirs in exchange for half the rancho. Greer agreed, the brothers went to work on the case, and finally, years later, the patent was issued. The Soto heirs were declared the legal owners, and the Seale brothers were given twelve or fourteen hundred acres in appreciation for services rendered. Thus, the Greers and the Seales were the largest landowners in what was to become Palo Alto.

As for the Rose of Castile, according to Joe Greer, another grandchild of Cap'n John Greer and Maria Luisa Soto Copinger Greer, no descendants of the original bush taken from the Santa Clara mission in 1850 remain today. He lived until his death in 1989 in a small house on Encina, on a remnant of land that has been in the Soto family since 1835.

John Lucas Greer, 1852-1945. The Greers built the huge 22-room house about 1862 at what is now Churchill and Alma Streets; it was later moved to Embarcadero and El Camino (today's Town and Country Center), where Lucas Greer used to sit on the porch and watch Palo Alto grow. He led many parades and rodeos on horseback, and actually worked cattle in his 80s. By the time of his death the Greer property had shrunk to 12 acres. Courtesy Palo Alto Historical Association

The Last Will and Testament of Rafael Soto
20th February, 1839

In the name of Almighty God, Three and One, and of the ever-virgin Mary our Lady, I, Rafael Soto, native and citizen of the pueblo of San Jose de Guadalupe in the Department of the Californias, legitimate son of Don Ignacio Soto and of Dona Maria Barbara Espinosa, both now dead, declare that, being in full and complete use of my judgment, I do execute my last will and testament in the following terms.

I declare that I am a Christian, Apostolic Roman Catholic, in which faith and belief I have lived and wish to die. I believe in the great mystery of the most holy Trinity, the Father, Son, and Holy Spirit; that the second person who is the Son became flesh in the immaculate womb of our Lady the Virgin Mary, that He suffered, died and was resurrected to save us from sin. I believe in all that our holy mother the church believes and confesses. I name as my advocates and patrons the Most Holy Mary my guardian angel, and the saint of my name and devotion, to intercede with God, our Lord, that He may pardon my sins and have mercy on my soul.

First: I commend my soul to its Creator and my body to the earth from which it was formed.

Item: I declare that I am married to Dona Maria Antonia Mesa, legitimate daughter of Don Jose Dolores Mesa and Dona Maria Josefa Villavicencio; that she came to me without dowry, and I have not given her any dowry or gifts; and that in this marriage I have had the following children: Maria Luisa Gonzaga, Juan Capistrano, Maria de Jesus, Maria Francisca Cecilia, Maria Dolores, Juan Crisostomo, Francisco de las Llagas, Jose Guadalupe, Estevan, and one still unborn *a quien dejo encomendado mi entierro y sufragios.*

Item: I declare that the following persons are indebted to me:

Don Estevan Yguera, five pesos in silver.

Don Cruz Chavoya, five pesos, four that I paid to Julian Cantua in wheat, and one for the tongue of a cart that he broke.

Don Felipe Soto, five mares.

Don Gerardo Bojorges, one mare under three years old.

Don Natan N., thirty-two pesos which Senor Yncle took in beans with fifty *calabazas llevadas por Jeremias.*

Don Dolores Mesa, four fanegas of wheat which I paid for him to Dona Concepcion Romero, now dead.

Don Mariano Martinez, five pesos, four given to him by my comrade Carmen;, and one that I gave him.

Don Teodoro Flores, two fanegas of wheat.

Item: I declare the following to be my property:

Fifty head of cattle.
Two yokes of oxen.
One mule.
Eight broken horses and a mare.
A herd of six mares.
One cart fully equipped.
Four axes, two with long handles, and two hatchets.
One adze with a long handle, and one short one.
One auger for cart wheels.
A few carpenter tools.
180 fanegas of wheat.
Eight cart loads of corn in the ear.
Eleven fanegas of beans.
Two shotguns.
Three plows fully equipped.

One piece of property which I have in the form of a loan, for which I have petitioned the Superior Departmental Government. I leave Don Antonio Buelna as my trustee in charge of this property.

Item: I declare that I owe the following:

To Rev. Padre Fray Rafael Moreno for the tithes of this year, twenty fanegas of wheat, eight of corn, ten arrobas of flour, and three fanegas of beans.

One mass to Holy Mary and one to Saint Joseph.

To Don Salvador Garcia, ten pesos.

To Dona Concepcion Romero, now dead, four fanegas of wheat and two steers.

To Don Jose Maria Alviso, son-in-law of Corporal Crisostomo, ten pesos.

To Don Pedro Chavoya, two steers.

To Don Antonio Chavoya, seven pesos.

To Don Antonio Sunol, fourteen pesos.

To Dona Dolores Vasquez, ten reales.

To Dona Maria Archuleta, two pesos.

Item: I declare that I bought of William Richardson a piece of cloth, and paid for it three and a half tercios of flour, for which he has not yet rendered account.

Item: I leave as my legitimate heirs my wife, Dona Maria Antonia Mesa, and my children, Maria Luisa, Juan Capistrano, Maria de Jesus, Maria Francisca Cecilia, Maria Dolores, Juan Crisostomo, Francisco de las Llagas, Jose Guadalupe, Estevan, and one yet unborn.

Item: I name my wife, Dona Maria Antonia Mesa, sole administrator of my assets, both those that I possess and those to be received.

I hereby revoke, annul, and declare of no value or effect any and all other wills or codicils that I may heretofore have made, since it is my will that this alone be valid and have effect in law and equity, and to this end I pray the Senor Alcalde of this jurisdiction to give this instrument the authorizatrion necessary to make it legally valid.

And I, the Constitutional Alcalde of the Pueblo of San Jose de Guadalupe, acting as receiver with two assisting witnesses in the absence of a notary public, do certify and declare that this will was executed as written, the testator being in his right mind and dictating its terms; and it shall be considered a public instrument with full force and value according to the will of the testator, notwithstanding the lack of certain legal requirements. It shall be filed in the archive of this tribunal, noting that for want of the properly stamped paper it is written on three sheets of common paper. Twentieth of February, Eighteen Hundred and Thirty Nine. Citizen Prado Mesa was a witness.

Signed: Jose Noriega (rubric)
Signed: Jose Z Fernandez (rubric) Assisting Witness
Signed: Salvio Pacheco (rubric) Assisting Witness

Translated from the original manuscript by F.M. Stanger, San Mateo Junior College, December 1937. The original was in the possession of Lucas Greer, grandson of the testator, and son of Maria Luisa Soto Greer. Rafael Soto would normally have signed his will with an X, before the witnesses; no such mark appears here, suggesting that the will could have been written out a few days after his death, when the need for it became acute.

An Account of a Voyage on San Francisco Bay, by Captain John Greer

Sunday, January 13th, 1850

Sailed from San Francisco alongst with Mr. Jas. McEchin and one atendant upon a propsecting voyage in an open lanch, making with our sail a temporary covering from the Elements. at noon water and provisions on board weighed and made sail in the Direction of San Jose de Pueblo, intending for to explore the west side of the bay a strong breese and Favorable. against a strong ebb tide, Towards dark it was blowing very Fresh and considerable of a swell. night on blowing harder, we determined to run for some creek, being entire strangers on the Route. having no rudder it gave two oars considerable to do for to steer her. a rough swell on the Beam and shipping considerable spray. at about 8 o'clock succeeded in gaining a Lee let go anchor and *Bouncked*, under the sail for the knight.

Monday, Jany 14th

First part calm. Rowed towards a Bluff found [where we] [blurred] at noon. went on shore made a fire and cooked our dinner. in the mean time made a small Excurtion over a Beutiful Plain towards a Ranch known as [space left apparently to insert a name later] here we made ourselves acquainted as to our future Route. at 6 made sail when after rounding the Bluff point we grounded upon a mussel bank. [several words blurred on fold of paper] we made our house up. during the whole of the knight it Rained tremendiously. however we did not get wet little Francisco crawling upon the top of Mr. McEchin heads and points or rather in the division between us. passed the night it blew very hard during the knight but the tide ebed away leaving us high and dry we did not care for it. Towards morning as the tide came it moderated.

Tuesday January 15th

In the morning up anchor and made sail with a fair wind and tide. at noon Entered a creek, upon a large swamp a whale boat coming in shortly afterwards we maid sail into another Creek. as soon as to an anchor we took the small boat and proceeded Exploring made a landing about two miles from the lanch and after considerable dificulty Reached dry ground having waded through water ancle deep for about a mile got upon a car track persuing its Route for about a couple of Miles finding night coming on and no habitation in sight we Returned to our boat. when upon our track a couple of fine deer passed us, and considerable quail started. Reaching the Margin of the swamp at dark, we with a great deal of trouble Regained our small boat and to our no small consternation high and dry. we now directed our steps back towards a wood coasting along we fell in with a River. Made a large fire from Trees and Brush wood and sat down to dry ourselves. the night passed very pleasantly. a little instans ocured about 1 o'clock in A M. [the A is written over the in]. a troop of white horses came Runing down the Car Road snorting and at full speed. I imediately cried out what comes now. Mr. M—not knowing whether or not a Grizle Bear might be about after a litle Turned the horses whe[n] the[y] all made back the same track which releaved my Fears. Towards morning it Rained some and with all the great heat from the fire it was very Cold, and little hungry having eaten nothing since Breakfast Previous to our starting [Here the account ends.]

Courtesy San Mateo County Historical Archive

Chapter Notes

Mission Santa Clara Archives and Northrop's book provide genealogical data on the Sotos, the only rancho family included in Coffman's beautiful book, *Illustrated History of Palo Alto.*

Especially useful for the Canada de Raimundo story are two Gilbert Richards publications, *Crossroads,* 1973, and *Stable Story,* c1970. An extensive collection of Greer papers is on file at the San Mateo County Historical Association Archives, including typescripts of excerpts from his diary. The Greer obituary file at the Palo Alto Historical Association Archives contains much important information.

Wood and Miller mention the Sotos in their histories. Ballard includes them and the squatters in his notes, and Bancroft makes brief comments in Volume V. The elder Sotos' journey with Anza is documented in *Anza's California Expeditions,* Volume 4. *Historic Spots in California* offers the most thorough modern account of the Sotos and the squatters.

In her unpublished history of Palo Alto, written in the 1930s, Frances Rand Smith has facts from interviews with old-time residents. Unfortunately the copy held by the PAHA is incomplete and in disorder.

The San Francisco & San Jose Railroad, one of the earliest in California, opened on January 16, 1864, long before Palo Alto existed. The fare was $2.50 one way, compared with $32 for a long, jolting stagecoach ride. Peter Donahue, iron foundry owner, Judge Timothy Dame, and Auctioneer Henry Newhall built the line at a cost of $40,000 per mile. Leland Stanford attended the opening ceremonies; six years later his Central Pacific Railroad bought the S.F.& S.J. line. Big Tree Station was a flag stop; Mayfield succeeded in getting a depot, and its future was assured. The impact of the railroad was enormous. Besides speed, economy, and comfort, it offered sport, in the form of a hunting car holding 50 huntsmen with guns, ammunition and dogs. This photo shows the Iron Horse at San Jose, about 1866. Courtesy Palo Alto Historical Association

CHAPTER EIGHT

Mayfield

When foreigners began to drift into Alta California in the 1840s and then rushed in in the 1850s, a few wandered into this neighborhood. The redwood country to the south and west was settled first because wood was needed to build San Francisco. One enterprising Scotch-Canadian named James Otterson decided to open a wayside inn in 1853 on land that had been part of the Robles rancho. He thought a good location would be in what is now south Palo Alto where the main San Jose—San Francisco road intersected the road that led into the redwoods. He was right. A little town soon developed around "Uncle Jim's" Cabin. It was called Mayfield.

The town grew and thrived. Bayard Taylor, a young Pennsylvania journalist who passed through California in Gold Rush times, made a second visit in 1859. He wrote in *New Pictures from California* about a trip from San Francisco to San Jose.

He was so astounded by the changes a decade had brought that he includes the following conversation:

> "Where are the nine-league ranches of the native Californians," I asked.
> "They have been swindled out of them."
> "Where are the grizzly bears and coyotes?"
> "They have been killed off."
> "Where are the endless herds of cattle?"
> "Butchered for the San Francisco market."
> "Who cut down the magnificent trees that once stood here?"
> "The Pikes [a derogatory term for an immigrant from the midwest.]

When he reached Mayfield, Taylor stopped at Uncle Jim's, which stood near what is today the corner of El Camino Real and California Avenue. (There is dispute about its actual location.)

> ... we looked out for a tavern. The first sign we saw was "Uncle Jim's," which was enticingly familiar, although the place had an air of "Pike." Our uncle was absent, and there were actually four loafers in the barroom. That men with energy enough to cross the Plains, should "loaf," in a country ten years old, is a thing which I would not have believed if I had not seen it. The house betrayed its antiquity by the style of construction. Instead of being lathed and plastered, the walls and ceilings were composed of coarse white muslin, nailed upon the studs and joints. This is the cheap, early method of building in California, and insures sufficient privacy to the eye, though none at all to the ear. Every room is a Cave of Dionysius. Whatever is whispered in the garret, is distinctly heard in the cellar. There can be no family feuds in such a house.

Reporter Cora Baggerly Older and historian J.P. Munro-Fraser report a livelier atmosphere. They have written that Uncle Jim's Cabin developed a reputation for splendid hospitality. Otterson played host to stagecoach passengers traveling between San Francisco and San Jose, to lumbermen coming out of the redwoods and to vaqueros from the ranchos. Oxcarts and horse-drawn vehicles were often lined up outside. The sleek California rancho horses were tied up waiting to take their masters home. In a corral at the back there were sometimes two or three hundred head of cattle milling about, while their drovers took a break from the overland trek to the San Francisco market. Imagine the mix: Spanish-speaking vaqueros in serapes, lumberman in rough woodsman attire and a sprinkling of gentlemen from the city, all stopped for a spot of liquid refreshment.

A multitude of services was offered at the cabin. In addition to being an inn offering food, drink and lodging, it became the local post office. Sarah Ann Smith, Otterson's stepdaughter, was postmistress. The mailbag was delivered by stagecoach, letters addressed to Mayfield were withdrawn and laid behind the counter, and the bag was resealed and

Uncle Jim's Cabin, the first building in Mayfield, was built by Jim Otterson in 1853 as a tavern to serve stagecoach passengers. Later enlarged, the tavern is shown here in 1874, when the upstairs was used for dances and social gatherings. A bronze plaque on California Street marks its location as a Palo Alto landmark.
Courtesy Palo Alto Historical Association

continued its journey. Anyone expecting a letter simply riffled through the stack.

One room was used for both church services and dances. apparently it was a habit for young mothers to leave their babies in an adjoining room as they danced. A story has survived of an unnamed prankster who once switched all the clothes among these patiently waiting babies and then sat back to enjoy the pandemonium as the mothers returned to collect their offspring.

After Uncle Jim's Cabin came a butcher shop, owned by a Peruvian, Andreas Ramos. Outside stood a live oak whose branches allegedly covered half an acre. The slaughtered steers were hung from its branches, high up to escape flies and yellow jackets. Then C. J. Fuller's general store and George LaPiere's smithy opened. A small cabin was converted to a schoolhouse with Miss Mary Tice the presiding teacher. A Dr. Gunning started a medical practice in 1857. A town was emerging in the midst of the ranchos.

In 1853 Elisha O. Crosby had bought 250 acres from Secundino Robles for $2000 and named it Mayfield Farm. Crosby was an attorney, the one who handled Maria Antonia Mesa's land title case, among many others, a participant in the California Constitutional Convention of 1849, and in 1861 a U. S. representative to Guatemala sent by President Lincoln. According to a *California Historical Association Quarterly* article by Charles A. Barker, his mission was a last minute effort by Lincoln and Seward to arrange for colonizing American slaves in Central America.

It is probably from Crosby's farm that Mayfield took its name. Guy Miller, a Palo Alto historian, traced Crosby's life looking for clues as to why he chose the name. He found none. The best guess is that the land he bought in the springtime was beautiful with huge spreading oaks and yellow mustard, and so he chose a comparably beautiful name for his home.

William Paul, a Scot and a bachelor, arrived in Mayfield about 1856. He bought land west of El Camino, later known as Ayrshire Farm, from Robles' Rancho Santa Rita, and he bought Fuller's General Store. He built a house near Stanford Avenue and El Camino and started raising vegetables and running the store.

Above: The house of William Paul (right), 1809-1891, regarded as the founding father of Mayfield. Born in Scotland, he lived in Toronto, Rochester, N.Y., and New Zealand before settling finally on land he bought from the Robles family. He laid out the town of Mayfield and had it surveyed in 1867; his map appears in the Thompson & West Atlas (1876). His modest house was enlarged after 1875 by Peter Coutts, and still later became the home of David Starr Jordan, first president of Stanford University, who named it Escondite*, William Paul never married; he reportedly once owned a dancing school in Mayfield, and he was a county supervisor for four years.*
Courtesy Palo Alto Historical Association

Mayfield Post Office, July 12, 1886. Lizzie Weissbaar, Assistant Postmistress, looks on as Joseph Spaulding Sr. reads his newspaper. Courtesy Palo Alto Historical Association

According to an old story, he awoke one morning in 1867 to discover that someone was building a house immediately in front of his. Distressed by encroaching neighbors, he reportedly bought forty additional acres from William Ralston, contacted the Santa Clara County surveyor, laid out streets and lots, filed a map and became the father of the town of Mayfield. The streets, Sherman, Grant, Sheridan, and Lincoln, the original name of California Avenue, remind us that the Civil War was still fresh in memories.

The grand coup which spurred Mayfield's growth was the relocation of the railroad station from today's Churchill Street to the heart of Mayfield. Today this stands as the California Avenue Station. Plans for a railroad had begun in the early 1850s, but high costs delayed its arrival in Mayfield until 1863 and its completion from San Francisco to San Jose until 1864.

It took two years of vigorous persuasion to achieve the relocation. William Paul promised to donate land for the depot. Sarah Wallis, who with her husband Judge Joseph Wallis had bought Mayfield Farm from Crosby in 1856, spearheaded the effort. In 1867 a grand ball at the new Mayfield Hotel celebrated victory.

Three industries provided for Mayfield's further growth into a town which eventually had a population of 1,700. A brewery was opened in 1868. By 1881 it was producing around 1000 barrels a year. The thirteen or fourteen (or twenty) saloons which eventually opened brought customers from far and wide. William Page and Alexander Peers brought the lumber business to town. Page married Sarah Smith, the postmistress; the road which bears his name was built to connect his lumber yard with his mill in the mountains. These two men were producing between 500,000 and one million feet of lumber annually in the 1870s. Lumbermen from La Honda and Searsville regularly came to Mayfield for its services. The cattle ranches had given way to grain and hayfields by the 1870s, and the farmers too used the town's services. Mayfield was in its most prosperous decade.

It seemed only logical for Senator Leland Stanford to approach the town fathers when he needed a town to provide housing and such services as grocery stores for students and faculty of the great university he planned. Palo Alto was a wheatfield and Menlo Park had a railroad station, a hotel and scattered estates of rich San Franciscans such as Timothy Hopkins. The Stanfords wanted Mayfield to abolish its saloons so that the town would have an appropriately sedate and wholesome atmosphere. The townspeople laughed and refused—they were skeptical of the grand plans for the emerging university, and they liked their

Above: Thompson's aptly named Pioneer Saloon in Mayfield, one of the taverns that brought Mayfield fame as a haven for tipplers.

Left: Mayfield citizens in shirtsleeves in front of the first Odd Fellows and Druids Hall in 1896. Courtesy Palo Alto Historical Association

liquor. Thus Stanford proceeded, through Timothy Hopkins, to buy land and lay out his own town, named after his own farm, Palo Alto.

The citizens of Mayfield continued their daily lives with the new university town being built beyond the wheatfield to the north. More services and amenities were added. Jasper Paulsen opened a livery stable, a shoemaker began doing business, and a billiard parlor, cigar store and lunch counter appeared. A roadside inn called The Little Vendome offered a friendly welcome. Concrete walks replaced the wooden ones around the depot, Wally's Barber Shop and Griffin's Candy Store. Everyone took great pride in the raising of the flag on the newly repaired and repainted town flagpole.

However, a close look at the saloons reveals that they had a darker side than spirited conviviality or ribald fun. Newspapers of the time often reported instances of violence. Borosi's Hotel was allegedly a stopping place for bandits in the '70s. The Cooney brothers, "outstanding gunmen" according to the newspaper, shot up the place about 1875. A saloon keeper named Granville Millsapp shot and killed a patron. There was a murder in French Hotel, another in Minch Saloon. One hapless young man was shot in the leg during Sunday night carousing in 1890. There were reported threats made against any who complained about the Chinese dens which stayed lively despite raids. It was this reputation that brought transients to town for some excitement and which caused the Stanfords to decide to build a new town for their university.

Students Discover Mayfield

It wasn't long before many of the citizens of Mayfield realized they'd made a rather large mistake. Stanford University opened as planned, and the students soon discovered Mayfield's saloons. In fact the saloons rapidly became part of university lore. But the professors and their families built their homes and did most of their shopping in Palo Alto's alcohol-free environment. The university officials became so outraged by the influence of the saloons on their students that they closed the "West Gate" on the main road from the campus to Mayfield. This, of course, served to further increase trade in Palo Alto.

Rivalry and antagonism developed between the two towns and between two factions within Mayfield. One group had a laissez-faire attitude; they considered Palo Altans to be snobs, resented Palo Alto's success, and insisted they liked Mayfield just the way it was. The other group was embarrassed by the town's seedy, boozy reputation and wanted to change it.

Ellen Elliott arrived from the East in 1891 with her husband Orrin, a Stanford faculty member, to take up residence. She described Mayfield as it was around the turn of the century.

> I supposed Mayfield was a neat, little flowery village ... Albert Fletcher drove ... me ... to Mayfield. I was all hope and cheerfulness, but how soon dismayed, for the village straggled aimlessly about, sprinkled with small one-story houses of the kind we called shanties in the East, and no style or promise anywhere. It seemed predominantly saloons: 14, I believe, with a few poor untidy shops.

The recollections of long-time Mayfield resident Mrs. Alexander Peers still showed her indignation and resentment when she was interviewed in 1928.

> Mayfield was a peaceful place until all the roughneck students from the university came down to racket around and the real estate men started saying the most outrageous things about Mayfield because they were so afraid that someone might buy a lot down here instead of in their newly laid out subdivisions. They said we had nothing but saloons here and that there was so much drunkenness that it wasn't safe for a woman to walk on the streets after dark. They told how our streets were flooded knee deep in water and did everything to discourage buyers. As a matter of fact, our streets *were* unpaved and muddy, but I can remember when the grain field which is now Palo Alto was completely covered with water from an overflow of San Francisquito Creek.

Sometimes this rivalry took virulent forms. This angry anonymous letter appeared in the *Weekly Palo Altan* on February 8, 1895.

> ... Palo Alto would like to put up a southern gate, called the Gate of Destruction, put a 50 foot high screen atop it, then a wall as high as the screen, keep it closed always, not just at night ..."that the sanctity of our town and the chastity of our people may not be contaminated by the degradation of these neighboring tribes [from Mayfield]" ...

Such was the mood and atmosphere after Mayfield rejected the opportunity to become the university's town. Palo Alto was thriving, and Mayfield was stagnating. Joseph Hutchinson, Mayor of Palo Alto for eight years, offered this explanation for the difference between the two towns. He spoke to the Mayfield Board of Trustees in 1904.

> [On a visit to Mayfield] ... forty years ago ... I was particularly interested in [a certain building in Mayfield] because I was told there was a dead

> Chinaman in there. As we came here this evening, there was that identical old building. It had no doubt the same coat of paint that it wore forty years ago, and for all I know it may have had the same dead Chinaman. This is no reflection on the town, but during the last forty years you have grown very little.

In 1933 Jasper Paulsen, the livery stable owner, reflected on the reason for Mayfield's lack of growth.

> ... No liquor clauses in deeds has been the salvation of Palo Alto. In Mayfield I've seen as many as 25 men lying drunk at the sides of the road. Mayfield was a disgrace with houses, streets, and saloons in deplorable condition.

Since the saloons were the main source of revenue for Mayfield, a long-enduring debate developed in town about abolishing them. In 1893 a petition was circulated to close the bar in the Mayfield Hotel. It failed. When the Croall den on Lincoln Street changed hands that same year, the new proprietor promised to try to make it more respectable. In 1894 there was an attempt to pass a law forbidding the sale of liquor within two miles of Stanford University. It failed. There was a petition against wholesale liquor licenses and against Charley Wright's delivery wagon. In 1895 Mayfield petitioned the county to revoke the license of Patsy Green's liquor den.

As the discussions and petitioning continued, so did the saloons. Students, construction workers, transient farm workers and travelers continued to seek their solace and refreshment. In 1901 the *San Francisco Chronicle* reported on their influence on Stanford's students.

> There is a tavern in the town of Mayfield with a back room where beer drinking can be carried on in safety, and this room is the scene of much revelry on Friday and Saturday nights. It is only a bare little apartment with beer steins along the walls by way of decoration and a pile of empty cases in one corner. But tradition has made it the most famous spot in the region of the university. For the past ten years that ugly little room has made university history. It is mentioned in all the student songs.
>
> Oh, there's the road to Mayfield
> As plain as plain can be
> And if you want to see a wreck
> Just take a look at me.
> For I've been to Mayfield
> And tasted of the beer
> And that is why my eyes are weak-
> I need to rest a year.

Ellen Elliott also made an observation.

> Stanford's callow youths frequented Mayfield's saloons more than Menlo Park's. A group had a special table with a cult and traditions, a table where they could sit and slop their liquor and carve their distinguished names on top.

In the next sentence she wrote, "Palo Alto was horribly Puritan."

Then on July 7, 1903, the citizens of Mayfield voted to incorporate their town. The incorporation papers were filed with the secretary of state on July 17, 1903. The faction in favor of progress was winning, and Mayfield seemed to have a second chance to grow and thrive. An active campaign to improve the town began.

One of the first orders of business was an ordinance prohibiting the sale of liquor except at hotels where meals had to be served with the liquor. There would be no licenses issued to saloons and only two to breweries. The ordinance was to take effect January 1, 1905.

That day dawned, and the saloons opened for business as usual, cautiously at first and then boldly. Customers dropped in. There were no arrests. The *Palo Alto Times* reported drunks everywhere. The next day there were arrests, fines and re-arrests. On the third day of the new year, Mayfield was dry. The saloons moved to Menlo Park and so did the students.

It was a time of optimism and enthusiasm for Mayfield. Congratulatory letters arrived from neighboring communities and from David Starr Jordan, president of Stanford. If the main source of revenue was gone, Mayfield's citizens hoped for a more stable source of income, homeowners.

A campaign to attract new residents began. Inducements were plentiful: a chance to buy property at low prices (around $200 an acre) early in the inevitable boom, the unparalleled beauty of the land, greater proximity to Stanford than any other town, and excellent prospects for any kind of farming—cattle, berries, hay, apricots, poultry. Promotional materials were distributed throughout the state. There was even talk, perhaps only partly in jest, of annexing Palo Alto. It was predicted in the *San Jose Mercury* on April 21, 1907 that one day San Francisco would encompass the entire peninsula and that its geographic center would be Mayfield. "Mayfield will be the actual axis of the peninsula," the paper said.

Above: Joseph Rosenblum's drygoods store at the corner of El Camino and California supplied Mayfield's growing population; the latest style seems to be pullover shirts that lace up the front. Maurice and Dan Rosenblum look very pleased with their stock.

Right: A well-dressed, proper family in Mayfield sits down to Sunday dinner with starched linens on the table, soup plates stacked and ready, and a fruitbowl as centerpiece. Courtesy Palo Alto Historical Association

Mayfield was far more than just rowdy saloons: Segbers' and Spellman's Dancing Academy, 1888.
Courtesy Palo Alto Historical Association

Visible changes began to appear around town. An ordinance for cement sidewalks passed in 1907 and one for sewers in 1908. The water system was expanded. College Terrace, Sunnyside and Evergreen Park were annexed. Houses were painted and numbered for door-to-door mail delivery. A Boy Scout troop was formed; the band even got new uniforms. Brochures of florid prose calling Mayfield the Uncrowned Queen continued to circulate.

And then began the saga of Main Street, one final problem which brought an end to the little town. Remember that a feeling of inferiority had existed for many years in the townspeople and that there were two factions with differing opinions about the direction the town should take. These attitudes had moderated somewhat after incorporation, but as rising property values leveled off and growth slowed, old feelings and hostilities returned.

Main Street, today's El Camino Real around California Avenue, was well traveled in the second decade of the century. About $40,000 worth of paving was done in 1912. Because of poor workmanship and constant use, it deteriorated quickly. Townspeople complained that Mayfield was called the town of a thousand bumps throughout the state. Neighboring towns were scornful and made jokes. Coming so soon after the saloon era, this street problem was disheartening.

So why didn't the town trustees just repair the street? A feud arose between progressives and conservatives, and the council was unable to take positive, decisive action. Formation of an assessment district of property owners was voted down. The state highway commission refused to make repairs. An election to give the street to the state failed. A huge argument developed over a plan to disincorporate the street and leave repairs to the county. One side argued that this move would save the town the cost of repairs; the other side was afraid such a decision would cause the town to lose control of water and sewer mains.

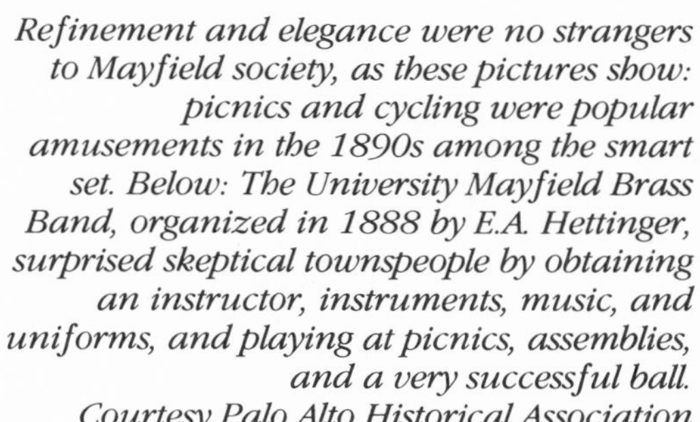

Refinement and elegance were no strangers to Mayfield society, as these pictures show: picnics and cycling were popular amusements in the 1890s among the smart set. Below: The University Mayfield Brass Band, organized in 1888 by E.A. Hettinger, surprised skeptical townspeople by obtaining an instructor, instruments, music, and uniforms, and playing at picnics, assemblies, and a very successful ball. Courtesy Palo Alto Historical Association

There was a stalemate, bitterness increased and the street's condition worsened. And the town government couldn't resolve the problem.

Finally a compromise was hammered out in which the commission, the merchants, the university and the county all paid to have Main Street repaired. Repairing the divisiveness that had developed was not so easy. The sense of inferiority because of the taverns, the statewide embarrassment over the bumpy road, and the endless bickering that an ineffective city government could not resolve meant the eventual end of Mayfield as a viable town, especially with such an energetic, organized neighbor as Palo Alto creeping ever closer.

Mayfield drifted along for another decade, sending out brochures touting such benefits as its pure artesian water and a bigger water system, its new street lights, its better fire equipment and its new town hall. The West Gate, leading from Stanford to Mayfield, was reopened in 1913. Two new industries came to town: The Bayside Canning Company, which seasonally employed 250-300 and produced 70,000 cases of fruit annually, and the Parkinson Brothers Safety Ladder Company, a small enterprise which manufactured a ladder of the brothers' own design.

The Annexation Fight

Unfortunately, the discord and deterioration continued. Town Clerk W. H. Myrick had reported on February 4, 1909 that the town was in financial difficulty. Income from property assessments and business licenses didn't replace that from liquor licenses. There was urgent need for repairs of streets, culverts, and street lights, the many necessities of town life. The public water system sustained a loss despite a study showing it to be well run. A petition to lower the salaries of town officers circulated.

Mayfield's prestige had reached a new low. Many citizens were embarrassed by their town's inability to solve its problems. Now the town argument was: Shall we join Palo Alto? Or shall we try harder to improve on our own? A third faction asked, "Or shall we just love Mayfield the way it is?" In 1918 an annexation attempt was begun and abandoned.

Even the repairs to Main Street didn't last. On July 31, 1921, the *San Francisco Examiner* poked fun at Mayfield, calling it a bouncing Bumpville.

> If the bumps grow any larger, it won't be long before they'll [motorists] have to wind around the edges in order to make the grade over the heights.

By this time Palo Alto had virtually reached Mayfield on the North and East; Stanford University, of course, was to the West. The pro-annexation group had powerful arguments: better fire protection, law enforcement and garbage collection; lower water, sewer and electric rates; less stringent requirements for mortgages; a lower tax rate; and a chance to become part of a thriving town and put petty bickering behind them.

The annexation election was preceded by a bitter, emotional campaign. The *Mayfield Weekly News* was anti-annexation, and it rallied many, especially long time residents, to its side. There were speeches, handbills and newspaper articles. The vote was set for October 8, 1924. Five hundred ninety of Mayfield's eligible voters turned out at the polls. Annexation was defeated by 26 votes. A big party, including 40 cars parading down University Avenue in Palo Alto, celebrated the defeat.

Four months later the advocates of annexation began again. A committee that was as non-partisan as possible was established to study the proposed merger. It reported benefits to both towns from an annexation. Stanford was thoroughly in favor of a merger. This time the vote was set for May 8. Policemen guarded polling places. One woman voter was knocked to the ground. There were accusations of ballot box stuffing. By a vote of 357 to 288, Mayfield elected to join Palo Alto.

Now it was Palo Alto's turn. The anti-annexation set here warned that accepting Mayfield would mean increased taxation and additional bond issues. Stanford controller Almon Roth mentioned that the university might establish a fashionable residential neighborhood in the hills near Mayfield if the measure passed. Emotions were running so high in Palo Alto that people changed vacation plans to stay home and vote. In a record turnout on July 2, 1925, Palo Alto voted to annex Mayfield by the overwhelming vote of 1094 to 441. On July 6 the appropriate papers were filed with the Secretary of State.

The population of Mayfield was 1700, and Palo Alto had 9000 residents. Mayfield had 16 miles of roads (5 were paved), and Palo Alto had 44 (28 paved). Mayfield's assessed valuation was one million dollars; Palo Alto's was eight million.

The Town of Mayfield Passes into History

The little town of Mayfield passed into history. Its name isn't even used as a neighborhood designation any more. What was once Mayfield is now the area around California Avenue. Yet it has not disappeared quite so completely as the Indian villages and the ranchos.

If you remember the bawdy saloons, keep too as a contrasting memory this picture of Mayfield which

Above: Mayfield Grammar School, built in 1867, shows civic pride of early residents. The four-room school was sold and moved in 1898, and converted into a brewery. Right: B. Mayer's Drug Store, with B. Mayer, F.M. Hilby, and Peter Mayer ready to dispense the latest remedies. The bottles alone in this 1888 picture would be worth a fortune today. Courtesy Palo Alto Historical Association

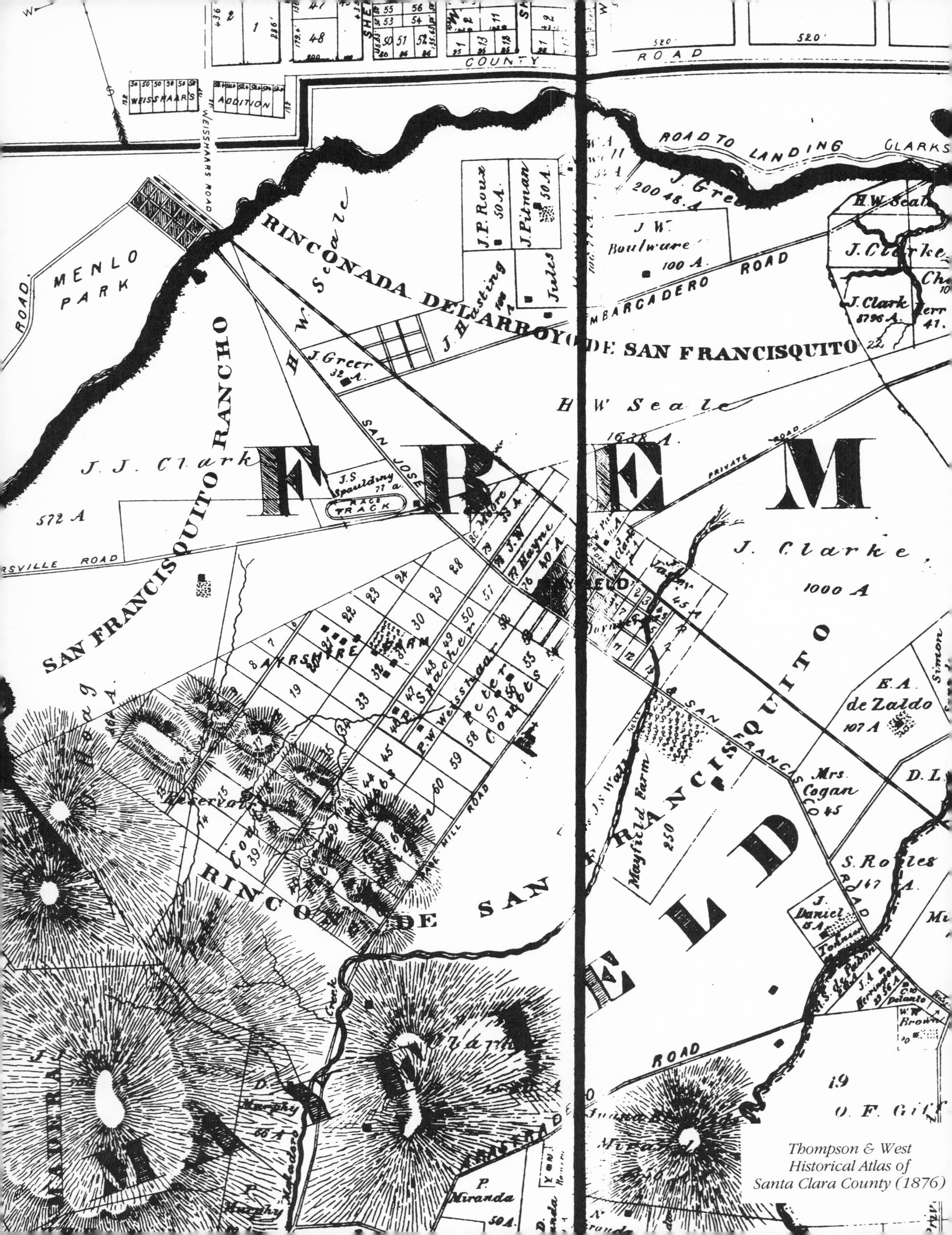

Thompson & West Historical Atlas of Santa Clara County (1876)

Mayfield residents enjoy the sunshine outside the News Depot and barber shop, January 16, 1904. Courtesy Palo Alto Historical Association

Birge Clark, long time Palo Alto resident and architect, includes in his memoirs:

> There were many small one-story houses with rustic siding and shingle roofs. They nearly all had a front porch and calla lilies in the yard. The calla lilies were probably because they seemed very exotic to the newly arrived Easterners or Europeans who settled Mayfield.

As the Rose of Castile was a reminder to Maria Luisa of the Sotos' Spanish heritage, to the citizens of Mayfield, the lilies were a symbol of a new life in a gentle climate.

Chapter Notes

The Palo Alto Historical Association files at the main Palo Alto Library house a voluminous, important collection on Mayfield. PAHA historians have clipped and filed articles on the town from early local newspapers such as the *Weekly Palo Alto*, the *Mayfield Daily Republican*, and the *Mayfield Weekly News*. Occasionally Mayfield news reached the *San Francisco Chronicle* or *Examiner* and the *San Jose Mercury*. Countless articles from the *Palo Alto Times* through the years record Mayfield's events. Especially interesting are interviews with old-time Mayfield residents.

Also on file are various sales and promotional brochures and a collection of letters to and from various individuals. T. B. Scott's undated, unpublished version of the town's history and W. H. Myrick's letters and notes are important.

Charles Barker's June 1948 article in the *California Historical Society Quarterly* provides useful information about Elisha O. Crosby.

The earliest published writer to record his impressions of Mayfield is Bayard Taylor in his 1859 *New Pictures from California*. In *It Happened This Way*, 1940, Ellen Elliott's brief descriptions eloquently capture her impressions. In 1982 memoirs, *An Architect Grows up in Palo Alto*, Birge Clark writes in rich detail of his turn-of-the-century boyhood in the College Terrace section of Mayfield. He also has offered his professional commentary on the architecture.

Joseph Hutchinson's speech appears in the *Palo Alto Times* of August 17, 1904, and Jasper Paulsen's comments are in the *Times* of December 21, 1933. The Nov. 10, 1901 *San Francisco Chronicle* contains the article about Mayfield's taverns.

All the local histories from Munro-Fraser and Sawyer through Wood and Miller up to Coffman and Cogswell (in a PAHA *Tall Tree*) briefly include Mayfield. There is virtually total agreement about the basic facts, a surprising occurrence in historial research.

By far the most outstanding reference is *Mayfield: Its Development and Annexation*, an unpublished manuscript written in 1957 by Robert C. Gobolic. It is housed in the PAHA Archives.

CHAPTER NINE

Five Early Settlers

Sarah Wallis

When Sarah Armstrong Montgomery Green Wallis, age 19, arrived at Sutter's Fort after immigrating to California in 1844 with the Murphy-Stephens party, she sat in on children's classes in reading and writing. From this fact historians have concluded that she probably was not a highly educated woman. Yet she became a fundamental force in the social and civic life of Mayfield and in the women's suffrage movement in the state. She bought the 250 acre Mayfield Farm from the Crosbys in 1856 and built a mansion where she and her last husband, Judge Joseph Wallis, lived for 20 years. Today it is called Barron Park.

Her first husband, Allen Montgomery, with whom she traveled west, abandoned her in San Francisco shortly before the Gold Rush. In October, 1849 she married her second husband, Talbot Green, for whom Green Street in San Francisco is named. He has been recorded as a scoundrel. A personable, popular young man, he came to California with the Bidwell party in 1841. When the travelers had to abandon their wagons and walk over the Sierra, Green cached a mysterious chunk of lead which he had been protectively carrying.

In 1851, respected and wealthy, Green was a candidate for mayor of San Francisco until a shady past was discovered. He was denounced as Paul Geddes, an absconding bank clerk and bigamist from Pennsylvania who had abandoned wife and children and headed west with gold bullion disguised as lead. Escorted to the wharf by a group of citizens, he left town without his wife Sarah, who was six months pregnant, vowing to return with a cleared name. He never came back, but eventually he did send her money.

Sarah took in boarders for a while, divorced Green, and in 1854 married Joseph Wallis, who had come to California in search of gold. He studied law, became a Justice of the Peace in 1857 and a state senator in 1862.

In 1856 Sarah took ownership of Mayfield Farm from Elisha Crosby, apparently in settlement of a debt. To take title in her own name was highly unusual for a woman in those days. The Wallises built a large and elegant home, surrounded with orchards, many trees and flowers. From there she conducted her civic and cultural affairs. The pinnacle was a party in 1877 with President Ulysses S. Grant in attendance.

Although famous for her parties, she was also a champion of various causes. She is credited with bringing the railroad station to Mayfield. She started the first women's club in Mayfield and spoke up at various public meetings, another unusual activity for a woman. She lobbied the legislature in Sacramento for women's rights issues: bills allowing property rights for women, access to state colleges for women and allowing women to practice law.

In 1870 she became president of the California Women's Suffrage Association. Susan B. Anthony herself was entertained at Mayfield Farm. In *The History of Woman Suffrage*, Elizabeth Cady Stanton wrote, "The most successful meetings ever held in Santa Clara County have been at Mayfield." Mrs. Alexander Peers, longtime Mayfield resident, remembered the crowds and brass bands many years later.

Perhaps ambition outran means, or there were financial reverses of another sort. In 1878 Sarah sold the Wallis mansion to Edward Barron, a San Francisco financier, for $35,000. He added another story to the house and more acres to the estate. Sarah moved to a modest but elegant house at Grant and Ash in Mayfield. She died in straitened circumstances in Los Gatos in 1905, six years before women won the right to vote in California. She is buried in an unmarked grave in Union Cemetery in Redwood City.

Today, on La Selva near the site of Sarah's house, there is a state historic plaque honoring her. The house itself burned on Thanksgiving weekend in 1936. When the plat for the sub-division was filed on September 10, 1925, it was named for Edward Barron.

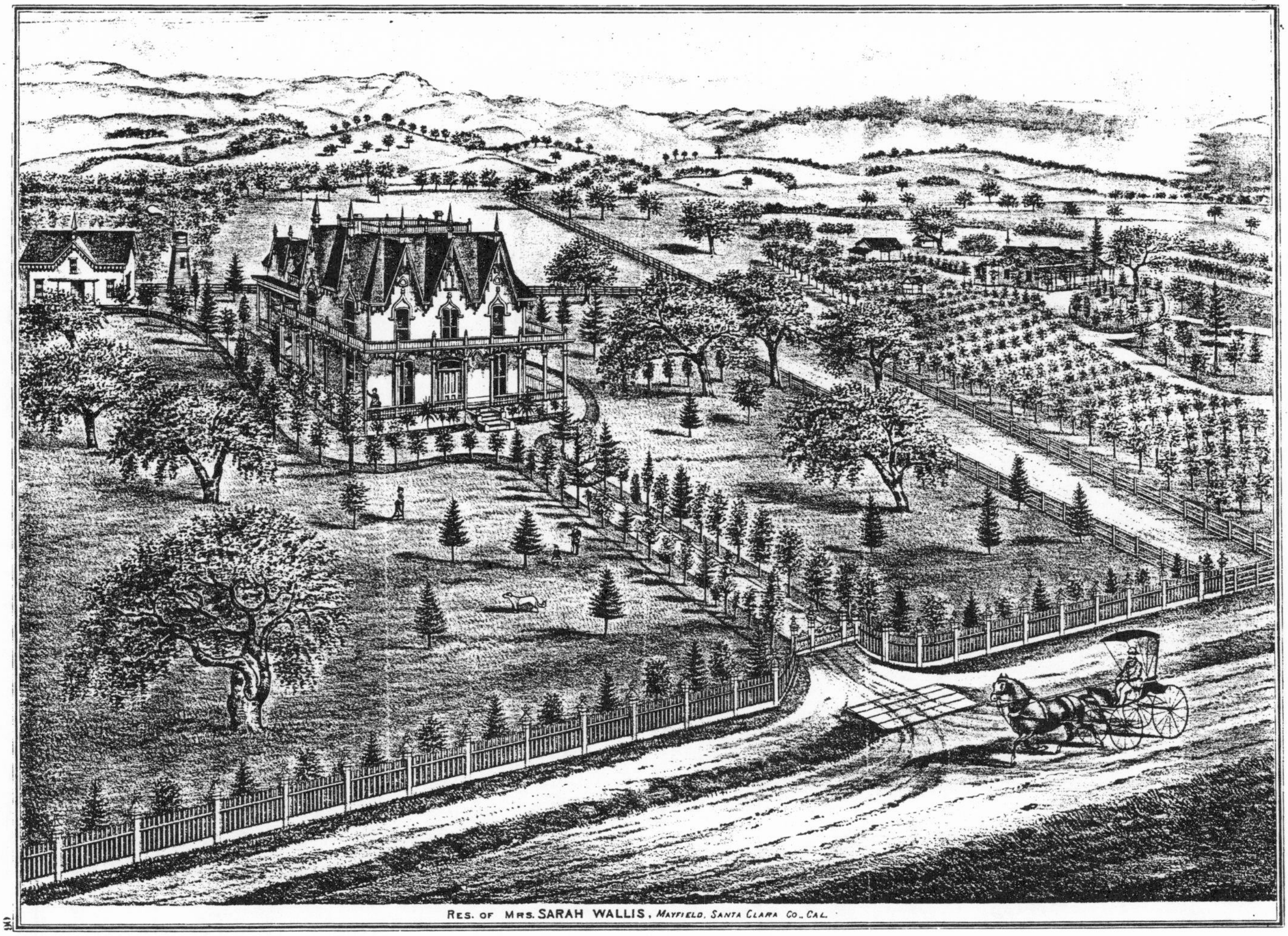

RES. OF MRS. SARAH WALLIS, MAYFIELD, SANTA CLARA CO. CAL.

Above: Mayfield Farm, Sarah Wallis's estate on La Selva Street. The splendid Gothic house, with seven gables and then some, was not splendid enough for Edward Barron, who built an octagonal cupola on top after he bought it in 1878 (left). The magnificent building burnt in 1936; its like will not be seen again.
Courtesy Palo Alto Historical Association

Peter Coutts

No story of old Palo Alto could be complete without at least a brief mention of Peter Coutts, the mysterious Frenchman. He arrived in 1874, a suave, singularly handsome foreigner with snow white hair and a military bearing. He was thought to be about 60, although his youthful appearance and springy step belied his age. It was also apparent from the very beginning that he was very well educated and extremely wealthy. He created quite a furor during his brief stay, and when he disappeared six years later, it was amidst wild rumors which only grew more extravagent over the next decades.

He brought with him his invalid wife, who was rarely seen, his son Albert, his daughter Marguerite, and the children's governess, Mlle Eugenie Clogensen. Altogether he bought about 1200 acres of Rancho Rincon de San Francisquito from William Paul, Jeremiah Clarke and others. His estate, called both Ayrshire Farm and Matadero Rancho, extended from the main Stanford campus south to Page Mill Road and to the summit of the foothills. Curiosity was piqued at once when all the land was purchased in the name of the governess. The rumors began.

He immediately began improvements, reportedly spending more than $40,000 a year. For the family home he converted William Paul's existing two-room, wooden house into Escondite Cottage. A nine-room L-shaped building with four fireplaces, two baths and a 65 foot hall, it was patterned after Le Petit Trianon at Versailles. The walls were covered with French chintz in pale pastel designs on soft gray backgrounds. The oldest building on the Stanford campus, it has undergone many changes and served many uses over the century of its existence, including being the first campus home of Stanford's first president, David Starr Jordan.

Coutts built perhaps a dozen brick barns for his purebred Ayrshire cattle, stables for his racehorses, a dairy, a wine cellar, and a two-story brick building for his collection of rare books. There were poultry yards and pigeon lofts. The kennels for his pack of beagles were situated on the site of today's Inner Quad near Memorial Church. There was a chalet in the Swiss style for a caretaker. At the corner of what became Stanford Avenue and El Camino, he built a race track complete with stands from which to watch training exercises for the horses or a parade of his exquisitely manicured cows.

And of course there was "Frenchman's Tower," which figures so importantly in the legends. Still standing immediately beside Old Page Mill Road, it is 30 feet high, with a few narrow, arched windows at varying distances from the ground, a crenelated top, and no door or apparent way of entry. Local historians have never deduced its purpose. It lent a certain charm to the view and perhaps was the convergence point of a network of irrigation tunnels, or merely a marker for the southwest corner of his property. The speculation was that this tower was a fortress containing an arsenal.

Ayrshire Farm, the great estate constructed by Peter Coutts on William Paul's old farm, had grown to 1242 acres by 1876, when this view was made. Courtesy Palo Alto Historical Association

The landscaping was splendid. There was an artificial lake with uncut sandstone walls, a fountain in the center and arched rustic bridges. A poplar-lined drive led from the lake to the top of Pine Hill where the foundations for twin palatial chateaux were laid.

All this in six years, and then in 1880 Peter Coutts and his family suddenly left. Curiosity was intense. Rumors were rampant: Coutts had been discovered by French secret service agents who had been searching for him because he had absconded with five million dollars; Frenchman's Tower had been built as a lookout to watch for authorities; the tunnels which were allegedly for irrigation were actually escape routes. Or they were underground vaults for his fortune. Or the tower was a stronghold and arsenal from which to make a last stand against authorities. There was half a million dollars hidden in the tunnels. No, there was a million! And the governess, Mlle Eugenie Clogensen ... well, she was actually the Empress Eugenie. (Empress Eugenie, wife of Napoleon III, did live in exile after 1870.) One version tells of French detectives finding Coutts, accepting $20,000 in gold to search elsewhere for a year and then returning to take the Frenchman into custody.

Needless to say, these stories were found mightily interesting by Stanford students when they arrived a decade after the Coutts family left. It is said that both Mrs. Stanford and David Starr Jordan loved retelling and embellishing the stories of the mysterious Frenchman. Generations of student explorers sought the lost treasure. In 1916 one Raymond Bevier reported finding an ancient musket in an underground vault. And that was it for treasure. No other trace has ever been found. Or found and reported.

What is believed to be the real story of Peter Coutts didn't emerge until the 1920s. His real name was Paulin Caperon. He was a wealthy banker and publisher of a newspaper opposed to the policies of

Napoleon III. He and others who were similarly disenchanted with the government left France to avoid harrassment. Since Coutts worried about both his and his wife's health, he had purchased the land in the name of the governess to avoid possible legal entanglements for his children, should both parents die. When the political difficulties were resolved, he took his family back to their homeland and built his chateau on the shores of Lake Geneva at Evian les Bains instead of on Pine Hill. In 1882, in a deed signed in London, he and Mlle Clogensen sold his estate to Leland Stanford for $140,000. Coutts died in 1889 and is buried in Bordeaux.

His granddaughter Marguerite married an American soldier in World War I and returned with him to Los Angeles after the war. It was she who told the true story of the mysterious Frenchman.

Courtesy Stanford University Archives

George Gordon

The name of George Gordon is barely known in Palo Alto today, and yet if he hadn't been a leading citizen of the area for a few years in the 1860s perhaps the entire course of its history would have been different.

Having come to California in the Gold Rush and amassed a fortune with various enterprises in San Francisco, he bought about 650 acres from the numerous squatters and litigants of Rancho San Francisquito for around $250. This was in 1863. He then proceeded to create a country estate for his family.

It is this estate, called Mayfield Grange, that Leland Stanford bought to form the nucleus of his Palo Alto Farm, the heart of today's Stanford University. Had Gordon not consolidated the various properties into one large one, perhaps Stanford would have looked elsewhere for his stock farm.

George Gordon was considered a spellbinder, a promoter, a speculator who developed South Park in San Francisco, the city's most fashionable address in post Gold Rush years and now enjoying a new life as architects and designers move in to restore old buildings. Gordon's origins are shrouded in mystery. There was alcoholism in his family beyond doubt, but whether it created the tragic legend that has existed for 100 years is doubtful.

The legend involves Gertrude Atherton, novelist and daughter-in-law of Faxon Atherton, founder of the town bearing his name. Mythmakers speculate that she used the Gordon family as the prototype for her tragic novel, *Daughter of the Vine.* In her fictional story, James Randolph, scion of a wealthy English family, marries a common uneducated bar maid while on a drunken spree. Embarrassed by the plight in which he has placed himself, he flees with his wife, eventually landing in Calfornia.

They have a daughter, Nina, and Randolph becomes the wealthy developer of South Park in San Francisco. At their country estate, Mrs. Randolph, embittered by being hidden away from English society, not only takes to drink, but repeatedly feeds her young daughter tiny quantities of whiskey until she, too, is addicted.

In the book, tragedy builds on tragedy. Nina tries to stay away from alcohol, but her mother encourages her indulgence. Nina falls in love with Dudley Thorpe but sends him away for a year. She has a baby she adores, and it dies.

When Thorpe is delayed in returning, Nina despairs, grieves and marries a distant cousin, whom she despises, to save Thorpe from what she now perceives as the disaster of marrying her. She returns to drink, the cousin dies, and she and her mother dissolve into drunken orgies. All of this is more than James Randolph can cope with; he ages rapidly and dies. Years later, Nina and Thorpe meet in a San Francisco cemetery, and she dies in his arms. The family and its fortune have been destroyed; their final possessions are sold at auction.

For a century this high tragic melodrama was told and retold as the Gordon story. Perhaps the rumors grew partly from the ghostly remains of Mayfield Grange, subsequently owned by Mrs. Gordon's family, the Clarks. Marcus Boruck in *Illustrated Spirit of the Times* wrote about Mayfield Grange in the early 1870s.

> [Gordon] sickened and died and afterwards there was an apparent fatality attending the place he had cherished with so much care. As the years rolled on, it fell into neglect and there were strange stories ... of the people who lived there [the Clarks]. The flowers and shrubbery were choked with weeds, the house was becoming dilapidated and the ownership lapsed to those who had no eye for beauty.

In 1976, Dr. Albert Shumate did extensive research on the Gordon family for his book, *The California of George Gordon.* He does write of parallels between the Gordons and the fictional Randolphs. In fact and story the fathers were highly visible, successful men. There is strong evidence to suggest that Mrs. Gordon was indeed an alcoholic. And their daughter Nellie did have an unhappy marriage and a baby who died, and she died herself in 1874 at the age of 29.

Gordon had died in 1869 at age 50, just six years after his purchase of Mayfield Grange and three months after his daughter's wedding. Mrs. Gordon died of chronic hepatitis three months after her daughter's death.

Upon her death the Gordon fortune passed to Mrs. Gordon's brother, John Clark, reportedly a drunkard, who died in 1876 at 47. He had married a former Gordon maid who inherited her husband's estate.

Despite these similarities, Shumate found no evidence of the main thrust of the legend: that the mother made an alcoholic of her own daughter. In this case, fiction was probably stranger than fact.

It was Mrs. Clark who sold Mayfield Grange to Stanford in 1876 for $170,000. She returned to her home in Ireland and died two years later.

And who was the real George Gordon, spellbinder and creator of the 650-acre Mayfield Grange that used to occupy Stanford's main campus? Shumate's research indicates that in all probability he began his life as George Gordon Cummings, a "tea and colonial broker." He and his wife, who appeared more educated and refined than a bar maid, came to California during the Gold Rush in a company organized by Gordon.

He accumulated his wealth in a variety of enterprises: chiefly a sugar refinery, an iron works and real estate. He wrote frequent letters to the editors of San Francisco papers on topics ranging from waterfront issues to the Civil War; he was usually involved in some kind of litigation concerning one or more of his interests. He was a speculator of tireless energy, not above perpetrating clever schemes of questionable honesty to further his fortunes. Words such as "knave", "humbug", "one of our greatest citizens", "good-hearted" and "persuasive eloquence" appeared in contemporary accounts of his activities.

Shumate cites an excerpt from the *Bulletin* of August 25, 1884: "It would hardly be an exaggeration to say that from the day of his [Gordon's] arrival continuously to that of his death, compassing a period of just twenty years, he was among the foremost of our citizens for public spirit and business energy, enterprise and sagacity."

The part of the Gordon story that is especially important to Palo Alto is Mayfield Grange. By 1865 George Gordon was one of the richest men in San Francisco. Only six persons or organizations there had larger fortunes than he. He originally envisioned his rancho purchase as a summer home. The family lived there in sumptuous style. They spent freely on clothes, jewels and extended trips to Europe. Their lavish house parties astounded local residents. To celebrate Mrs. Gordon's birthday in 1868, a private train brought 400 of their friends down the peninsula for a large feast in the English manner. The music lasted until 4 a.m.

To Gordon goes the credit for laying out the beginnings of the estate that became Stanford's Palo Alto Farm. He laid out Eucalyptus Avenue, today's Governor's Avenue, brought in water for irrigation and planted a large vineyard. He built the various barns and outbuildings required for a country gentleman. The house itself had high ceilings, broad balconies, fine views and a fountain in front. The Stanfords made elaborate additions to the house which stood on the site of today's Children's Hospital at Stanford until 1965, when its wood provided fuel for the Big Game's bonfire.

We can thank George Gordon for creating an estate that enticed the Stanfords to our area. And while large chunks of the century-old Gordon legend probably aren't true, it is true that within a few short years after the Gordons' purchase of Mayfield Grange, the entire family had died at early ages, and the last of their possessions were sold to the curious who sought a remembrance of the once flamboyant and powerful family.

The Seale Brothers

The Seale brothers, Thomas and Henry, sold the 700 acres that became old Palo Alto when the first streets of the town were laid out in 1888. As were so many of the early inhabitants of this land, they were larger-than-life figures, well known in their era but unknown today. They had land dealings with heirs of the rancheros and with Anglos. In the former case, they were given a vast amount of property in return for a favor, reflecting a characteristic Spanish/Mexican attitude toward land at that time. In the latter case, three people ended up dead over a land dispute, a demonstration of quite a different philosophy.

Thomas and Henry, along with their brother Joseph, came to California via Panama in the early 1850s. They became grading contractors in burgeoning San Francisco, supposedly doing the first grading of Montgomery Street. They enter Palo Alto's story about 1853.

When they were looking for pastureland for their draft horses, they met Captain John Greer, second husband of Maria Luisa Soto, son-in-law of ranchero Rafael Soto and prominent citizen of the area.

The Seales soon learned of the immense difficulty the Soto heirs were having in obtaining United States confirmation of their 2200-acre ranch. The ownership documents weren't clear enough, and the Soto heirs didn't understand the American procedures. In short, they were experiencing the problems that caused California land to be locked in litigation for decades after the United States took over.

Thomas Seale offered to try to secure a clear title for the Soto heirs in exchange for half the rancho. Thomas passed the problem on to Henry, who presently succeeded where the Soto heirs had failed. The rancho was confirmed to Rafael Soto's descendants in 1865, and true to their word, they handed over half their land.

During these years Thomas became involved in another land dispute, this one over land which both he and brothers Paul and Richard Shore claimed as their own. In January 1859, when the Shores began to build a house on the land in question, a heated argument developed between them and Thomas Seale.

Eyewitness accounts differ, but we know incendiary words were exchanged, more people arrived on the scene, a scuffle occurred, either one or two pistols and an axe or hatchet materialized, a dog may or may not have jumped on a participant, but in the end Paul Shore was shot and killed by Thomas Seale. Being a good and upstanding citizen, Thomas surrendered himself and his hired man Alexander Robb to the authorities in San Jose where they were indicted and where the dispute continued.

Thomas Seale, 1826-1907

On March 28, 1859, Richard Shore and another brother, Thomas Shore, as well as supporters of the defendants Seale and Robb, gathered outside the courthouse. After another angry skirmish, Samuel Crosby, a Seale friend and brother of E. O. Crosby of Mayfield Farm, was dead. Posey Fergusson, an innocent bystander from Grass Valley, was also killed.

An investigation after the shootout concluded that a Crosby bullet had killed Fergusson, and Crosby had been killed by several bullets from Shore guns. The Shores fled and were never prosecuted. Thomas Seale was eventually tried and found innocent. Nevertheless, the Shore brothers promised to get even. Thomas Seale left for Nevada and shortly thereafter settled in Australia.

Meanwhile brother Henry, who was six foot three with fiery red hair and beard, married, built a large house on Webster near Oregon Expressway, raised race horses and became a friend of the Stanfords. He had a fish pond stocked with golden carp and a race track near today's Churchill and Waverley. He had a pass, probably for granting right of way across his property, to ride the San Francisco to San Jose railroad and to send small freight and telegrams at no charge. In 1887, the year before he died after a day at the races in Sacramento, he sold Timothy Hopkins 700 acres of his ranch for, according to most accounts, a mere $60,000.

Henry Seale built this impressive Greek Revival house after his brother's exile to Australia, but Thomas returned to live in it after Henry's death. The house, on Webster near Oregon Expressway, later became an orphanage, the Maude Booth Home. It was destroyed in 1937. Courtesy Palo Alto Historical Association

The coda to this story involves the long-standing grudge the Shores held against the Seales. After several years, Thomas Seale returned from Australia to San Francisco, where he worked for Stanford's California Street Cable Railroad. When Henry died, Thomas returned to what was by then Palo Alto and took up residence on the remaining Seale property, still about 600 acres. Rumor was that the Shore brothers were still looking for him, and that for the rest of his life he turned pale upon mention of their names.

According to a manuscript by T. B. Scott, a longtime Mayfield resident, when Thomas Seale died in 1907, Thomas Shore, an old man himself by then, unbuckled the gun he'd worn for half a century and said to his son, "Sorry I never had a chance to use it."

Chapter Notes

The Stanford University Archives holds maps, photos and deeds pertaining to Peter Coutts and his estate. David Starr Jordan writes of him in *Days of a Man*, 1922. Both Roy Ballard and T. B. Scott interviewed people who knew him. The Ballard notes and manuscript are on file at Stanford; Scott's manuscript is in the PAHA files. An unpublished manuscript by Geoffrey Bilson is in the history room at the main Redwood City library. Various newspapers through the years have told and retold his story, notably the *San Francisco Call* in October 1882 and April and May 1908 and the *Palo Alto Times* on September 6, 1935 and July 24, 1947.

The definitive article has long been considered to be one by Edward M. Pallette in the *Stanford Illustrated Review* of December 1925. Today the recognized expert on Peter Coutts is Dorothy Regnery, Portola Valley historian. She has written about him in her splendid book, *An Enduring Heritage*, 1976, and in the *Stanford Historical Society Newsletter*,

Volume 5, Number 3. She has researched in Switzerland and France as well as locally to unearth the truth behind the legend.

Both Mrs. Regnery and Women's Heritage Museum volunteers have done important research on the elusive Sarah Wallis. An excellent article by Mrs. Regnery, "Portrait of Sarah," appears in the December 1986 issue of *The Californian*, the magazine of the California History Center Foundation at De Anza College.

No Wallis photographs, diaries or letters are known to exist. She is, however, one of the few women included in Bancroft's *Pioneer Register*, Volume 4, p. 743. Mrs. Alexander Peers, longtime Mayfield resident, reminisced to a *Palo Alto Times* reporter on June 14, 1928 about Sarah. Older includes her in the 1918 newspaper series.

Thomas and Henry Seale appear in both the Wood and Miller histories of Palo Alto as well as in the Older newspaper series. Phyllis Butler includes portions of their story in her 1975 book, *Valley of Santa Clara, Historic Buildings, 1792-1920.* Eugene T. Sawyer tells of the Thomas Seale trial in his 1922 *History of Santa Clara County* as does the *San Francisco Herald* on April 12, 1859 and on April 23, 1859. In the PAHA files a 1949 manuscript by Claudia Walker, a letter from W. H. Myrick and a manuscript by T. B. Scott contain important information about the brothers.

George Gordon is briefly mentioned in the Wood history and in *Historic Spots in California.* Roy Ballard tells his story in the *Sequoia* of May, 1895. Samuel Dickson's 1949 *San Francisco Kaleidoscope* contains a heart-rending version of the Gordon legend. An outstanding reference is *The California of George Gordon*, 1976, by Dr. Albert Shumate, former president of the California Historical Society.

MAYFIELD DRUG STORE BERNARD MAYER, PROPRIETOR.

GRIMLEY'S HOTEL & LIVERY. PETER GRIMLEY, PROPRIETOR.

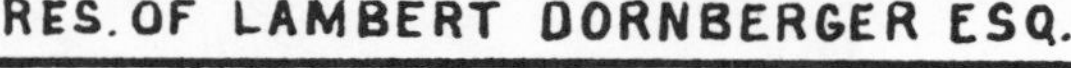

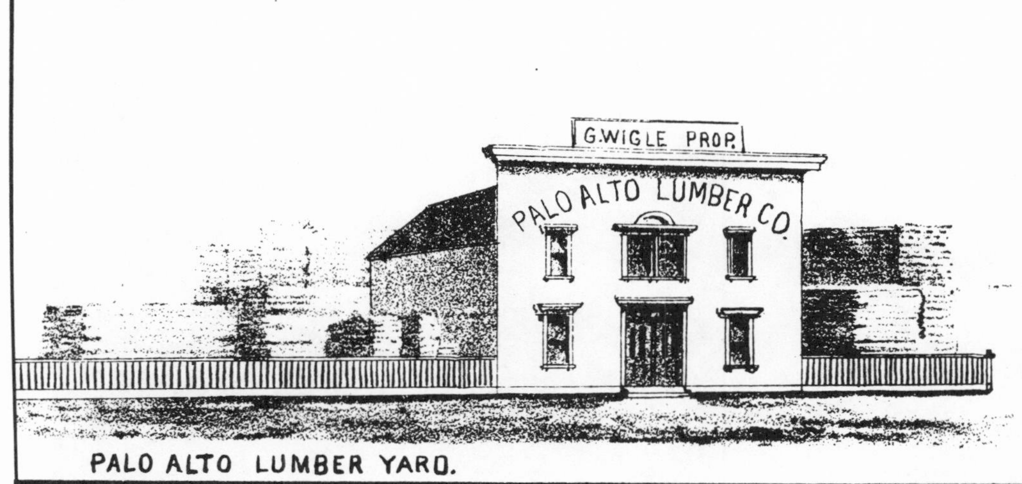

Mayfield had all the amenities by 1889, when these pictures adorned a brochure promoting a new town called Palo Alto (now College Terrace). Courtesy Bancroft Library

Leland Stanford in the 1860s. Courtesy Bancroft Library

CHAPTER TEN

The Stanfords Build a University and Create a Town

It's hard to imagine today how sparsely settled the south San Francisco peninsula was during the last half of the nineteenth century. Local historian Roy M. Cloud claims that the *total* population of all of San Mateo County in 1860 (at the outbreak of the Civil War) was 3,214. Most of the Indians had died of smallpox and other European diseases, and Santa Clara Mission, once the center of social and spiritual life, was already falling into disrepair. A person could ride for miles without seeing another soul.

With neither the exciting gold finds of the Mother Lode nor a great harbor to attract ships and settlers, the peninsula lay quietly waiting for the era when it would become important to California. Gradually, disappointed miners, traders and others looking for arable land and a pleasant climate did indeed wander down the bay and discover the land that was to become Palo Alto.

On January 10, 1885, a reporter for the *San Francisco Monitor* waxed eloquent about the improvements the settlers had made:

> Over immense stretches of swampland...once useless as veritable quagmires, may be seen the deep furrows of the plow, and the long even drains and ditches that in sections run to the bay and appear like so many streaks of glass in the morning light.

Little did this reporter, or anyone else, guess that this land would some day support a number of small, modern cities, with Palo Alto as the nexus. In these communities, residents would invent the vacuum tube amplifier basic to radio design, and then computer chips and other technologies indispensible to contemporary life.

It is fair to say that Leland Stanford singlehandedly changed the fate of the region. This man, with his wife Jane Lathrop, founded the university that bears their son's name and subsequently laid out the town of Palo Alto on the nearby wheatfield.

Stanford was born March 9, 1824 into the family of a farmer who supplemented his agricultural income by running a series of inns catering to stagecoach traffic in Albany County, New York. One of eight children, Leland was chosen by his father for legal training. In 1841, the boy attended Clinton Liberal Institute near Utica and later transferred to the Methodist Cazenovia Seminary, near Syracuse. According to Norman E. Tutorow, author of the meticulously researched biography *Leland Stanford: Man of Many Careers* (1971), Stanford received perfect marks in philosophy and was generally a good student, but did not graduate.

At age 21, Stanford joined the eminent law firm of Wheaton, Doolittle, and Hadley in the city of Albany and studied to be an attorney on the job. He passed the bar in 1848 and, though he was offered Doolittle's place in the firm, decided instead to move west to set up his own law practice with a partner in the small, promising town of Port Washington, Wisconsin. Two years later he married Jane Lathrop.

In a glowing article in Sacramento's *Evening Bee* (June 21, 1893), a reporter describes the next significant event in Stanford's life: "...a circumstance transpired which some will regard as providential, giving an entirely new direction to his thoughts and energies, a fire [destroyed his extensive law library] and nearly all his worldly possessions." In fact, Port Washington had not boomed the way Stanford had hoped and he was glad for the opportunity to return to Albany in 1852 and consider his next move.

In Albany, he read letters from his five brothers who had gone to California to seek their fortunes. Within weeks, Stanford, 28 years old, was on a steamer headed for San Francisco, leaving his bride at home in Albany with her parents.

Oscar Lewis, author of *The Big Four* (1938), points out that "...this Argonaut of '52 had no intention of mining; he had come west to join his brothers in a less romantic but more stable calling: the grocery business." Josiah, oldest of the siblings, had opened a store in 1850, and later founded a central store in Sacramento. As each of the brothers arrived, Josiah set them up manning branch stores in the gritty mining camps. With his brothers' help, Leland became part-owner of a one-room store at Cold Springs, a camp between Hangtown and Coloma, "then mostly inhabited by Chinese," according to Lewis. Leland later moved to Michigan Bluff and, when Josiah and another brother Philip moved to San Francisco, Leland, a canny businessman, bought out the flourishing Sacramento store. Lewis says that Stanford Brothers "was a wholesale house of standing; dealing in groceries, liquors, tobacco, flour, and produce and the usual miscellany of miner's supplies and equipment."

One fateful day, Stanford accepted 76 of the total 93 shares in the Sutter Creek Lincoln Mine as payment for a merchant's debt. Stanford wanted to sell the low-yield mine for $5,000, but the former owner, Robert C. Downs, talked him out of the sale at the last minute. Stanford re-hired Downs to manage the mine, and soon it began producing handsomely. In 1872, Stanford and the other owners did sell—for $400,000—and Stanford realized about half a million dollars profit from the transaction and his dividends through the years. Stanford finally had the means to enter the big time in the booming economy of California.

Enter it he did. With three other Sacramento partners—Collis Huntington, Mark Hopkins, and Charles Crocker—Stanford built a transportation empire and became a multimillionaire. Called The Big Four, these daring businessmen formed the Central Pacific Railroad and laid track where there had previously been only Indian footpaths and wagon trails.

Probably their most spectacular success was in May 1869, when they completed the western half of the first railway between the east coast and west—celebrated with the famous gold spike. But that was not the last of their ventures. Quickly, they acquired the San Francisco to San Jose Railway. They constructed a rail line from San Francisco to Portland through the Sacramento Valley, and then another line from San Jose to San Diego under the name of the Southern Pacific.

Estelle Latta, in her 1958 book *Controversial Mark Hopkins,* describes the dramatic rise of the transportation empire:

> ...the four gentlemen from Sacramento and San Francisco proceeded to absorb, to buy, to steal, to build, and to manage every other form of transportation then developing. Street car lines were acquired, steamship companies controlled, docks and warehouse stock purchased.

Oscar Lewis claims that as the four men built their enterprise, power struggles developed within the group:

> Of the Central Pacific's Big Four, Huntington, of course, was easily the dominating figure. But Huntington, until late in life, avoided whatever would make him personally conspicuous, choosing to sit in the wings while others carried out his wishes before the footlights. Crocker, energetic and blustery and physically domineering, was essentially a subordinate, a man to take orders and carry them out, and Hopkins never rose, nor ever desired to rise, above his position as the keeper of the company accounts.
>
> There remained Stanford, who had all Huntington's craving for leadership and much of his ruthlessness, but who lacked the other's adroit cunning and his talent for moving in a direct line to a desired end.

Lewis argues that Stanford, a man devoted to attaining power, lost out to Huntington over ultimate control of the company. So Stanford turned instead to other egoistic activities, including politics.

Lewis's line of reasoning is somewhat simplistic, however. Stanford was interested in renown long before meeting Huntington. Stanford had run unsuccessfully for district attorney in Port Washington as early as 1850, and sought other prominent political posts in California. He became a leader in organizing the Republican Party in California, campaigned for Abraham Lincoln for President, and was elected California governor in 1861. Stanford's influence kept California in the Union during the Civil War. He was elected to the U.S. Senate in 1885 and re-elected in 1889.

When he had the means, Stanford did turn to the trappings of power with an elegant lifestyle that caused gossip, even in San Francisco, a town accustomed to overnight millionaires. In 1875, the Stanfords built a house that particularly caused tongues to wag. Lewis says:

> Stanford startled San Franciscans by encircling two acres of sand on the crest of Nob Hill with a thirty-foot wall [still holding up the hill along Pine Street between Powell and Mason] and constructing a mansion [on the site of today's Stanford Court Hotel] that dominated the city like the castle of a medieval hill town.

Opposite, above: The Stanfords' Stock Farm, where champion racehorses pastured. Below: The employees of the Stock Farm in the 1880s. Courtesy Palo Alto Historical Association

But Stanford's rivals were not far behind. Mark Hopkins built a mansion next door, now the site of the Mark Hopkins Hotel, with a granite wall that overshadowed Stanford's. Charles Crocker moved in next, on the site of today's Grace Cathedral, with a palatial building that topped them all in grandeur. Collis Huntington and James Flood were next door neighbors on the north side of California Street.

Oscar Lewis claims:

> [With] its noble isolation gone, Stanford lost his first interest in the Nob Hill house, and his thoughts focused on a larger enterprise. The Palo Alto farm, a nine-thousand-acre block of foothills and oak-studded meadow... An army of workmen made camp among the oaks, and descriptions of the wonders of Palo Alto began to appear regularly in the press. The residence ...had 'all the luxuries of a beautiful manor;' the two racetracks and the trotting park were 'rolled and sprinkled daily;' its lines of stables, attended by the farm's hundred and fifty employees, were brightly painted studies in perspective.

Historian Roxanne Nilan, Curator of Stanford University Archives, points out that it was not unusual for ambitious men of the nineteenth century to raise horses as a sign of their success. Stanford, like his colleagues, wanted to have the accoutrements of a successful merchant prince.

Biographer Tutorow emphasizes that Stanford bought the Stock Farm because his doctor had earlier recommended a more relaxing life away from the rigors of business. Stanford had invested in horses in Sacramento and built a stable in San Francisco in 1874, quickly gaining a reputation as a good judge of horseflesh. Says Tutorow:

> Partly to give his son the appreciation of farm life that he had acquired as a boy and partly to take up serious breeding and training of race horses ...Stanford decided to buy a farm.

Whatever his reasons were, Stanford soon had a prestigious but hardly relaxing place to pursue his hobby. Trotters at the Palo Alto Stock Farm set 19 world records. Electioneer, a stallion Stanford bought even though colleagues advised him against the purchase, sired nine world champions. (A statue of this elegant-looking horse stands now at the site of the former Stock Farm.)

Throughout his active life, Stanford demonstrated his love of the new and different. He developed the Vina Winery in Tehama county and experimented with wine-making. He brought paintings and other European art treasures to the West Coast. He delighted in showing visitors to his San Francisco home his mechanically operated orchestra, called an orchestrion, and a collection of mechanical birds that chirped when he pressed a hidden button.

At the Stock Farm, he planted eucalyptus trees and helped his young son—who had been born a year before the gold spike was placed—build a miniature railroad with 400 feet of track laid in the farm's arboretum. To determine whether or not a horse has all four legs off the ground simultaneously while in mid-gallop, Stanford had Eadweard Muybridge, a photographer, set still-photo cameras at intervals along the Stock Farm track. As the horse passed, the pictures snapped, proving that a horse *is* momentarily airborne in stride. Moreover, Muybridge's technical innovations for the experiment led to the concept of motion pictures.

But tragedy struck in 1884 when, during a family trip abroad, young Leland Jr. died of typhoid in Italy. Leland Sr. and his wife were overcome. To channel their grief, they decided to build a university near their farm as a memorial to their only son.

The cornerstone was laid on May 14, 1887 as a brass band played and Jane was moved to tears of joy. Still in the midst of construction, the university opened for its first classes four years later on October 1, 1891.

Although women did not yet have the right to vote and were seldom allowed a higher education, Stanford welcomed them—along with young men—without restriction. According to Palo Alto architect Birge Clark, the grades needed to enter the university were relatively low (just above a B average). Respected faculty arrived at Stanford from Cornell and other established schools, and the Stanfords set out to provide a top education aimed at even the poorest Californians. No tuition was charged.

But not everyone was convinced that this enterprise would succeed. There is about as much need for a new university in California as for "an asylum for decayed sea-captains in Switzerland," sneered an editorial in the *New York Mail* and *Express.*

Indeed, even the new, eager faculty sometimes gulped back disappointment when they caught their first glimpse of the college. Ellen Coit Elliott, wife of the university's first registrar, records her first impressions:

> Then at a dramatic gesture from Dr. [David Starr] Jordan [the university's first president] we looked toward the foothills and saw *The University,* our goal, the source and end of our destiny. What—to me, excited, tired, wistful, homesick, full of fanciful imagining and hopes—was an anticlimax! My heart sank ...For I had expected the university to be beautiful, imposing, adequate to high thoughts and noble purposes; and what I saw, some distance off across a dry, dun waste, was a

1900 STANFORD HOME
Wing at far left now part of
Convalescent Home

The Stanford house at the Stock Farm, shown here in 1900, was restrained in style, rather like an English manor house. It was badly damaged in the 1906 earthquake, but was rebuilt and used as a convalescent home. It was finally destroyed in 1965, its remnants burned in the Big Game bonfire of that year. Courtesy Palo Alto Historical Association

> low, bare line of buildings, plain and stiff, unrelieved by greenery, lying against hills of the same dusty hue, not an arcade or a court or the least mitigation of their commonness. They appeared to me exactly like a factory...I made no moan. I don't remember that anyone said anything.

Local residents read the newspapers and wondered. They came out to the university site to watch and comment. Writes Ellen Elliott, "This show of beginning was regarded by many [Californians] with skeptical, if intense curiosity. Some grumbled because there was no preparatory department; some criticized the architecture; some hinted darkly that the whole project was only an intricate scheme to make more money for 'the Senator.'"

Leland Stanford was undeterred; he and his wife continued their grand plans. Earlier, they had even decided that the new university should have an accompanying college town to provide a clean-living place for student housing and other services.

Though Leland and Jane personally believed that moderately sipping wine prevented alcoholism, they thought that a completely dry town would pose the least temptation to the young people. After unsuccessfully trying to talk leaders of nearby communities into local prohibition, they decided to carve out their own new city, one that would prohibit the sale of liquor within its boundaries.

A Town of Teetotalers?

Whiskey may not be the root of evil, but it—or rather its absence—was certainly the root of Palo Alto. For his greatest project, Stanford University, Senator Leland Stanford and his wife Jane Lathop wanted to create a healthy, moral environment for the incoming students. This meant no liquor in the college town where the students would live, shop, and find recreation.

In 1887, as the new university was on the drawing board, the Senator and his wife asked civic leaders of the small town of Menlo Park to the north to shut down the bar at the thriving Menlo Hotel and to declare the rest of the town dry as well. The leaders politely said no. The Stanfords turned to Mayfield to the south and asked citizens to board up the fourteen saloons that gave Mayfield its particular raucous ambiance. These citizens laughed and said no.

So Senator Stanford, who had not become a frontier millionaire by being easily deterred, decided to create his own dry town, Palo Alto. Real estate flyers advertising lots went out across the country and people flocked to buy parcels of the field that would be the city. Clauses in each deed stipulated that the property must revert to the university if intoxicating liquors were ever sold on it.

In 1908, a drunken Stanford student returning from a Menlo Park saloon was shot and killed when mistaken for a burglar as he entered the wrong house in Palo Alto. The Stanford Academic Council subsequently banned liquor on campus. In 1909, a California state law forbade the sale of liquor within a mile and a half of Stanford University and the University of California campuses.

Thus, while most of the West became notorious for its hard-drinking, hard-fighting style, Palo Alto was an island of sobriety. At least officially. Unofficially, the citizens, even instructors living in the area called Professorville, were known to tipple on occasion.

Those who wished to serve wine or Scotch in their homes contacted the grocer, Goldberg Bowen in San Francisco, to have a case or two shipped express. Out of deference for Palo Alto's blue laws, the shipper usually marked these boxes "books." Thomas Angell recalls that one day near the turn of the century, the phone rang for his father, Professor Frank Angell. A clerk at the university requested that Dr. Angell please pick up his "box of books" because they were "leaking."

Though citizens privately winked at Palo Alto's anti-liquor charter, restaurants and stores remained bone dry as long as forty years after Prohibition ended in 1933. Even large chain groceries offered their customers nothing stronger than 3.2 percent beer.

From the 1930s and into the '50s, Palo Alto's city council protested liquor license applications, even though a 1934 amendment to the state constitution took control of liquor from the local arena and gave it to the State Board of Equalization. Merchants persisted and in 1953, the town's first liquor store opened on Middlefield Road and Loma Verde.

Commercial property owners closer to campus also pressed for liquor licenses. In 1972, real estate dealer Melvin Mack, who then owned the historic President Hotel (now called President Apartments), wanted a liquor license to boost patronage of Henry's Restaurant, located in the building. Palo Alto attorney Frank Lee Crist Sr. broke the deed restrictions by arguing before the Superior Court of Santa Clara County that "conditions had changed" since the Stanfords originally restricted liquor on town property, *and* the Stanford Faculty Club had quietly served wine and other spirits for years right on campus. The leaky books were exposed at last, and Henry's Restaurant obtained the first of many Palo Alto restaurant liquor licenses.

Editors of the *Palo Alto Times* wanted to show a celebration of Crist's legal victory by photographing him taking the first official drink. Crist recalls wryly that the whiskey did not arrive on time, however, so the first official alcoholic toast in Palo Alto was actually water. One would like to think that the Stanfords would have smiled at this.

Leland Stanford directed Timothy Hopkins, the adopted son of fellow railroad magnate Mark Hopkins, to purchase the fields along El Camino, the wide, well-travelled dirt road connecting the old missions. Stanford advanced a loan to Hopkins and on October 28, 1887, Hopkins bought 697.55 acres from Henry W. Seale and later a smaller parcel from the successors to Maria Louisa Greer. He paid either $60,000, as recorded by a number of historians, or $300,000, as he claimed later in life. Hopkins subdivided the land and named the streets. Herbert Hoover, a member of the first freshman class, helped survey the beeline of the new town's University Avenue leading into Palm Drive to the magnificent arch to be built at the center of the University's quad.

The following three pages are from a brochure advertising University Park, the original name of today's Palo Alto. Timothy Hopkins bought the land for Stanford and drew up the map in March 1888. Meanwhile, plans for a different settlement called Palo Alto (now College Terrace) were being drawn up (see pp. 96-99). Courtesy Bancroft Library

Leland Stanford Jr. University

—AND—

UNIVERSITY PARK.

THE act by which Senator Stanford so grandly endowed the Palo Alto Institute of Learning will, in the years to come, rank as one of the great events in the history of the State of California, and, for that matter, the United States. Since the death of his only child, Leland Stanford, Jr., it has been the sole aim of the Senator's life to found an institution of learning in this State, which should be equal to all, and, if possible, excel, the best colleges in the world. To this end he draughted and secured the enactment of a law for the protection of all endowments that may be made in the future for educational institutions in California. Since that time his attention has been largely paid to the perfection of his plans for the founding of the great educational center. By the deed of trust, he conveys for the benefit of the institution 83,200 acres of land, comprising some of the most valuable estates in California, the products of which will go toward the fulfillment of his wishes.

There will be no branch of the arts, sciences or mechanics that will not be taught, and to these educational advantages, male and female will be equally entitled.

The institution by the munificent salaries it will be able to pay, will draw to its force of educators, the most famous and talented professors on the globe; and the splendid climate of the section of country in which the University is situated, will in no small degree, tend to induce the great professors of the East and Europe to accept chairs in its departments.

Thorough instruction will be given in painting, sculpture, drawing, design, etc. A grand conservatory of music, under the direction of the most famous masters of Italy and Europe, which will afford the best musical education to be had in the world, will be one of the particular features of this institute of technics. There will also be a school of Mechanics, which will turn out all grades in this class, from the common artisan to the scientific civil engineer and master machinist, and include instruction in all grades of scientific draughting and architecture. One of the important branches of the institution will be a School of Agriculture, to which will be attached a farm, the soil and climate of which will produce any of the agricultural or horticultural products of the temperate or semi-tropic zones. Among the valuable adjuncts of the institution are to be a splendid museum, and libraries containing the best works pertaining to the various departments of learning. And this is not all.

When the time comes, as it eventually will, that University Park and vicinity becomes an educational center, the intention of Senator Stanford is to erect buildings for preparatory schools, in order that people residing there may have facilities for educating their younger children up to the standard at which pupils will be admitted to the higher courses.

University Park is a tract of beautiful oak-park land, immediately opposite and adjoining the grounds of the Leland Stanford Junior University, and has been subdivided into villa blocks, comprising about five acres each, capable of subdivision into ample building lots, and is offered for sale at reasonable terms, by the block, half block, or quarter block or lot. The land has been subdivided in the most artistic manner, with broad avenues intersecting each other at picturesque angles. The Middlefield road, upon which is built the Menlo Park Villa of the late J. C. Flood and other beautiful residences, has been extended through the entire tract, and constitutes one of the main avenues of the property hereby offered for sale. Immediately adjoining the tract on the northwest, is the beautiful residence and grounds of Timothy Hopkins, Esq., Treasurer of the S. P. R. R. Co. Each block has a frontage of 1,800 feet upon the streets or avenues, the blocks being 500 x 400 feet. The great majority of the blocks are covered with a beautiful growth of live oak trees.

The ground is ready to be built upon, without grading. It is situated at such an altitude above the level of the bay, which will provide for perfect drainage and sewerage.

As will be seen by the accompanying map, the main avenue from the University, (100 feet in width, passing through one-half mile of ornamental grounds), intersects the Southern Pacific Railroad at a point where the main avenue of the town meets it. Here is soon to be constructed a fine stone depot, from which the University will be reached by means of a cable road.

W. M. MACMILLAN & CO.

have for sale the choicest of the Villa Sites in this University Town.

OFFICES, 621 MARKET STREET,

Palace Hotel Entrance, San Francisco.

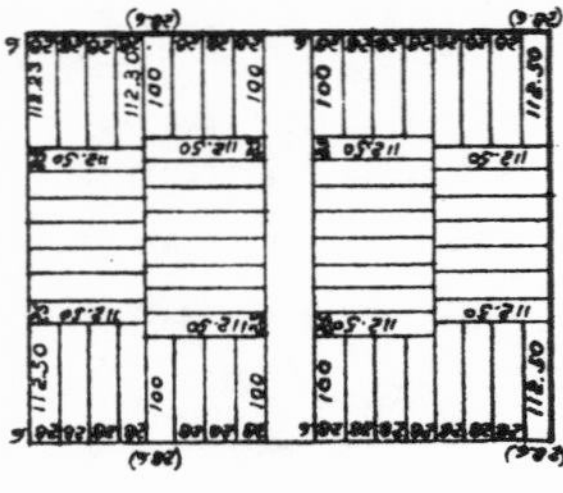

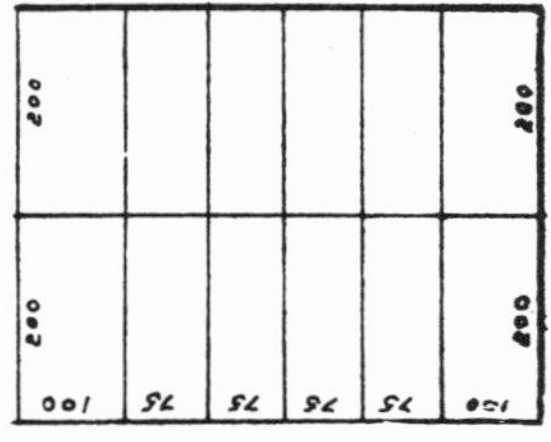

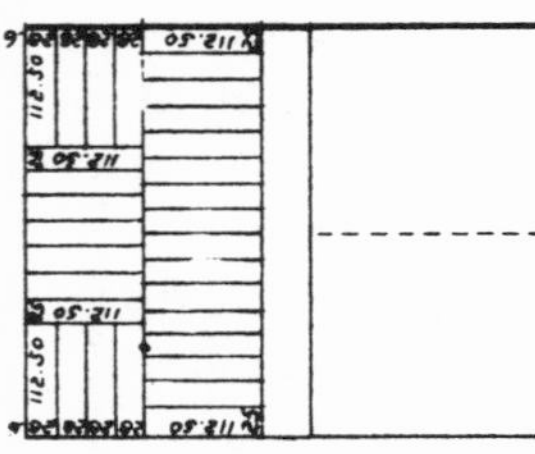

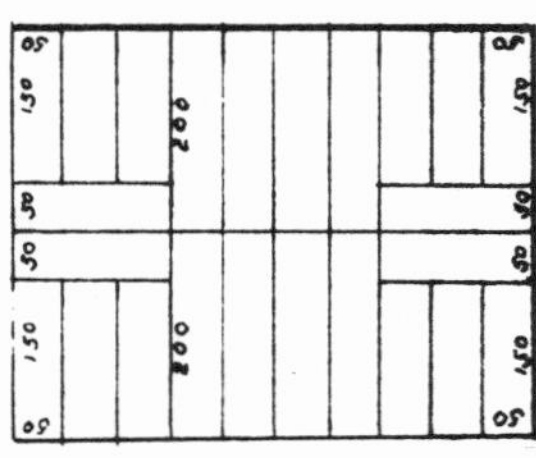

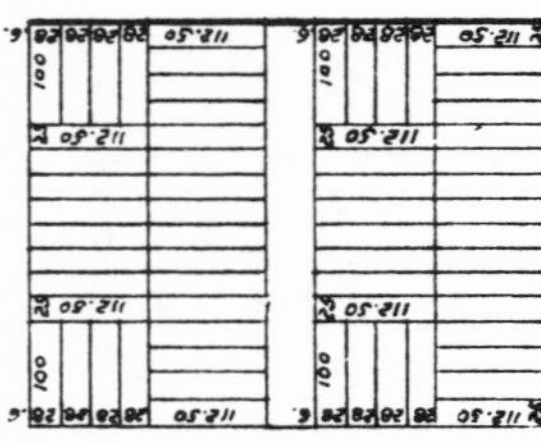

52

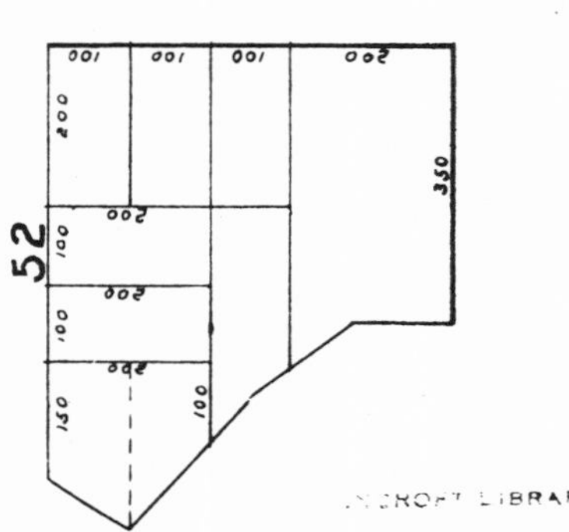

5

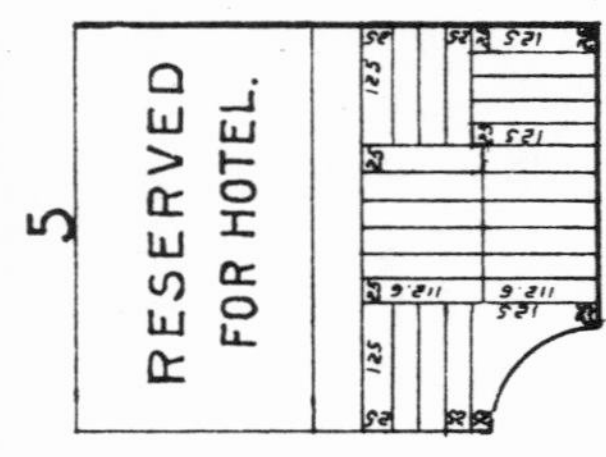

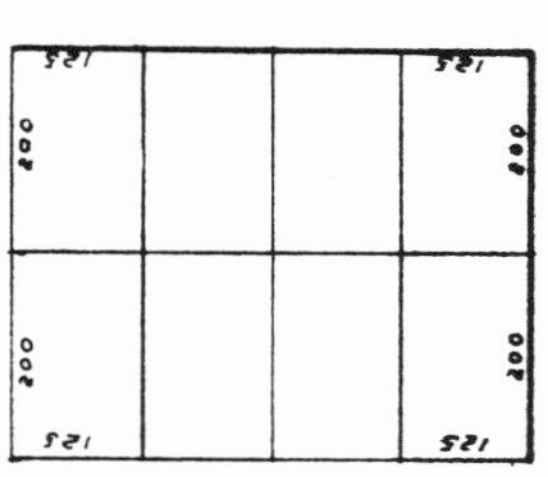

4

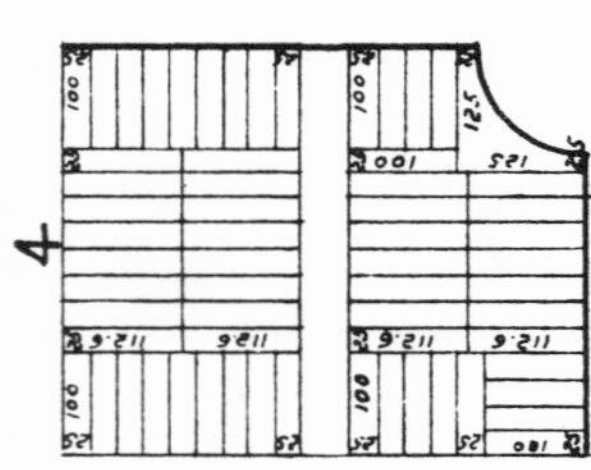

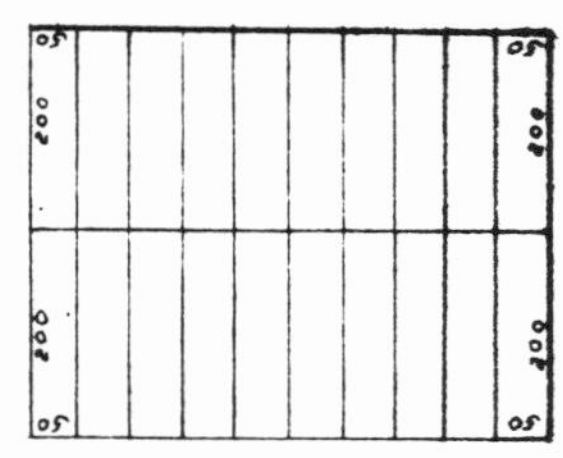

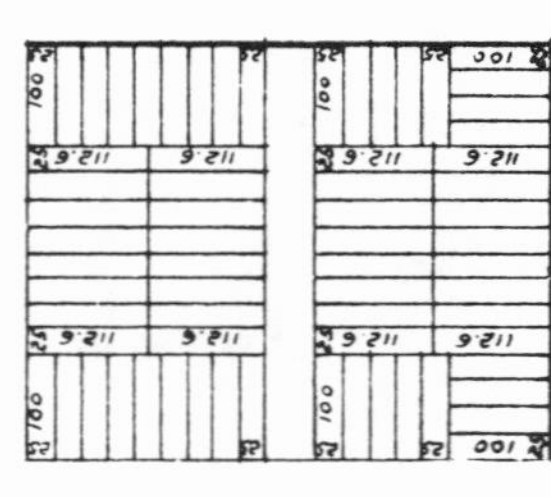

THIS ELEGANT PROPERTY

WHICH WE OFFER

FOR SALE AT TERMS

TO PLACE IT

Within the reach of all Persons

DESIRING A

SUBURBAN HOME

IS SITUATED IN

University Park,

THE TOWN OF THE

Leland Stanford Jr. University,

AT PALO ALTO,

And is located in the heart of the Finest Climatic Belt in California, on the

COAST DIVISION of the SOUTHERN PACIFIC RAILROAD

BETWEEN

San Jose and San Francisco,

And within thirty-five minutes' ride of the Metropolis.

FOR PARTICULARS, APPLY TO

W. M. MACMILLAN & CO.

621 MARKET STREET,

Palace Hotel Entrance,

SAN FRANCISCO, - - CALIFORNIA.

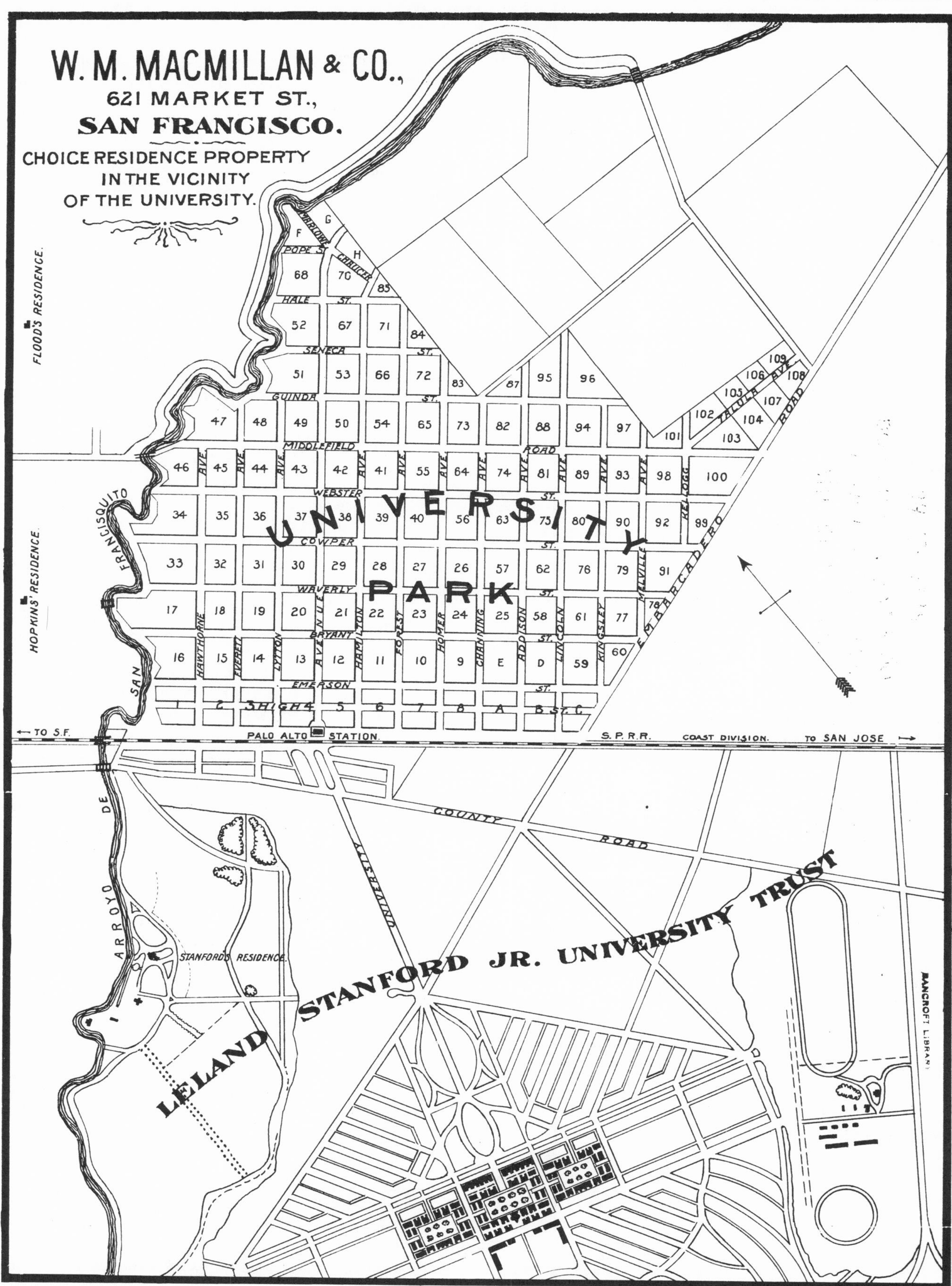
W. M. MACMILLAN & CO.,
621 MARKET ST.,
SAN FRANCISCO.
CHOICE RESIDENCE PROPERTY
IN THE VICINITY
OF THE UNIVERSITY.
FLOOD'S RESIDENCE.
HOPKINS' RESIDENCE.
UNIVERSITY
PARK
SAN FRANCISQUITO
ARROYO DE
MIDDLEFIELD ROAD
WEBSTER ST.
COWPER ST.
WAVERLY ST.
BRYANT ST.
EMERSON ST.
HIGH ST.
HALE ST.
SENECA ST.
GUINDA ST.
POPE ST.
CHAUCER
EMBARCADERO ROAD
HAWTHORNE AVE
EVERETT AVE
LYTTON AVENUE
HAMILTON AVE
FOREST AVE
HOMER AVE
CHANNING AVE
ADDISON AVE
LINCOLN AVE
KINGSLEY AVE
MELVILLE AVE
KELLOGG AVE
TALUCA AVE
PALO ALTO STATION
← TO S.F.
S. P. R.R. COAST DIVISION. TO SAN JOSE →
COUNTY ROAD
UNIVERSITY AVENUE
STANFORD'S RESIDENCE.
LELAND STANFORD JR. UNIVERSITY TRUST
BANCROFT LIBRARY

Advertisements for lots in the non-alcoholic community appeared in newspapers throughout the west. A flyer on the university and College Terrace circulated about 1890 by the Carnall-Fitzhugh-Hopkins Company touted Palo Alto:

> ...in his remarks to the Trustees when they received the deed to the property, Senator Stanford said substantially: 'The reasons for selecting the Palo Alto estate as the location of the University are its personal associations—which are most dear to us—the excellence of its climate, and its accessibility. It also furnishes a sufficiently diversified soil, with a topography which admirably fits it as a place for agricultural education. The endowment of the lands is made because they are of themselves of great value...'

Stanford must have realized that peninsula real estate would one day be a valuable commodity. This idea was not lost on real estate agents, who soon swarmed to Palo Alto to begin selling lots. Lucas Greer, son of rancho owner Captain John Greer, recalls those heady days of the first real estate sale:

> It was in a huge army tent pitched where the first block of University Avenue is now situated. There was a good-sized crowd of people from all over the state, drawn largely by the excitement of the new university. From there on, the town built up right away. Soon there were business houses and a hotel. Lots on that first block sold for $100. On the second block down from the railroad, lots sold for $50, and after that they were $25 apiece, going north and south.
>
> There was a red-headed fellow in town then by the name of McMillan...He certainly was a livewire. He sold a lot of property here, and then suddenly he dropped out of sight.
>
> Once he gave me some advice, and the words still ring in my ears. He said: 'Greer,—you beg, borrow and get all the money you can get together and put it into property. You'll be a millionaire.'

Prophetic words. Little did Greer and the other pioneers realize that Palo Alto would become a town of over 56,000 people, and that a quarter-acre of downtown land would one day be worth well over five *thousand* times the original price.

As 1893 opened, the university was in the midst of its second full academic year, and the town itself had grown to a population of 400. According to Ellen Elliott, the townsfolk still came to the university to gape at the "'tramp perfessors'...to behold this embryonic faculty eating its dinner out under the arcade, seated in a row on the curbstone."

Spring came. The orchards surrounding Palo Alto began to bloom. Palo Altans continued to watch Leland Stanford and his wife with awe and curiosity, and with a note of sadness as the Senator's health declined. Ellen Elliott describes an early visit from the Stanfords:

> A big carriage with beautiful horses and burly coachman drove across the gravel and stopped at the steps. Mr. and Mrs. Stanford had come. They would not go in to be more formally received but sat down cozily with us on the porch. It was the half-light of early evening. We found them kind-hearted, unaffected people carrying their large frames with simple poise. She was dressed in silk or satin of creamy white, with lace and jewelry, but seemed unconscious of her garments. He appeared somewhat feeble, with his cane and slowness of walk. They were grave, yet full of eager pleasure at our coming [the arrival of the faculty] and at the unfolding of their plans. We felt their urge and happy desire to see [first president] Dr. Jordan's work initiated and help him with it in every way. Mr. Stanford was still a member of the U.S. Senate; some called him "The Senator" and some old-timers said "Governor," for he had been war governor of California in the '60s. He seemed to us an aging man, feeling his age, ready to be rid of burdens and care if he could successfully transfer his wealth...We were sorry for him and loved him.

Ellen Coit Elliott's intuition of his death was correct; one June night just after commencement in 1893, he died in his sleep. So before the new century could be ushered in, both town and gown were to enter a new era without the imposing presence of Leland Stanford himself.

The burden he left fell primarily on the shoulders of Jane Lathrop Stanford, a woman of *Iron Will*, as described by Gunther Nagel in his excellent biography of her by that name. Not long after the eulogies for her husband were said, Jane Lathrop Stanford faced financial ruin. Though at the time, feminist ideals were openly scoffed at by many men and women, Jane Lathrop Stanford wielded all the power within her reach.

Gunther Nagel describes her dilemma and unflinching courage in an admiring tone:

> The wife who had lived long in the shadow of her famous husband emerged a lone woman of unsuspected perceptivity and will—and she needed it all. With the Senator's estate in probate, funds for operating the university were not immediately available, and to make matters worse, the country was in a financial panic which bankrupted every major Western railroad save the Southern Pacific Company, which held the Central Pacific and allied lines. Cruelest of all, the

Right and below: The Stanford Quadrangle rose with a speed that amazed skeptical Mayfield residents in 1888. Sandstone came from a quarry near San Jose. Courtesy Palo Alto Historical Association

government initiated a suit attempting to establish the estate's liability for $15,237,000 in railroad construction loans not yet due. While the suit was pending, the estate could not be distributed, and a decision favorable to the government would bring an end to the fruit of Senator and Mrs. Stanford's labor and dreams—Stanford University....

The [65-year-old] widow began her newest duty with one resolve indelibly etched in her mind. The University would be kept open, nothing would swerve her from her purpose. When told point-blank 'The University must be closed!' by a grim-visaged gathering of San Francisco's leading attorneys and bankers, she was undismayed. 'Do you think I believe that my husband's carefully laid plans can wholly miscarry?' she replied. They would learn what one determined woman could do.

Indeed. The probate court allowed Jane Lathrop Stanford a household allowance of $10,000 per month while the question was being settled, and this cash had to be derived from the family's businesses. Though Jane Lathrop Stanford had not previously managed the family's assets, she set about, like a

Opening Day, Stanford University, October 1, 1891: David Starr Jordan delivers his inaugural address as Stanford's first president, shielded by a parasol. Leland and Jane Stanford, sheltered by the great arch, sit beneath a portrait of their son, Leland Jr., for whom all this was a memorial. Courtesy Palo Alto Historical Association

Silicon Valley executive during hard times, to contain costs and raise income. Her goal was to keep the entire $10,000 per month rolling in, and to use most of it to support her beloved university. In the past, her household expenses alone had been $10,000. She cut staff, sold the $500,000 brandy inventory of money-losing Vina Winery and laid off 150 employees there. By streamlining the wine and brandy-making operation, and leasing some of the acreage, Jane Stanford turned Vina into a profitable business by 1895.

Meanwhile, she requested that the judge declare the professors and other staff of the university her "personal servants." Thus she could give them the "household" money allotted to her by the courts.

She gathered up all her fine jewelry and tried to pawn it to keep the University afloat. Though able to sell only six strings of pearls at this time, her strength of purpose was not lost on Palo Altans and others as she they watched her cajole and occasionally bully people into helping her keep the university alive. Even university president David Starr Jordan, her longtime ally, found the penury and stubbornness trying at times, but he and others maintained their respect for her ability to achieve her goals.

The first major aim—of getting the estate out of probate—was realized in March, 1896, when the U.S. Supreme court rejected the federal government's claims against the Stanford estate. Students and faculty were jubilant. David Starr Jordan, exhilarated by the victory, told partying students that they could do anything in their revelry except "tear down the buildings or paint the professors," to which the students responded by painting the post office red, a color that was declared a vast improvement by Dr. Jordan.

The endowment of the University, as stated in the founding Grant of 1885, consisted of the Gridley Farm (19,000 acres in Tehama county), the Palo Alto Stock Farm (8,800 acres), and the Stanford Vina Ranch (55,000 acres). The Stanfords accurately calculated the total worth at about $20 million, but little of this would be owned outright by the university until Jane Stanford's death.

Thus, she practiced stringent economies. Her refusal to accept help from outside sources was understandable since she held the nineteenth century view that accepting monies for her personal charity—the university—was unseemly. Yet her opposition to fund raising at times exasperated even her closest allies. For example, in 1895, she turned down the offer of the 4,000-volume Hildebrand Library, saying that the University could not afford it. When she found out that the university trustees had bought it anyway and paid for it out of their own pockets, she castigated President David Starr Jordan.

Through all the budget battles, Jane Stanford kept her university open. As the university's financial troubles eased, she again had money for her philanthropic contributions to worthy causes in Palo Alto and elsewhere.

From the outset, she supported the kindergarten movement in the West. She subsidized Palo Alto's own first kindergarten, kept as a private school in the Mayfield home of Miss Frances Hamilton (until support through monthly subscriptions for a free kindergarten was organized by the Women's Christian Temperance Union). Irma Zschokke writes of a visit by the imposing but kindly benefactor:

> I remember the time Mrs. Stanford's carriage drove up in front of the kindergarten in Mayfield and the coachman assisted her in getting out and escorted her in. She sat in a chair close to where I was standing, and even today I can still hear the rustle of her black taffeta-silk dress as she picked me up and sat me on her lap, took a piece of candy from the box held by the coachman, and quickly popped it into my mouth....

Leland Stanford, The Man

Though Leland Stanford had considerable popular support throughout his lifetime, he was by no means universally liked. Some Californians grumbled that Stanford and his partners in the Central Pacific, the Big Four, used unfair, strong-arm tactics as they rapidly built their railroad empire. An anti-railroad faction deplored such practices as Central Pacific's rebates, fixing of prices in favor of preferred customers. The complaints increased as Central Pacific officers seemed to bamboozle other businessmen into disadvantageous deals. In 1870, for example, Stanford beguiled Horace W. Carpentier, who owned most of the property along the Oakland waterfront, to sell his real estate to the Oakland Water Front Company. As it turned out, Stanford had hastily organized that company for the sole purpose of gaining Carpentier's deed and turning it over to the Central Pacific. According to Estelle Latta, author of *Controversial Mark Hopkins,* Oakland residents were in an uproar over this "steal" of the property.

The Big Four's power reached deep into the political structure of the state. According to Roxanne Nilan in her exhibit, "1885: The Founding of a University," the Big Four brazenly bought favors from politicians. In 1883, letters were made public from Collis P. Huntington to David D. Colton concerning "the cost" of "particular legislators and legislative measures favoring the railroad network."

The anti-railroad sentiment had reached such a high pitch four years earlier that a railroad commission had been established. According to historian Nilan, "Two of the three-member commission were promptly bribed, and the railroad's control of state legislation continued to exceed the state's power to regulate the railroad."

Leland Stanford was canny enough to keep a certain distance between his personal image and his role as president of Central Pacific. His ponderous manner and slow speech gave him a sincere, thoughtful air. Many Californians affectionately called him "The Governor" or "The Senator," honoring him for his terms in office. To his supporters, he was a man of integrity and intelligence.

This public image was enhanced by his university. Eleanor Pearson Bartlett, who co-founded Castilleja Hall, a private girls' school in Palo Alto, describes the kind of admiration he received from many:

> ...the University, that fabulous gold mine in the early days, which was believed to stand ready to hand out education, places, money, fairy chances of all kinds, with a real fairy godfather and godmother standing ready to wave the wand for every Cinderella and hand out a ring for every Aladdin. You cannot, any of you, imagine the rosy mist that floats around it all in those magic two years before the Senator died.

Stanford's friends revered him as a Renaissance man eager to try new ideas. In addition to breeding prized trotters on his Palo Alto Stock Farm and experimenting with winemaking, he became a patron of the Metropolitan Museum of Art in New York in 1883, and the next year acquired a collection of duplicates of Cyprian antiquities from the museum's Cesnola Collection for the Stanfords' planned museum. He and his wife made plans for an art school, to be housed in their San Francisco mansion which, unfortunately, was destroyed in the 1906 earthquake. He cultivated orchards and gardens on his various properties and his wife proudly served California produce at their exquisite parties in Washington, D.C., where they lived part of the year as he carried out his Senatorial duties.

A re-examination of Stanford's life shows a complicated man. He was capable of genuine tenderness toward his son Leland Junior and took pleasure in helping the boy develop his own interest in historic artifacts. Stanford started a number of projects to improve California's future. When he died in 1893, just two years after his university opened its doors to the first class, there was an outpouring of grief from personal friends and acquaintances. Yet the other side of his personality, the side that makes many historians declare him ruthless, cannot be entirely buried. The business practices of Central Pacific were considered so unethical that rebates, for example, were outlawed by the Elkins Act of 1903 and the Hepburn Act of 1906, along with regulations of the Interstate Commerce Commission. And the ICC in other ways finally tamed the railroads in the early twentieth century.

Robber baron *and* philanthropist, Stanford will be remembered in all his guises for his vision. He saw a nation criss-crossed by railroads, and he saw a great university in the wilds of California. He was also a man of enormous energy, who accomplished more than most people could in two lifetimes.

Leland Stanford built a model railroad for his son, near the Stanford house at the Stock Farm. Shown here in 1894, the track looks forlorn, a constant reminder of the great tragedy of the Stanfords' life, and of a father's love for his son. Courtesy Palo Alto Historical Association

Jane Lathrop Stanford

Jane Lathrop Stanford, who saved Stanford University from financial ruin soon after its opening, was a woman of contradictions. Historian Roxanne Nilan, Curator of Stanford University Archives, points out that Jane believed strongly in the values of hearth and home. "Of all the walks of life a woman may be destined to travel," writes Jane, "there is none higher, or more beautiful, or influential, than that of a loving intelligent wife and mother." Yet Jane herself became one of the most powerful people in California. Jane could be sentimental and tender, yet was capable of devising clever strategies to save the things she loved. She was deeply spiritual, yet personally committed to no particular denomination. Even her reputation remains obscure; most people have forgotten that without Jane Lathrop Stanford, her husband's name would not have become so illustrious.

Jane's personality was enigmatic. She was born Albany, New York, on August 24, 1828, and grew up in a time when female domesticity was the ideal. Jane married Leland Stanford when she was 22 and became his devoted and publicly-silent helpmate.

Through their married life, Jane supported Leland's business and political endeavors. Childless for years, she devoted her time to charitable causes, such as child care centers, and to entertaining her husband's cronies. Finally, at age 40, she gave birth to a healthy son, Leland DeWitt Stanford (at age nine, the boy asked to have his name changed to Leland Stanford Jr.). Jane and Leland were delighted to be parents. As her husband's empire grew, Jane devoted herself to her son, a robust, likeable boy, and to interests associated with his education, such as developing an antique art collection. Although the Stanfords maintained a mansion in San Francisco and a country home at their Palo Alto Stock Farm, they also leased a house in New York, anticipating that Leland Jr. would attend Harvard University.

She and her husband were devastated in 1884 when Leland Jr., then 15, died of typhoid in Italy while the family was on a European trip for business and health, and to give the boy an educational experience. Within weeks, Jane and her husband decided to build a memorial to their beloved son. On their way home from Europe, they stopped to visit Cornell, Yale, Harvard, and Massachusetts Institute of Technology to ask administrators for advice on their plans to found a major educational institution and an art museum. Harvard president Charles W. Eliot strongly supported the idea of creating a university offering humanities as well as sciences. A major university seemed appropriate to the Stanfords since their son had been almost college age when he died.

The Founding Grant for The Leland Stanford Junior University was signed November 11, 1885. At the university's gala opening in October, 1891, Leland called his wife to the speaker's stand. He opened his notes and she linked her arm with his, shading him with her parasol. Her own speech remained folded—she was too shy and overwhelmed to speak.

Two years later, as a deep business depression hit the country, Leland died—leaving his estate in disarray and his business empire and the university on the verge of collapse. Then, Jane Lathrop became one of the most quoted voices in the West. Through years of litigation and business recession, she surprised almost everyone by keeping the university open. Today, it rivals the Ivy League colleges of the East.

Jane's unique perspective on issues of the day emerged as she battled for her university. According to Roxanne Nilan in her excellent article on "Jane L. Stanford" in the February 1979 issue of *Sandstone and Tile,* Jane argued that women could not simultaneously combine career with family, but rather had to choose one or the other. Yet the first two names in her prized autograph collection were

Elizabeth Cady Stanton and Susan B. Anthony. In April, 1888, Jane hosted the International Council of Women in her Washington D.C. residence, and these two feminists were honored delegates. Roxanne Nilan points out that from then on, Jane corresponded with Susan B. Anthony, showing in her letters an acute awareness of the need for women to control their own property.

Jane's greatest contribution to women was to open the doors for higher education. Stanford University originally accepted any qualified student, male or female. This caused quite a stir among educators. Women flocked to the university so that by 1898, they made up 40 percent of the student body. Then, in a move that shocked and mystified her supporters, Jane limited female enrollment to 500. She was no fool and she realized that in the 19th century, educating men meant educating those who would control society. She also did not want Stanford to become known as a women's school since that would not be a fitting tribute to her son. Despite tremendous opposition, she held firm. Perhaps that is why Jane, who helped so many women rise above solely domestic lives, later became erroneously known as a retiring housewife who wanted women to stay at home.

Another myth, particularly dear to Stanford undergraduates, is that Jane was sentimental, and a religious fanatic. The pre-1906 facade in grand lettering dedicated Memorial Church to her husband. Students thought this maudlin. Today, they joke that she was so overcome by her son's death, she preserved his last meal. Pranksters have erected a sign saying "Leland's Last Breakfast" in a small room at the campus museum housing Leland Jr.'s bicycle and other effects, an inside joke that must bewilder foreign visitors.

In fact, this museum is devoted to European art treasures, which the Stanfords collected during their travels, and to contemporary art. Historian Roxanne Nilan emphasizes that though Jane—and her husband—did consider the fad spiritualism of the Victorian Age, Jane had a clear-eyed view of any organized religion. "Don't think that I believe," Jane writes, "that any particular creed or that even the church itself is capable of making saints of some folks. Such things are not matters of creed ...I mean that men and women should be sound at the core, whatever their doctrines may be."

The one thing that contemporaries agreed upon was that Jane Lathrop Stanford paid attention to detail, and that an incoherent argument or sloppy work was not likely to meet with her approval. According to the 1984 pamphlet, *Stanford from the Beginning,* Charles E. Hodges, university chapel architect, claimed that Jane could read blueprints like an expert. He reported that she would climb the scaffolding of the church with him, holding onto his coattail. "She invariably carried a parasol," he said. "It was notched at the lower end. She would run it into the carving and if it did not come up to the mark, she would ask me to have it cut deeper."

On February 28, 1905, Jane died while on vacation in Hawaii after taking an elixir of bicarbonate of soda with a heart stimulant. She was 77. The first coroner's report indicated that she had been poisoned, but Cooper Medical College physicians, asked by David Starr Jordan to conduct a second autopsy, concluded that she died of a ruptured coronary artery. Her death records were subsequently destroyed in the 1906 California earthquake.

So Jane's death was as ambiguous as her life was contradictory. Though she was born almost a hundred years before U. S. women gained the right to vote, she developed a commanding presence that influenced some of the most powerful people in California and across the West. How her reputation was reduced to that of a teary-eyed mourner is one of the great mysteries of history. Perhaps as Stanford University celebrates its centennial, the real Jane Lathrop Stanford, one of those important people with a talent for rising to the occasion, will be discovered once again.

The brochure from which these details are taken, published in 1888, suggests that there may already have been some confusion about which development was to be called Palo Alto. The map and the beautifully drawn aerial view (pp. 98-99) try to erase all doubt, as does the page at right, which also shows us that "hype" is nothing new. The confusion was not settled until 1892, when University Park officially became Palo Alto, and the development shown here became College Terrace. Courtesy Bancroft Library

"THERE IS NOTHING LIKE IT."

PALO ALTO

The University Town

It is within four blocks of Mayfield Station, on the Southern Pacific R. R.; it is now within one hour of San Francisco, and by the time table of the near future will be only forty minutes; it is nearer the Stanford University Buildings than any other land; it is surrounded on three sides by the University domain, A PARK OF 7,000 ACRES; it is fronted and traversed by the only public roads leading to the University Buildings;

It is the only land adjacent to the University that occupies higher ground than the railroad and that commands a view of the University buildings and grounds; its higher elevation gives it better climate, better drainage and more certain healthfulness than any lands of the vicinity; it is assured of an abundant water supply; it is entitled to water from the mains of the Menlo Park Water Company and from the Manzanita Water Company, Senator Stanford's enterprise; it is already a growing town; homes and business places are built and are building; its streets are all graded and turnpiked; its parks are laid out and enclosed; its titles are valid and unquestioned. All that have heretofore purchased of its lands have made handsome profits. All that now buy there will surely partake of the same fortune.

SECOND AND LAST GRAND SALE

600 Building Lots* — *At Auction on the Grounds

Saturday, May 25, 1889, at 1 o'clock P. M.

THE CARNALL-FITZHUGH-HOPKINS CO. AGENTS IN CHARGE

WM. BUTTERFIELD, Auctioneer — **624 MARKET STREET** (Opp. Palace Hotel) **SAN FRANCISCO**

THERE IS ONLY ONE PALO ALTO

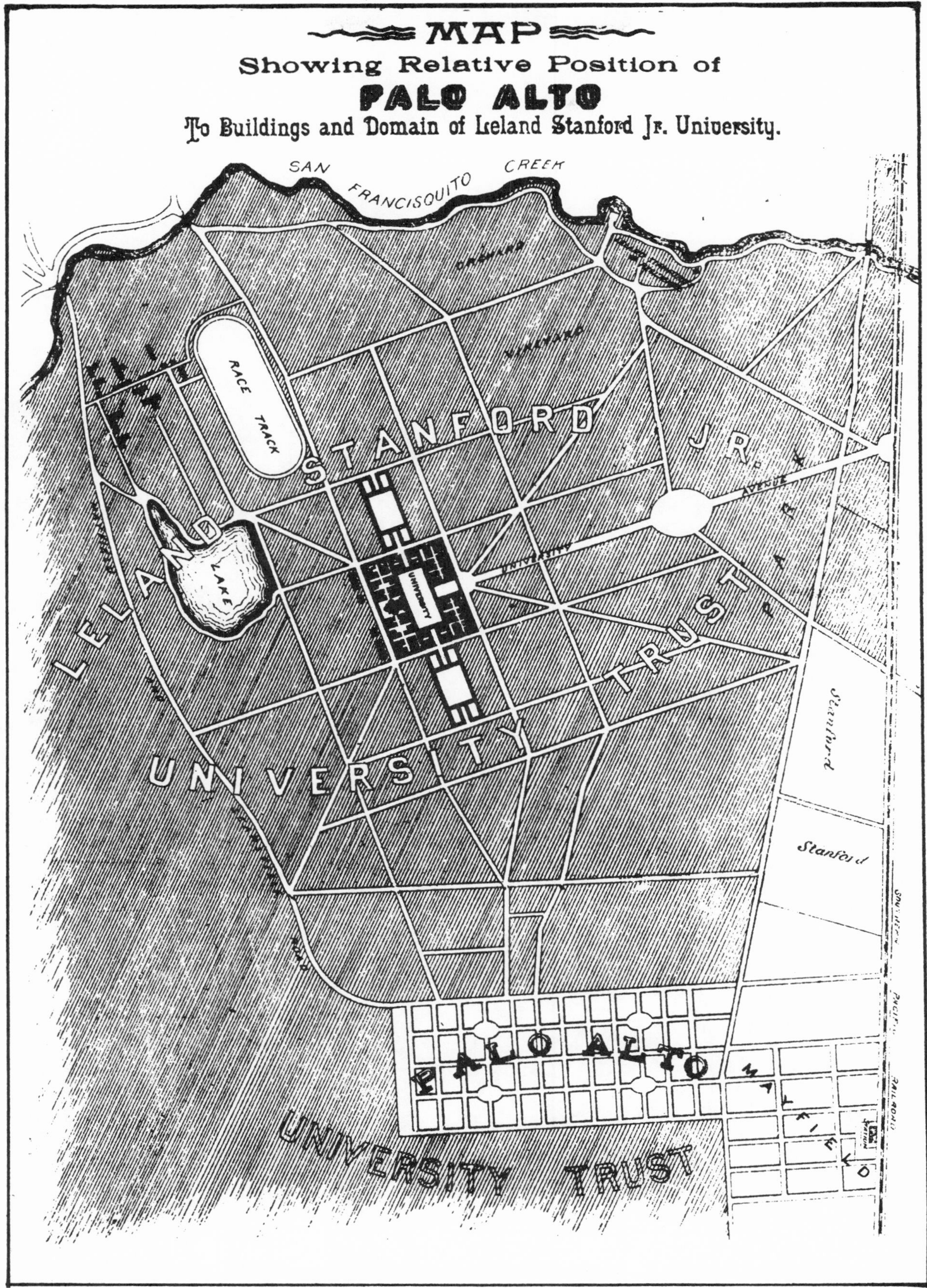
MAP
Showing Relative Position of
PALO ALTO
To Buildings and Domain of Leland Stanford Jr. University.
SAN FRANCISQUITO CREEK
ORCHARD
VINEYARD
RACE TRACK
LAKE
UNIVERSITY
UNIVERSITY AVENUE
LELAND STANFORD JR. PARK
UNIVERSITY TRUST
Stanford
Stanford
PALO ALTO
MAYFIELD
UNIVERSITY TRUST

STANFORD UNIVERSITY MEM
1.
2.
4.
6.
7.

HAPEL.
3.
5.

World News

During the period from 1887, when Timothy Hopkins bought the first 700 acres of land that became Palo Alto, until 1894, when the City of Palo Alto was incorporated, the Victorian Age was in full flower. Yet seeds of the coming twentieth century were already germinating around the world. Palo Altans eagerly absorbed the new ideas, learning of them through Eastern newspapers that arrived overland, sometimes days late.

When Thomas Edison invented the first motor-driven phonograph in 1887, Palo Alto was still lit by kerosene lamps and was so quiet that it was called a "nine o'clock town."

Far away in Chicago, skyscrapers for the offices of the burgeoning number of white-collar workers became possible in 1887 as the new Tacoma building proved that a steel-skeleton structure could carry tons of weight into the sky. According to a May 18, 1893 article in the *Sequoia*, local construction was also impressive:

> Palo Alto is humming with the boom. Two doctors have erected and moved into a cottage just this side of the post office; a drugstore will be built to help them; the carpenters have finished their Presbyterian Church; the new lumber yard is fairly established; and a third one is expected for next week; two large buildings whose ground floors will accommodate a dentist's parlor, a tin shop, the post office, a clothing store, while a number of students will occupy the rooms above and a barber shop are fast being hammered into shape; the hardware store is drying its first coat of paint, several insurance and real estate firms have come to town; eight new residences are underway and the University Book Store will open an ice cream saloon next week.

Three years earlier in 1890, George Eastman had brought out the first "Kodak" box camera, and amateur photographers brought the word "snapshot" into the language. Also in 1890, the first moving-picture film (*The Great Train Robbery*) appeared in New York, spawning a whole new entertainment industry.

In science, Sigmund Freud was in the midst of his groundbreaking studies of the subconscious, publishing *Studies on Hysteria* in 1895. Charles Darwin died in 1882, with the evolutionary theory he set forth in *On the Origin of the Species* (1859) still widely debated.

Americans and others were also beginning to discuss the ideas of German social philosopher Karl Marx, whose seminal work, *Das Kapital*, was published in English for the first time in 1886.

In Palo Alto, few conversations, whether trivial or profound, took place over the phone. As late as 1896, Palo Alto had only three telephone subscribers—a real estate office, a butcher, and Parkinson's Lumber and Hardware.

In art, the Impressionist Exhibitions in Paris (the eighth and last was in 1886) had begun re-shaping the world's sensibilities, and Vincent Van Gogh was creating some of his most famous images. Auguste Rodin had just completed "The Burghers of Calais," one of his most important sculptures, breaking with the Beaux-Arts style. Palo Altans, so busy producing basic services for their fledgling town, could little have guessed that one of the world's foremost collections of Rodin's works would be owned and exhibited by Stanford University a century later.

In 1888, Guy de Maupassant wrote *Pierre et Jean*, and Emile Zola published *La Terre*; in Britain, Victorian poet Alfred Lord Tennyson was just completing the *Idylls of the King*. But the old guard was about to give way to authors who anticipated "modern" writing. Americans Herman Melville (*Moby Dick*) and poet Walt Whitman (*Leaves of Grass*) were already finishing their last works. The "casual" style of Samuel Clemens (Mark Twain) had introduced a distinctly American way of writing. Twain had been a newspaperman in San Francisco, and his funny tales of life in the West, such as "The Celebrated Jumping Frog of Calaveras County," first published in 1865 in the *New York Saturday Press*, helped form easterners' images of California.

Palo Altans read the work of Mark Twain serialized in San Francisco newspapers, and they learned about local events in the precursor to the *Stanford Daily*, which began publication September 19, 1892. The first issue of the *Palo Alto Times* appeared in 1893.

In music, Gilbert and Sullivan extravaganzas reigned as the popular choice, while Peter Tchaikovsky's *Nutcracker Ballet* premiered in 1892 in St. Petersburg, thereby making a permanent imprint on American Christmases. Johannes Brahms, German composer and master of the Romantic style, was producing some of his best work at this time, while Frenchman Claude Debussy ("Afternoon of a Faun," 1894) and his contemporaries were already starting some of the experimentation that would change the music of the twentieth century.

In Palo Alto, Women's Club members gave whistling and singing recitals at regular meetings, such as Miss Nellie Werry's solo "Love's Golden Dream O'er" on April 3, 1896.

In politics, the contemporary world was beginning to take shape, for better or worse. Nikita Krushchev was born in 1894, one year after Senator Stanford died. France established a protectorate over Laos, and British Prime minister W. E. Gladstone introduced a bill for Home Rule in Ireland in 1886.

Entertainment in America was already becoming a big industry. The Barnum and Bailey Circus toured the large and small towns of the United States. The first professional football game in this country was played at Latrobe, Pennsylvania.

The first Big Game between Stanford and University of California, held March 19, 1892, was played at the Haight Street Field in San Francisco and cardinal red became Stanford's team color. A persistent legend says that student Herbert Hoover forgot to bring the football, but Stanford records show that he was not student body business manager until 1893-94 and so probably forgot the game ball for the third, not first, Big Game.

Overhand pitching, newly introduced, helped make baseball the national pastime. The *Redwood City Democrat* published "a digest of the new baseball rules of 1889" on March 14, 1889 for local enthusiasts, including:

> Players must come in from the field and seat themselves on the player's bench at the conclusion of their half in the field.
>
> Foul tips will not be out.
>
> Four balls, instead of five, give a base.
>
> The umpire shall not reverse his decision on the testimony of any player or bystander.

Chapter Notes

Many articles about Leland and Jane Lathrop Stanford and their university can be found in the archives of the Palo Alto Historical Association.

Historian Roxanne Nilan, Curator of Stanford University Archives, has written carefully-researched literature for her exhibit, "1885: The Founding of a University." The definitive work on Leland and Jane Lathrop Stanford and Stanford University will be *The Family Album: A Photographic History of Stanford* by Margo Davis and Roxanne Nilan, published November 1989 by Stanford University Press. Nilan, author of the text, deals with all the mythology about the Stanfords from the vantage of someone who knows the sources well. She puts Stanford University's history in the context of its times.

Stanford News and Publications Service published *Stanford: A Centennial Chronology* in 1985, edited by Karen Bartholomew, assistant director of the News and Publications Service, and Roxanne Nilan. This 31-page document contains an enormous amount of factual material about Stanford, and presents it in fascinating detail.

"Stanford From the Beginning," a pamphlet written by Peter C. Allen, provides a quick overview of the university's founding.

An important biography is *Leland Stanford: Man of Many Careers* by Norman E. Tutorow (1971). Tutorow has tracked down practically every available scrap of material about Stanford and presented it in a graceful prose style.

A classic source of information is Oscar Lewis's *The Big Four* (1938), which is a readable but largely undocumented account of the lives of Mark Hopkins, Collis Huntington, Charles Crocker, and Stanford. An almost unknown book, *Controversial Mark Hopkins* by Estelle Latta, outlines the aggressive business practices of the Big Four.

Ellen Coit Elliott's account of the first year at Stanford, *It Happened this Way* (1940), gives touching descriptions of the feelings of the first faculty members at Stanford. Similarly, Eleanor Pearson Bartlett provides a poignant account of "Beginnings in Palo Alto," in *The First Year at Stanford* (1905).

Gunther W. Nagel's biography, *Jane Stanford: Her Life and Letters*, gives a view of her life from an admirer. Roxanne Nilan's article, "The Tenacious and Courageous Jane L. Stanford," in the winter 1985 issue of *Sandstone and Tile*, is a penetrating study of this remarkable woman.

The role of liquor in the beginnings of Palo Alto is given in many sources, including Woods' history. Mary Grant's article, "Dry Palo Alto Springs a Leak," in the October 18, 1958 issue of *Peninsula Living*, illuminates the forces and counter-forces of Palo Alto's prohibition. The anecdote on the "leaky books" was written for the Palo Alto Historical Association files by Thomas Angell in April, 1970. Finally, attorney Frank Lee, Sr. himself provided information and humor about his own role in breaking the liquor covenant in a telephone interview on July 14, 1989.

"Lucas Greer Recalls Interesting Events of Fledgling Community," published in the April 19, 1939 issue of the *Palo Alto Times*, conveys the excitement of the first real estate sale. Irma Zschokke's unpublished autobiography, a clear remembrance of growing up in Palo Alto, can be found in the archives of the Palo Alto Historical Association.

CHAPTER ELEVEN

Bigotry in Palo Alto, A Sad Tale of the Chinese Community

By at least the 1870s, waves of racial prejudice swept California. Unfortunately, the Mayfield-Palo Alto area was not immune to ugly racist attitudes that shock contemporary sensibilities. Blacks, Filipinos, Japanese, and Chinese experienced discrimination here.

As in many California towns, there is very little evidence of blacks living in Palo Alto before 1925. The first major migration of blacks to the area was during World War II. But two or three black children appear in Channing School photographs between 1897 and 1910 (see the frontispiece of this book, where Etta Harris appears left of center). One can assume that one or two black families must have lived in Palo Alto during its earliest decades. They probably endured *de facto* discrimination typical of the times. In May, 1923, Dollie de Mesa urged fellow Mayfield residents in a *Palo Alto Times* editorial to "come forward and buy property [on the block bounded by Sheridan and Grant Streets] in order to prevent the Negro influx [from another part of the Palo Alto area]."

Filipinos also came under attack. In January 1921, a delegation headed by Mrs. Havens, M.C. Havens, Mrs. H.B. Bird, Mrs. and Mrs. J.A. Taff, and Mrs. Harriott E. Morales presented a petition to the Palo Alto Chamber of Commerce protesting the establishment of a club for Filipino students in Palo Alto. The petition (which was finally denied) concluded:

> Therefore we feel positive that this settlement of Filipinos at 711 Cowper Street is but the forerunner of a large Oriental colony set down in the midst of one of the best residence districts of Palo Alto. We ask you as the most representative body of Palo Alto citizens to devise some plan to remove the menace and restore the block its old character of a street of homes and families.

The Japanese experienced the same insulting discrimination in Palo Alto that they met in many other parts of California. University of Santa Clara professors Gary Okohiro and Timothy Lukes completed an 18-month research project in 1984 chronicling the lives and working conditions of early Japanese immigrants who farmed in Santa Clara Valley. Timothy Lukes told a *Mercury News* reporter in a June 13, 1984 article that, "Even the reform politicians, the so-called progressives, were racist, calling for clean government and anti-Japanese laws at the same time." In Palo Alto, strong anti-Japanese sentiment led to such blatant racism as that of a January 7, 1920 *Palo Alto Times* editorial lamenting that "the energetic campaign against land ownership by Japanese [was failing]." Such groups as the Palo Alto Anti-Japanese Laundry League met from 1900 to 1910.

Though it should be noted that not all local citizens espoused racist views—for example, in the 1890s, many Palo Altans supported Jane Lathrop Stanford's dismissal of Professor Edward A. Ross partly because of his anti-Japanese stand—other Palo Altans took every opportunity to vent their prejudices. The Chinese community, located along El Camino south of what is now College Terrace, bore the brunt of local racist attitudes. Perhaps the Chinese suffered the most because they were the largest, most visible minority group to come to early Palo Alto.

An editorial in the November 3, 1893 issue of the *Live Oak* reveals the depth of anti-Chinese feeling:

> No saloons for Palo Alto! No Chinese for Palo Alto! Clean town, clean morals ... The cry in other towns: 'The Chinese Must Go!' In Palo Alto, the motto is: 'The Chinese must not come!

An editorial in the November 8, 1893 *Palo Alto Times* shows that the feeling was broad-based:

> We are solidly determined that that vile combination of bad odors, bad women and bad habits known as Chinatown shall not find a lodgment within our [Palo Alto] limits. There is a place for everything—even for a nuisance, and the place for a Chinatown is as far as possible from Palo Alto ... [The other night] it was learned that a certain citizen had built a shanty for a Chinese wash house, and had leased it to a Chinaman for five years. A large delegation of citizens

Mayfield School graduating class, circa 1919, shows that both integration and assimilation were making some progress. The teacher, Kate Smith, is at center; the Asian girl is not identified. A more obvious minority is the young man, whose name is Pearson. Courtesy Palo Alto Historical Association

> immediately waited on him and protested against his plan ... [Cancelling the lease] was soon arranged with the Chinaman, and the danger averted.

A brief look at the complex history of Chinese integration into California society shows how some Anglo Palo Altans acquired their prejudices.

Eliot Mears points out that the Chinese originally came to California for the same reasons other nationalities did, as Forty-Niners seeking gold nuggets. He cites, Ta Chen writes in *Chinese Migrations* (1923):

> The state of California, which contained three-fourths of the Chinese immigrants until after the exclusion law was passed, was settled by men drawn by the lure of gold ... who had no intention of earning a living as laborers or domestics. They came to make no less than a fortune.

Like most Forty-Niners, however, the Chinese for the most part did not strike it rich. Instead, they found jobs, particularly in California wineries and lumber mills, and working on the railroads being laid across the West by Leland Stanford and his colleagues. At first their cheap labor was encouraged, and by 1867, 50,000 Chinese—primarily Cantonese from Southern China—had been induced to come to California.

Soon, conflict arose in the fight for California jobs. Racism grew. In 1877, San Francisco, as well as some smaller towns, experienced a number of anti-Chinese riots. The anti-Chinese sentiment culminated in 1882 with the Chinese Exclusion Act which, with subsequent acts, stopped Chinese immigration. In 1913, the first Alien Land Law passed in California effectively made it impossible for Asians, who were not allowed citizenship, to own land. Racism that would be unthinkable today was institutionalized.

In the Palo Alto-Mayfield region, the hostility was not limited to angry letters to the editor and scare tactics. Outright violence sometimes broke out, as evidenced in this May, 1899 article in the *Palo Alto Times*:

> A party of Palo Alto young men, out for a lark last Sunday evening, when a short distance south of Mayfield met a couple of quiet and inoffensive Chinamen on the road. The pent up exuberance

> of their natures, which had been accumulating in the temperance town for some time must have vent, and they thought there was an opportunity. So the rig was stopped and three or four of the party jumped out and proceeded to beat and pummel the Chinamen without the least cause or provocation ... A resident of the vicinity passing a short time afterward found the Chinamen in the road and brought them to town. They entered a complaint before Justice Van Buren.

Unfortunately, this was not an isolated incident. Bruce Cumming writes in the unpublished manuscript, *History of the Palo Alto Police Department*, that when Samuel W. Charles was appointed Justice of the Peace for the Palo Alto township on September 6, 1901:

> One of [his] first significant cases involved 9 grammar school youths who were charged with assaulting a Chinese vegetable vendor. The boys threw stones and one hit the man and inflicted a severe scalp wound. Abusing the Chinese was apparently a common practice in these times.

Anti-Chinese sentiment was so ingrained that some of Palo Alto's leading citizens felt free to espouse it publicly. John F. Parkinson, president of Palo Alto's first Board of Trustees, wrote an editorial in *The Citizen*, a Palo Alto Weekly newspaper he owned and published, headlined: "People's Law Must Be Obeyed." Parkinson rants:

> *The Citizen* stands ready with the community to say that the Chinese merchants, laundrymen,

In this portrait of an illustrious Chinese-American family, the father, Nam-Art Soo-Hoo, was a Presbyterian minister and founding editor of the Chinese daily newspaper in San Francisco. Son Peter Soo-Hoo (standing) graduated in civil engineering from Stanford (1908), then returned to China to build the Canton-Hankow railroad. After the 1906 earthquake he walked to San Francisco to help his family; it took three days to get there. The other children, Lily, Clara, Lincoln, Andrew, Pauline, and Nettie, earned degrees from American universities and became university professors or engineers. Of 11 children in all, six returned to China to teach or work. Courtesy of Ruth Fok

"Chinaman Jim," gardener at the Squire house on University Avenue.
Courtesy Palo Alto Historical Association

> etc., are not wanted in our midst and cannot prosper in this community. We predict for the Chinaman absolute, utter failure, and it will take him but a short time to discover it and he will go the way of others.

The ominous tone of Parkinson's letter is not spelled out. An anonymous editorial in the December 29, 1903 issue of the *Palo Alto Times* is more explicit:

> Citizens of Mayfield are meeting with difficulties in their effort to change the location of the Chinese quarters. It is not easy to find land upon which to place them and such tracts as can be had the Chinese will not accept. The people in our neighboring town [Palo Alto] have about come to the conclusion that the proper thing to do is to prosecute the Chinamen for their frequent infraction of the law and for sustaining nuisances and thus make it unprofitable for them to stay where they are. It would be best for Mayfield if the Celestials could be eliminated entirely and it would be an improvement to have their places moved away from the county road.

Though the Chinese were not dislodged from their homes, the campaign against their working and residing in the area did not stop. In 1905, Mok Wo, Ah Fong and their agent, B.F. Hall, applied to the City of Palo Alto for a license to open the Cardinal Restaurant at 209 University Avenue. John D. Boyd, Clerk of the Town of Palo Alto, denied the request "without ceremony," as reported in a July 29, 1905 article in *The Citizen* headlined "No License for Chink Beanery." B.F. Hall persisted on behalf of his client, and eventually, the restaurant opened, establishing a small niche for other successful Chinese businesses in Palo Alto.

Yet the California state land laws and renewed immigration acts, including the law of 1924 that excluded, in effect, all Asians, made it impossible for Chinese to fully partake in the riches of California. According to Connie Young Yu, in an article "Our Bicentennial Story" written for the October, 1976 Chinese/American Conference held in Palo Alto, from 1910 to 1940, many Chinese trying to immigrate were detained for long periods on Angel Island and some were deported.

Yu points out that it was not until 1943 that Chinese "saw the beginning of equal opportunity." That year, the exclusion acts were repealed, an annual federal immigration quota of 105 set, and naturalization privileges extended to all Chinese. Also, the valor of the Chinese during U.S. military service in both world wars and Chinese-American contributions to war industries lowered racial barriers across the country.

J.F. Parkinson, lumberman and first postmaster, was a prominent figure in Palo Alto for 40 years.
Courtesy Palo Alto Historical Association

The Leung family of Palo Alto: from left, mother Jungsee, son Jimmy, father Kee, son Peter Hin, in 1922. Hin Leung became an architect and worked for Birge Clark. Courtesy Jimmy Leung

Ruth Fok, a Palo Alto resident for 33 years, and former member of the Commission for the Status of Women in Santa Clara County, agrees that it is best not to cover over problems of prejudice, whether "blatant or covert." In a 1989 interview, she described her family's personal contact with discrimination in California. Because of the Asian Exclusion Acts, her mother, California-born Lily Soo Hoo, was stripped of her citizenship when she married William Z.L.Sung, a graduate student from China, at Oberlin in 1921. Mrs. Fok says with quiet sorrow, "We Chinese didn't have a chanced to become second or even third-class citizens. We weren't allowed to be citizens at all."

She adds, "I have lived a long time and I have seen prejudice between races, within races, and between sexes. It is not a problem confined to one area or group. It is a human failing." She and her husband Samuel faced discrimination themselves when they were looking for a house in Palo Alto in the 1950s, finally buying from builder Joseph Eichler. "For me," she says, "prejudice does not cause rancor; what I feel is a deep sadness."

Kee Leung, a successful Palo Alto businessman, lived through California's era of discrimination. In 1897, he came to Palo Alto to work as a cook at the Phi Delta Theta house on campus. As reported in a 1948 *Palo Alto Times* feature by Rosa Jensen:

> Men from the stock farm and workmen on the new university ate there with the students, paying around ten cents a meal. Summer, [Leung] worked for Charles Dobbel, who had a tourist camp and rest home in Woodside ... In 1914, he started the City Cafe on High street and in 1920 moved it to the 100 block on University Avenue where he stayed six years. He then built and operated the Mandarin Grill and it is in the same building that he and his son Jimmy have their new restaurant, the Golden Dragon.
>
> Kee Leung was born in San Francisco 74 years ago. He belongs to the Chinese Citizens Alliance ... He built one of the first early apartment houses—the Palm Court Apts. on Cowper. He has been active in bond drives in both world wars, and was captain of the Chinese citizens' group that was first 'over the top' in the Liberty Bond drive of 1918.
>
> Kee Leung has three children. Mrs. Helen Lew who lives in Oakland; a son, Hin, who is with Clark and Stromquist, architects of Palo Alto; and Jimmy, the only one born in California. Jimmy saw nearly three years of service, in the Ground Forces Training Command and later as mess officer of Bremen Port Command.

It would be pleasant to erase from history the kinds of conscious and unconscious bigotry Kee Leung and others have faced in their efforts to make a successful life in Palo Alto. However, by letting the record stand, perhaps we become more sensitive to the ways intolerance detracts from everyone's life.

Chapter Notes

The articles from the *Palo Alto Times*, *Live Oak*, and *The Citizen* were obtained from the files of the Palo Alto Historical Association.

The research by Timothy J. Lukes and Gary Y. Okihiro on Japanese pioneers has been published as a book, *Japanese Legacy: Farming and Community Life in Santa Clara Valley* (1985).

An understanding of the overall picture of Asian immigration can be gained from Eliot G. Mears' 1928 book, *Resident Orientals on the American Pacific Coast: Their Legal and Economic Status.* Connie Young Yu's concise introduction to the 1976 Palo Alto pamphlet for the conference "We ... Chinese Americans" co-sponsored by the Palo Alto Revolution Bicentennial Committee '76 and the Palo Alto Unified School District provides a good place to start research on the Chinese in California.

Top: the earliest picture (1892) of University Avenue shows the dirt track (far left) disappearing between oaks; High Street crosses it between two buildings. The simple but handsome real estate office sports a false front, bracketed cornice, flagpole, and veranda. Below: by 1894 the town had sprouted many commercial buildings, and houses were popping up in the distance. Two buildings in top picture appear in this view of High Street and University, looking north. Courtesy Palo Alto Historical Association

CHAPTER TWELVE

The New Town Grows

Most cities grow unevenly, by relatively slow increments, expanding according to economic changes. Palo Alto, however, arrived full-blown, an idea conceived by Leland and Jane Stanford. The grid of Palo Alto's main streets was recorded in San Jose on February 27, 1889, and those who bought lots found themselves contending with loneliness and raw land.

Recalls Marguerite Weichselfelder, an early resident: "The land was mostly hay or wheat fields, with scattered houses. The fields were good places to hide when playing hide-and-go-seek or run, sheep, run. When the hay was cut, haystacks provided play places. It was fun to see how far you could tunnel under without having the haycock cave in." These early residents quickly realized, however, that despite the hardship of starting over in the middle of nowhere, they had a rare opportunity to build a city from nothing in one generation. They made the most of it. Their creative approach to municipal affairs still influences the city of today.

The First Years

On June 14, 1890, Anna Probst Zschokke, a widow, and her three young children came to Palo Alto from Santa Clara with their household goods piled into one buckboard wagon. Anna's husband, a pharmacist and doctor, had died of tuberculosis, leaving her a plot of land in Palo Alto. He had planned to build a family home near Stanford University, where he hoped their oldest son Theodore would attend when he came of age. The widow, Palo Alto's first resident, camped under the oak trees with her children while a house was built on Homer Avenue.

Anna Zschokke was a remarkable woman who left her imprint on Palo Alto's schools and other institutions. Born in Germany on September 30, 1849, she came to Terra Haute, Indiana when she was three years old. Her father taught German in a nearby normal school. He had a strict rule that his five children speak no English—only perfect German—at their dinner table. Anna's love of learning, her self-discipline, and her ability to get things done are characteristics that she imparted to the new town.

As the story of Palo Alto unfolds, Anna Zschokke takes a prominent role. Physically, she was quite diminutive. Her grandson Fremont Zschokke describes her in an October 9, 1988 oral history ably conducted by Betty Rogaway, longtime member of the Palo Alto Historical Association. Says Fremont:

> [My grandmother Anna Zschokke] was a real short woman ... she was about maybe four feet ten ... No fat on her, she was pretty busy, and pretty industrious. But she always wanted to be a little taller. So she had long hair and she would always wind it up into kind of a psyche and put a hat on top of it. Which was ... to look a little taller than she really was, so ... it would shape up here and [she] put a hat on it.

Anna's size did not stop her from setting to work in the new town. Her daughter, Irma Zschokke (Crawford), remembers:

> The windmill and tank rising above our oak tree was built prior to our move. We settled at once in a tent under a tree next to our lot, then into the two-story, newly-built barn, then into our new house. The platform around the tank had several beehives which soon expanded to twenty hives providing much work and an income for my brothers which they used mainly for guns to go hunting with ... Our house was the first one to be built in the town of Palo Alto. We soon had a lawn with a border of roses and a row of fruit trees. Beside our driveway our fence was promptly covered with grape vines taken from our Santa Clara vine ... the streets were graded through the fields. Some hops were already staked out in what was then called 'Timothy Hopkins' Wheat Field.'

This 1893 view shows the Bank of Palo Alto looking like a wedding cake at the corner of University and the Circle, where a similarly-shaped building stands today. Large building at near left is Hall's Drug Store.
Courtesy Palo Alto Historical Association

> Alas, many of the new houses meant the chopping down of my favorite trees, so I often arrived home in tears. [Mother] could only blame this on progress, and described our town of the future which sounded like bad news to me.

That winter of 1890-91, only five other families lived in the heart of the fledgling town. The Arragons used an abandoned barn as a dwelling. Homes for the other families—Lynch, Gillan, Kimball, and Anderson—were in various states of development.

Dust

In the next years, the university's quadrangle rose slowly from the dust. Palo Altans came out to watch, and the dust thickened the air and gathered on their shoes. Ellen Elliott recalls, "The dust—the most perfect dust in the universe, lying gray and powdery over everything—'got on our nerves,' and we brazenly desired some old-time mud ... [there were] mosquitoes and a form of beast not mentioned in polite company (fleas)."

After touring the university, Palo Altans drove their buggies back to their own construction projects. New houses had to be built in town for the 76 families that inhabited Palo Alto by the next year. Writes Eleanor Pearson Bartlett, co-founder with Lucy Fletcher of Castilleja Hall, a private school for girls, and author of "Beginnings in Palo Alto" in the 1905 book *The First Year at Stanford*, "Palo Alto [in 1891] was a pioneer settlement, indeed. If I remember rightly, 'down town' consisted of Parkinson's lumber yard, with a tiny shanty for a post office at one corner, Mrs. Yale's little thread and needle shop ... The Sunday school assembled on benches under the big oaks by the station." This "station," according to David Starr Jordan, was originally just a railroad car that served as a depot until an open shed was built in 1891, then enclosed and heated.

Anna Zschokke recalls that early visitors could not see the university or the town when they first alighted from the train. "Finally the traveller would decide to follow the faint streaks discernible in the waving grain, or perchance the weeds or stubble meant for a street, and get utterly bewildered among the trees, for there were many more of them at that time."

University Ave. in 1894 had wooden plank sidewalks to protect the ladies' boots from mud and dust. Bicycling never has gone out of fashion in Palo Alto. Courtesy Palo Alto Historical Association

Even when visitors discovered the town, they found the streets a nightmare. Notes Eleanor Bartlett:

> But my chief recollection is of the roads ... One dreary stretch of dust in the summer, and an unending chain of black mud holes in winter, with no sidewalks at all. The first sidewalk we had was constructed by voluntary subscriptions on the part of the property owners, and ran up Waverley Street, with a side branch off to us. Occasionally an absentee owner refused to pay, and it ambled across the street to some more public-spirited person on the other side. It was a simple affair, just two planks following all the natural ups and downs, just too narrow for two persons ... It was quite a feat to get from one end to the other, without succumbing to mud on either side, or the crack that yawned fearfully between. But the dismal state of the roads was compensated for, as far as beauty went, by the trees that still shaded them.

Somehow, newcomers found their way and brought business to the new town. In September, 1891, Miss Alice Horton opened Palo Alto's first restaurant. The next month, Palo Altans began patronizing the city's first bookstore, opened by H. W. Simkins. Thus the early Palo Altans were able to indulge both of their consuming interests—eating and learning.

Other entrepreneurs moved in. According to historian Arthur Coffman, from 1890 to 1894, the number of buildings in Palo Alto rose from six to 165, and the population boomed to 700. Although Palo Altans could still hear the rasp of saws and the rhythm of hammers drifting from the university across the hayfield, it was time for them to think about their own schools, grading of the streets, water services, and all the other necessities of a small town set in the wilderness of California.

Before the century was over, they argued heatedly over city-owned versus private control of water, gas,

Hill & Yard took many of the early pictures of the town. This 1894 view shows their studio on the north side of University betwen High and Emerson. Posters advertise cigars. Courtesy Palo Alto Historical Association

and electricity utilities. They campaigned for strong secondary schools and effective medical care. They debated securing land for open space, and they battled over Prohibition, women's suffrage, and minority rights. In these controversies, their clashing hopes and dreams mirrored those of citizens in small towns throughout the State of California.

Their approach to realizing those dreams was quite different, however. While other small western towns—and even the big ones like San Francisco and Los Angeles—struggled with inadequate water systems and disorganized city services, some Palo Altans quickly showed their individuality by lobbying for municipal ownership and management of water, electricity and gas. Later, the city even experimented with municipal provision of medical care. Gradually, the town developed centrally-controlled services. In this sense, Palo Alto was one of the first modern municipalities in the west. Citizens of other towns were not so sure that the experiment worked, and editorials appeared in western newspapers saying that the citizens of Palo Alto were akin to socialists.

Palo Altans refused to listen; they were busily establishing one of the highest standards of living west of the Mississippi.

A Dry Town Needs Water

Actually the story of bringing water to this town situated next to a brackish bay begins not with a brilliant communal idea, but with a Rube Goldberg kind of plumbing. By December, 1892, there was such an urgent need for water in the new town that, for the use of his livery stable, H.G. Wilson sank a 175-foot well and erected a 14,000-gallon wooden tank. A similar tank can still be seen at Hawthorne and Alma Streets. As a service to his neighbors, Wilson laid pipe to nearby developments.

A few individual homeowners sank their own wells and pumped water up to tank houses. The most famous tank house was built in Professorville, the section of town now bounded by Ramona, Kingsley, Waverley, and Addison Avenue, where Stanford faculty were beginning to settle. Near the home of Charles Benjamin Wing, Professor of Civil Engineering at Stanford, this tall tank house built over a cooperative well was maintained by Professor Frank Angell, who headed the Psychology Department, Charles D. ("Daddy") Marx, a Professor of Structural Engineering, W. W. Thoburn, a Methodist minister and Professor of Biology, and Wing himself. This water "system" pieced together by the academics to serve their homes broke down one night, and it was rumored in Palo Alto that the only person who could get it running again was a local handyman. Palo Altans were proud of the practical ingenuity of ordinary citizens.

Drinking water for homes without wells was provided, according to Birge Clark, architect, by a "horse-drawn tank wagon [that] went along the alley from which professors had to dip out their drinking water with a bucket. The area of Palo Alto between the creek, Embarcadero, Middlefield, and Alma developed in almost identical fashion [as Stanford] except that 'Professorville' rapidly became a little more dense, but there were the same tanks and

Looking north on Emerson at University, where the new Ledyard building sports a domed turret and striped awnings. Across the street is Parkinson's Lumber Co. Courtesy Palo Alto Historical Association

windmills, and backyard privies."

Town leaders, notably Stanford professors Charles D. Marx and C. B. Wing, saw that the problem with water could be solved only by municipal intervention. Eventually, this led them to believe that broad services should be centrally controlled.

C.D. Marx is known in engineering circles as the man who declared that the Golden Gate Bridge was economically and financially not feasible. However, his forthright, early criticism certainly helped strengthen the early design plans of the bridge. And it was this willingness to take a position that made Marx's contribution to early Palo Alto so significant.

To put his plan of municipal ownership of utilities to work in Palo Alto, he and his supporters realized that the city had to be legally incorporated. They campaigned vigorously for incorporation, and on April 9, 1894, the 750 residents of Palo Alto voted to become a city. Official papers were filed with the state on April 16.

A huge bonfire to celebrate the official birth of the town was built at the corner of University Avenue and High Street. Stanford's band marched in and, with their inimitable raucous and casual style, apparent even in their first performances, helped the town celebrate its incorporation.

Armed with the city charter, the city leaders campaigned for a $40,000 city bond issue to buy out the private companies that haphazardly supplied water to the region and to install a public water system. The *Palo Alto Times*, founded as a weekly in 1893, campaigned in favor of the bond by becoming a daily four months before the election. On May 9, 1896, the bond issue passed.

Electrifying the City

Palo Alto's night watchman, G. D. Dunsmore, not only kept the tiny town secure, at dusk he lit the glowing kerosene lamps that illuminated the business district at night. In December, 1896, however, that part of his job was eliminated as electricity came to Palo Alto, and the two-block business section was strung with incandescent lights. Thus began the saga of the municipally-owned electrical company. Palo Alto was just about ready to move into the next century.

Electricity was supplied to Palo Alto for 20 cents per kilowatt-hour by the Peninsula Lighting Company of Redwood City, under a 23-month franchise that was later extended. Marx and Wing argued publicly that this was too high. They claimed that the city could build a plant that would supply electricity for *half* the going rate. Officers of the privately-owned Peninsula Lighting Company wanted the city's concession, but the town trustees asked E.C. Moore, city engineeer, to cost out a new plant and, amazingly, the price came to $12,000, the exact amount of the money in the treasury, a surplus left from an 1898 sewer bond.

One hundred and thirty residents signed a petition for such a city-owned business. Moore set to work, using a Corliss steam engine and electric generator installed in the water plant building. Palo Altans soon began enjoying cheap electrical power from dusk until midnight.

First city water plant, at Newell and Embarcadero, 1900. Courtesy Palo Alto Historical Association

In 1900, however, the Redwood city businessmen tried to lure back Palo Alto customers by undercutting their own rates to eight cents per kilowatt hour. A price war was on.

Early Palo Alto civic leaders were not hampered by stodginess. They displayed creativity bordering on high-handedness in dealing with the city's early problems. But they also had a good sense of fun. During the price war, the private Redwood City company disregarded Palo Alto's city charter regulating franchises, and one Sunday strung lines into the City of Palo Alto. Since city offices were closed, no injunction could be obtained and the private company made a significant incursion into city territory.

Marx and his friends fumed. But not for long. Mysteriously, their rival's electrical wires and other equipment disappeared a few nights later and a notice appeared in the newspaper advertising where the equipment could be found—no questions asked, or answered. Thus, the Palo Alto group won, assisted by the nefarious characters—certainly not the town leaders—who had spirited away their competition's equipment.

Gas

The last major utility to fall to Palo Alto's municipal ownership was gas. The first Palo Alto trustees, John Hutchinson, D. L. Sloan, George Mosher, J.S. Butler, and C.D. Marx, wanted to install a city-owned plant, but they were defeated in a city election, and the franchise was awarded to the Palo Alto Gas Company, privately controlled by L.C. Low of Santa Clara. This private company equipped the city with a piping system that delivered gas purchased from Pacific Gas and Electric.

In 1912, however, city officials sought at first to control the rates, then to condemn the private plant altogether and gain control of the gas system. The railroad commission, which still established rates, set the value of the plant at $65,500. The private company appealed, asking for $15,000 more. To settle the matter, the president of the railroad commission invited Palo Alto officials to randomly examine the condition of pipes. Ever wily, city engineers looked for signs of decay on the soil and around nearby trees and managed to find only leaky and rusty pipes underneath. The Palo Alto Gas Company abandoned its appeal, and in 1917 the new gas plant was dedicated, and the City of Palo Alto finally owned all three of its utilities.

Opposite, top: J.F. Parkinson's first lumber yard, and the town's first post office, were in this tiny building on Alma Street in 1890-91. From right are Benon, the town's first banker; C.W. Jones, founder of Palo Alto Times; J.J. Morris, first real estate agent; Felix Rainer, Parkinson's bookkeeper; Alice Kelly, Acting Postmaster for Parkinson, and a Stanford student. Building also held the first telephone office, with one phone. Below: Parkinson's second, larger lumber yard, on University between Emerson and High, where a crowd has gathered to watch someone work—or to have their picture taken. Courtesy Palo Alto Historical Association

POST OFFICE
GERMAN AMERICAN
FIREMAN'S FU

THE PARKINSON
LUMBER HARDWARE CO
AGENCY
OOK STORE

Above: By 1898, University has a pool parlor and an imposing brick building (behind the bank) with striking window trim; it's still there. Left: Hall's Pharmacy, with living quarters above, dominated the first block of University on the north side in 1893. Next to it is a small, elegant building which was later moved to face the street and converted to a library.

Opposite: Two vital businesses were the blacksmith (top) and the livery stable, housed in a handsome building (right). The horse-drawn Palo Alto & University Bus served visitors arriving by train. Courtesy Palo Alto Historical Association

ANK OF PALO ALTO
A. 1892
THE BANK OF

MULLEN & HARMS.
BLACKSMITHING
& HORSE SHOEING
RED BELL

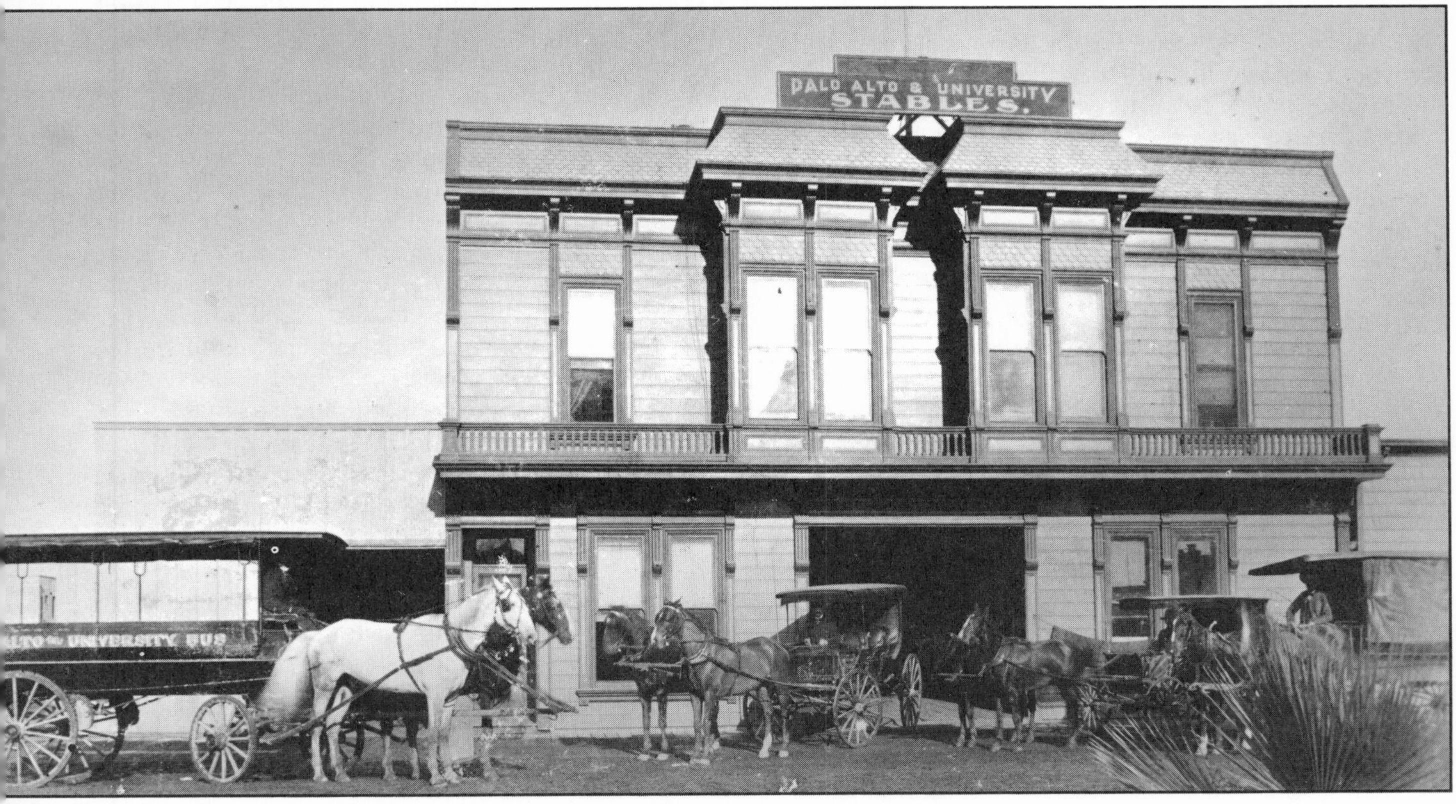

Palo Alto's first school, on Bryant, was built by volunteers in just three days in 1893, so that Palo Alto children would no longer have the long trek to Mayfield. The two classrooms were crowded, but by 1894 the much larger Channing School was ready to open. Courtesy Palo Alto Historical Association

Education

Palo Altans were deeply concerned with the education of their young children from the very beginning. In 1891, the only school was located in Mayfield. Palo Alto children walked to the two-story frame schoolhouse and, according to "Schools Wanted Here," an excellent pamphlet published by the Palo Alto Historical Association, children from neighboring ranches rode horseback to classes and left their steeds hobbled to the hitch-rail back of the schoolhouse.

> Al Mesa, of Palo Alto, attended primary grades in the frame Mayfield School and remembers such teachers as Mamie Dowd, Miss Zumwalt, and Miss Passmore, the drawing teacher from Stanford. Al, whose great grandfathers, Tom Miranda and Prado Mesa, were once the Spanish commandantes of Presidios Monterey and San Francisco, recalls playing 'Andy Over' across the school roof with a ball at opportune times when neither Principal McIntosh nor Mr. M. R. Trace was at hand.

By 1893, Palo Altans began agitating for their own school district. Anna P. Zschokke spearheaded the school drive. According to the Palo Alto Historical Association, by Anna Zschokke's own census, 54 school age children resided in Palo Alto. With John F. Parkinson, the lumberman who later became president of Palo Alto's first Board of Trustees, Anna Zschokke convinced the county superintendent of schools Lemuel Job Chipman that Palo Alto schools should be outside the Mayfield sphere of influence. Parkinson personally measured the two mile distance from Mayfield needed to fulfill new school district requirements, and Palo Alto men set to work. Writes Anna Zschokke's daughter, Irma: "A school was desperately needed in our town so the first one was built in three days [on Bryant near University Avenue] by all available able-bodied men. It had two large rooms with a wood stove placed halfway through the partition, allowing heat and noise to spread ... "

W. E. Norris, William Pluns and Frank Cramer, the first elected school board members, helped Anna Zschokke dedicate the new building. She writes: "On Admission Day [1893], we assembled at the school house to celebrate a flag raising with appropriate exercises. We were a happy crowd, especially the mothers of school age children who were there in force."

Seventy pupils had registered at the W. E. Norris furniture store for the first day of classes on Monday, February 12, 1893. Mrs. E. H. Powers rang the large bell hung in the cupola, calling the children to their lessons.

In the next months, the school population swelled. Palo Alto city kids mingled with those from nearby farms. According to the Palo Alto Historical Association, "Joe Vargas, tenant at the Greer Place, drove each morning with his springwagon load of 14 kids, eight being his own," to be instructed by such teachers as "Miss Mayme Bass and Mrs. Ellsworth L. Rich ... Miss Bass was principal."

The tiny building, crowded with two hundred children by the end of the next year, was either too cold, or, when the stove was heated, too hot. There were not enough texts or materials.

Yet, according to the Palo Alto Historical Association:

> The public grammar school was a going concern. Miss Bass asked, October 20, that a croquet ground be fixed for the children and offered to superintend the volunteer work in person and enthuse the workers. On October 27 the schoolhouse got a large box stove for heating the two classrooms, and on November 3 its team won a 16-10 football victory over Mayfield. By December 8 the school marms began selling 25-cent tickets for the December 22 Nortree Hall school library fund entertainment, in which 16 girls presented a wand drill and costumed youngsters performed in 'Ten Little Grasshoppers,' 'Rose March,' and 'Sleeping Daisies.'

Palo Altans, well aware of the school's inadequacies, passed a $15,000 school-bond issue for a two-story six-room schoolhouse in 1893 (with 45 favorable votes counted at the Norris Store), and school trustees acquired a site for the new building at Channing Avenue and Webster Street. By the next year, the grammar school pupils occupied the lower floor of the new Channing School and the town's 20 high school students studied under the direction of Miss Margaret Foster and M.W. Greer in the upper two rooms, paying tuition of $6 a month to the administration of Principal Granville Terrell.

But even the new school could not long accommodate the influx of children. Building schools to keep up with the population growth became a major community activity.

Anna Zschokke, who became known as General Whipper-In, built the first free-standing high school in 1897 at 526 Forest Avenue. Writes her daughter

Jane Stanford established a free kindergarten in Mayfield in 1887, when it still seemed likely that Mayfield would be the university town. Courtesy Palo Alto Historical Association

Irma, "But there was no high school building in the town's immediate plans ... So my mother mortgaged our home, bought a lot, secured a good contractor and built the high school of three rooms with good plumbing."

The mystery of how Anna Zschokke, a widow, had sufficient financial means to donate an entire high school to Palo Alto was cleared up in 1988 when Betty Rogaway asked Fremont Zschokke about his grandmother's funds. Fremont explained that the Zschokke family can be traced to the sixteenth century in Switzerland and somewhere along the line, a fund was set up to benefit anyone with the Zschokke name. Family members could draw from it during times of need, and those with extra resources replenished the account. So it could be said that an ancient Swiss family tradition helped bring Palo Alto's schools into being!

Anna Zschokke's building, including a wing for the study of science added later, served as the public high school until the city passed a $20,000 bond issue to finance a new school across the street on Channing, built in 1901.

Birge Clark, one of the illustrious graduates of that second high school, writes:

> The high school was in a four square two-story frame building standing where Channing House now is. It was virtually a prep school for Stanford—both because of the high percentage of professors' children attending it, and the fact that in those days the law required that a teenager attend high school only through the age of 16, which more or less coincided with the end of the first two years of high school, and anybody who wasn't going on to college would drop out of high school at that time. In my class of 42 in 1910, 38 entered Stanford the next fall. Don't think that we were all that erudite. It only took 15 "B" grades plus your principal's recommendation to get into Stanford in those days—if you were a boy, that is. Girls had been limited to 500 and people were entering newborn daughters' applications the day after birth.

In 1907, the $21,648 Lytton School was opened on the street of that name to accommodate additional high school students. Many Palo Alto residents affectionately recall taking lessons from Elizabeth Van Auken, who began teaching at Lytton School in 1912 and retired as principal in 1949.

Anna Zschokke left the legacy of an outstanding school system to Palo Alto children. All three of her children—and her grandchildren—attended Palo Alto schools and graduated from Stanford. She herself pursued an education by attending several classes at Stanford until her health required her to slow down. From then on, according to her daughter Irma, Anna maintained an enjoyable contact with Stanford as a guest in Professor Rentdorf's German classes, where she spoke German to his students.

Lirio Hall, 325 Waverley St., was a private school and a meeting place for religious and civic groups. Mrs. Willard, owner, sits on the porch; J.K. Hutchinson stands at the gate. The building was flattened in the 1906 quake.
Courtesy Palo Alto Historical Association

Left: Anna P. Zschokke with her daughter, Irma, and grandson. Mrs. Zschokke, one of the first to settle in the new town, was what people used to call "a go-getter." When she saw a need for a high school in Palo Alto, she had a four-room house built at 526 Forest (below) and lent it to the town for use as a school until Channing School could be built. A leader in social, civic, and cultural affairs, she left her mark on Palo Alto as few other people have. Courtesy Palo Alto Historical Association

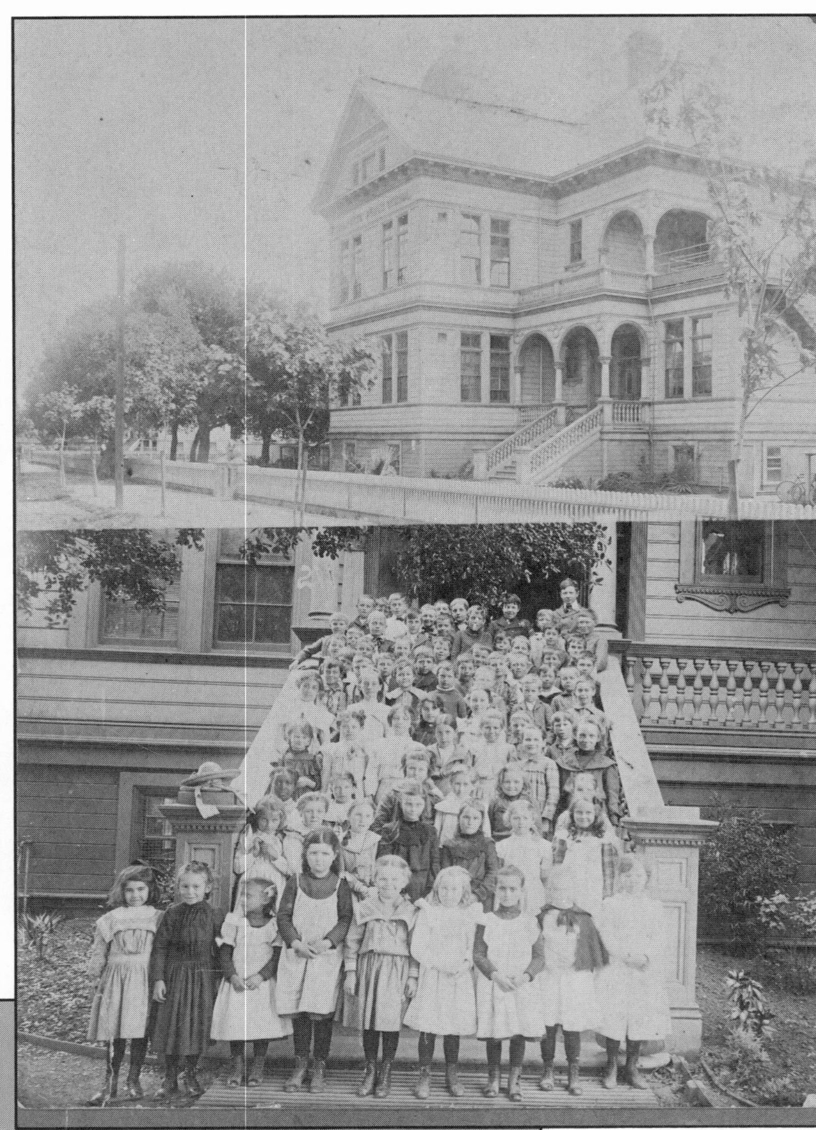

Right: Channing School, built in 1894, shown here in 1903 with a troop of promising first-graders on the steps; the school, which served elementary and high school pupils, was torn down in 1926. Below: The first public-built high school, opened in 1909, shows the new directions architecture was taking. Courtesy Palo Alto Historical Association

Christmas in Palo Alto in the Nineties

While much of the country reveled in the razzle dazzle spirit of the Gay Nineties, Christmas of 1893 was bittersweet for the 400 citizens of Palo Alto. Not only had the labor unrest and nationwide economic panic earlier in the year left them shaken, they were also still mourning their beloved Senator Leland Stanford, who had died in June, just two years after his university opened its doors. With the assets of his estate frozen in a legal battle, many doubted that his widow Jane Lathrop would even be able to keep the university open.

Nevertheless, these pioneers were able to capture the holiday spirit. The eldest daughter of a typical family was sent to the pie shop in the basement of Scroggs' big house on the northeast corner of Ramona Street and Lytton Avenue for mincemeat and pumpkin delectables.

With pies in hand, she would have to follow the wooden planks that were the fledgling town's only sidewalks. As Marguerite Weichselfelder recalls, the journey about town was most perilous when you tried to cross the deeply-rutted streets. "The boards sank in the slush, and there you were, sunk, too." Sometimes men rushing by on Christmas errands were stopped and enlisted in a battle to free a wagon stuck in the mud. "Though the team of horses struggled and pulled, they couldn't move it. Then the driver, angry and cursing, (had) to get out in the mud ... Once [the wagon] was pulled out, it left a big hole in the street."

Women lifted their crinoline skirts above the mud and hurried to the one butcher shop on University. Mr. Dulion, head butcher, a large man with thick curly gray hair, would stand at the end of the counter near a large chopping block and hand over holiday meat orders. A small child wandering in with his mother would be given a free "wienie," which he would eat immediately.

Meanwhile, the Presbyterian Church at Waverley and University, the hub of much of Palo Alto's social activity, was being prepared for its finest evening of the year. The Zschokke family was in charge of this event. According to Irma Zschokke, her brothers took special pride in cutting down the best tree in the hills. Irma herself helped decorate the towering evergreen with tinkling bells and exquisite wax angels with wings of gauze, sent by her Tante Leontine from Aurau, Switzerland.

Finally, the Christmas service would begin with prayers and Christmas carols. Santa handed out gifts to children, including sweet oranges that had arrived from Los Angeles via the railroad built ten years before by Senator Stanford and his colleagues. Through all the festivities, Irma Zschokke's mother Anna sat hidden behind the tree, carefully pulling a string to suggest a gentle breeze among the branches and to tinkle the bells. Since there was no electricity, wax candles were used, and Anna Zschokke prudently kept a bucket of water at her feet. But this night, there was no fire. Several of the wax angels melted a bit, but more would be sent from the Old Country.

At the end of the party, the church bells rang as parents rushed home to put sleepy children to bed and begin decorating their own trees. Soon, 1894 would begin, a year when the entire town would turn out for another celebration—the lighting of a huge bonfire at High Street and University Avenue to signal the official incorporation of the City of Palo Alto.

The Hamilton Stage Coach Company carried passengers between the railroad and outlying towns on the Peninsula.
Courtesy Peninsula Times Tribune

Transportation

The fate of Palo Alto was closely tied to the university growing nearby. Both town and gown depended upon the transportation industry. Not only was the little town conceived upon the philanthropy of transportation mogul Leland Stanford, but also its economy quickly became keyed to commuters. Palo Alto was strategically located along El Camino, part of the traditional inland route from Monterey to San Francisco. Yet, as many early residents noted, transportation problems arose just about as quickly as the population climbed.

Even before Palo Alto became a town, the stage-coach road along El Camino was rutted and unkempt. The overnight journey down the peninsula was so perilous that passengers from San Francisco often chose to go by steamboat or schooner down the bay to Alviso and thence overland to San Jose instead of risking the kidney-jolting ride down the old mission route. Several attempts to establish a railroad were begun and abandoned in the mid-1800s until finally, in October 1863, Leland Stanford himself came to Mayfield to officiate at the opening of a line to San Francisco. In 1891, the first Palo Alto citizens could board the train only by signalling for it to stop. By the turn of the century, however, four- and six-car passenger trains ran twice daily from San Jose to San Francisco, making the forty-mile part of the journey from Palo Alto to San Francisco in the astounding sprint of one hour and fifteen minutes.

Travellers within town, and particularly between town and campus, climbed aboard the surrey owned by Jasper Paulsen. One favorite driver, "Uncle John," Asa Andrews, was famous for his tall tales, entertaining travelers along the route between the campus, the train station and downtown Palo Alto. Paulsen soon provided regular service with a horse-drawn wagon called the Marguerite, which was painted red and had yellow wheels. The name is commemorated by the red Marguerite buses that still ply routes from campus to town.

The Marguerite, which could carry 32 passengers, hauled picnic parties up King's Mountain Road and could even be hired for special trips to San Jose and La Honda. Taxiing Palo Altans to work and play, the Marguerite gave the town a festive atmosphere.

After the earthquake in 1906, lines were laid for the "Toonerville Trolley," an electric streetcar similar to the ones that ran in Los Angeles and other towns all over the West. Students rode on the Toonerville Trolley, joking and playing pranks; Palo Altans on errands traded gossip and joined in the high jinks and fun. It was not until thirty years later that enough citizens had automobiles to render the Toonerville obsolete.

Top: Only a fence and a For Sale sign occupy the Circle in this picture from 1894, as a train steams north past the little station; at far right is the back of the little wedding-cake bank building. Below: An 1895 picture shows passengers ready to board. Courtesy Palo Alto Historical Association

Most private transportation at the turn of the century was by bicycle, but a shopper could carry few supplies on a bicycle or the original Marguerite. So the shop came to the customer. Explains Birge Clark:

> Every morning a groceryman in a one-horse buggy would come around taking orders, and in the afternoon would return in a two-horse wagon to make deliveries ... Another daily delivery was by the butcher which had a covered wagon in which hung a beef, half a pig, half a calf, etc., and the butcher would cut off your order right there at the tail gate of the wagon, perhaps fighting off flies. He also carried a lot of packages on the seat beside him for people who had 'standing orders' for a roast on Thursdays, steaks on Mondays, etc. Twice a week, a fish wagon came around, the driver of which blew a horn so people could run out and get a fish. A bread wagon from Thompson's bakery on the Avenue came twice or three times a week, something which he was still doing as late as 1920. A tank wagon with kerosene also came at least once a week and here it was remarkable as the driver and owner was blind, but the horse knew the route and the driver would get out and know just where in the backyard the owner's oil can was kept, and with his [smaller] can would find his way to the can, and if you needed more oil would proceed to fill your can up. For those people who did not get their milk locally ... the Wildewood Dairy and driver Billy would arrive early in the morning and with a five-gallon can walk into your kitchen and fill a pan or pans which had been left out for him.

Year around, news from the outside world was still brought primarily by train. Newcomers and visitors no longer stepped off into an open field, but rather were greeted by Palo Altans at The Circle, a curve of businesses that grew up on the east side of the train station. Large oak trees shaded the old men watching the comings and goings of the famous and not-so-famous.

Recalls Fremont Zschokke, Anna Zschokke's grandson, "But coming into Palo Alto on the train or whatever you were travelling in, you could smell the area. Trees gave a certain odor to the whole area and you always knew that you were coming into Palo Alto because there were [beautiful] oak trees on the campus, and on both sides of the highway ... "

Recalls Paul Gibson, a child at the time:

> Palo Alto was a friendly place where everyone knew practically everyone else; also what they did. Gossip travelled faster than the newspaper which only came out once a week. Everyone seemed to

A four-horse omnibus carried passengers from the station to the Stanford campus in the 1890s. Courtesy Palo Alto Historical Association

E.F. Weisshaar and W.C. Werry stand in the doorway of Palo Alto's first grocery store, on Alma Street, in 1892. Mr. Weisshaar, member of a popular Mayfield family, evidently came up to cash in on the booming new town. Courtesy Palo Alto Historical Association

> know when a leading citizen came in periodically on the ten p.m. train and almost staggered home up the main street or when a certain prominent horse and buggy was tied too long or too frequently in the middle of a vacant block not too far from the home of an attractive widow. In fact, some folks said "gossip" kept the town honest. In any event, Palo Alto was not a dull place and had its share of activities with Fourth of July celebrations, its volunteer band concerts, Stanford affairs, travelling stock companies, dog shows, merry-go-arounds, and hypnotists.

Not only hypnotists, but occasionally movers and shakers of the world stopped at Palo Alto on their way to Stanford. Says Gibson: "I think the most important event was in 1903, when President Theodore Roosevelt visited Stanford. A patriotic arch was erected over the University entrance gates and all the school kids were lined up on each side of Palm Drive waving American flags, and President Roosevelt and his party, with their high silk hats, were driven to the Stanford Museum and to Mrs. Stanford's home."

Even on an ordinary day, there was plenty to see and do at The Circle and in the growing town. Says Lester R. Morris, another early citizen:

> I used to rollerskate on the Boardwalks around the Circle. Sometimes we'd carry our skates to a roller rink which used to be an old furniture store on Bryant Street across from the old Fire House ... I recall there was a firehose cart always parked across from Castle's Plumbing establishment on Emerson Street. We kids loved getting hold of the big rope and helping the firemen pull it to the fire.

As the children played, Palo Alto slowly changed "from a village to a town," according to Paul Gibson, "and the business section began at The Circle, extended down University Avenue to Ramona and rapidly lost itself between Bryant and Waverley."

H.W. Simkins opened the first bookstore at 159-161 University Avenue. The first lending library began here. Courtesy Palo Alto Historical Association

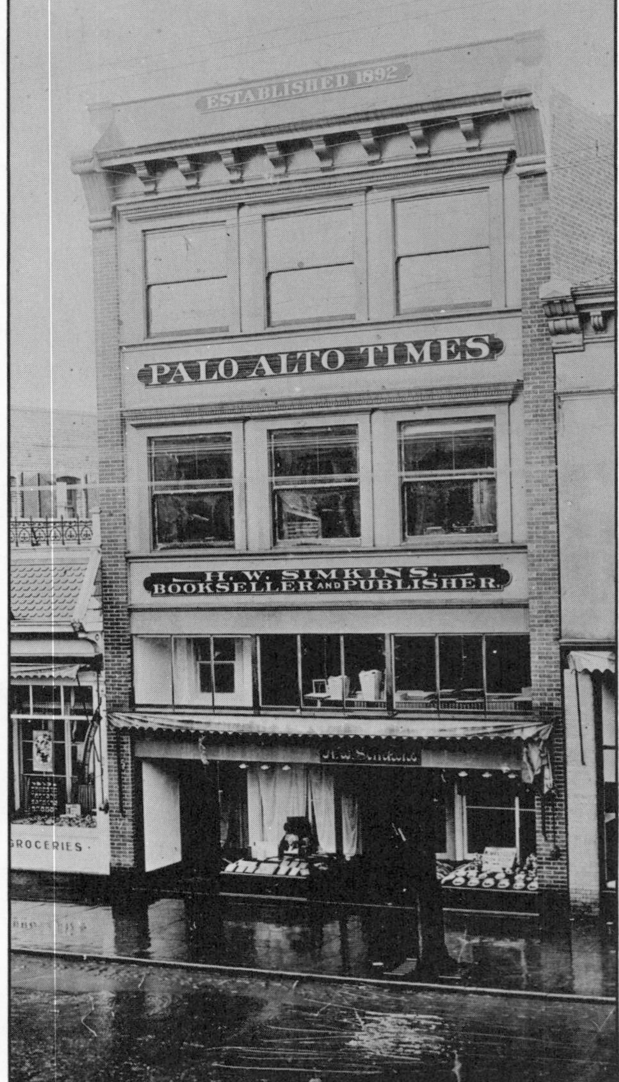

The Palo Alto Times, *established in 1892 in a small wooden building, built an imposing three-story brick building in the late 1890s, and rented the street-level store to H.W. Simkins. Courtesy Palo Alto Historical Association*

Marguerite Weichselfelder, an early resident, remembers the ambiance of one of the first business establishments, G. W. LaPeire and Son:

> [The store carried] a fine stock of groceries and other items. Older men usually sat around the pot-bellied stove in front, which was red hot in winter, cold in summer. They dipped their hands freely in the nearby oyster cracker barrel, chewed their tobacco and spat in the spittoons provided. At the back of the store the kindly grocer would be busy fixing his shelves when not waiting on customers.
>
> I remember best Ed LaPeire, with a black moustache. He was very friendly, would tell you about new things he had in stock that you might like. Sometimes he was grinding coffee in the big red coffee grinder. A person who bought a dozen cookies always got 13.

Palo Alto rose quickly in the wheat field next to Stanford University. People were attracted to the town's natural beauty and mild climate. But Nature is not always kind, even in Palo Alto, This was earthquake country, as residents soon discovered.

Waverley Street between Lincoln and Kingsley, 1902. The tall man left of center is Richard Keatinge, who paved many streets and sidewalks. His son Percy holds a wheelbarrow. Far right is Joseph Hutchinson, with son James on his shoulders, and daughter Katherine at left. Courtesy Palo Alto Historical Association

Chapter Notes

The Way It Was As Told By Those Who Were There, (1979), a collection of lively anecdotes about growing up just after the turn of the century by Marguerite Weichselfelder, Paul Gibson, Lester R. Morris and others, provides a more complete record of the texture of Palo Alto life than bare facts.

We are fortunate that Anna Probst Zschokke, and her daughter Irma (Crawford) took the time to write about everyday existence and special occasions in the new town. Irma's articulate autobiography, "Our Family Diary: 1886—1968," is augmented by Anna's article, "Pioneer History of the Town of Palo Alto," first published in the December 30, 1897 issue of the *Live Oak* and reprinted in the February 20, 1914 issue of the *Palo Alto Times.*

Betty Rogaway's carefully-constructed 1988 interview with Fremont Zschokke, Anna's grandson, filled in research gaps on the Zschokke family.

Background for understanding Palo Alto in the 1890s and early 1900s can be gleaned from Ellen Elliot (1940), Eleanor Pearson Bartlett (1905), and from two Tall Tree booklets published by the Palo Alto Historical Association, "Palo Alto: Its Background, Beginning and Growth" by Elinor Cogswell, and "From Portola to Palo Alto." Coffman and Miller were reliable sources. Bruce Cumming's *History of the Palo Alto Police Department* (1985) gives interesting tidbits, such as G.D. Dunsmore's job as night watchman and security guard.

The Palo Alto Branch of the American Association of University Women's 1977 booklet, "... Gone Tomorrow?: Neat Cottages and Handsome Residences" is a storehouse of information about architecture, the personalities of the homeowners, and the contemporary fate of the houses. The association has published "Exploring Palo Alto's Past: A Self-Guided Architectural Tour" (1977) and "Professorville" (1971) to provide historical walking tours.

Birge Clark's 1982 autobiography, "An Architect Grows Up in Palo Alto," shows the lifestyle and design of the new town. Clark's astounding memory, broad interests, and his affection for his fellows make this unpretentious work invaluable.

"Schools Wanted Here," a Tall Tree pamphlet by the Palo Alto Historical Association, is a good account of Palo Alto's school system as it emerged.

Transportation in Palo Alto is described in many works, including *History of San Mateo County* by Philip W. Alexander and Charles P. Hamm (1916), Allan Hynding's 1982 *From Frontier to Suburb: The Story of the San Mateo Peninsula,* and in Coffman, Miller, and the Palo Alto Historical Association's Tall Tree pamphlet, "Early Vehicular Travel."

MEMORIAL CHURCH, STANFORD.
COPYRIGHT 1906, PILLSBURY PICTURE CO.
NO 93.
LELAND STANFORD

CHAPTER THIRTEEN

The Earth Shook

On a cool Wednesday morning, April 18, 1906, the great San Andreas Fault shifted, sending violent tremors through communities all along San Francisco Bay. Palo Altans awoke with a start, then ran from their houses as the earth shook beneath their feet.

In a breathlessly-punctuated letter, Chris H. Christensen, a Palo Alto resident, wrote to his cousin Morris in Chicago a week later and described how the earthquake felt:

> Such excitement I have never seen in all my days. Wednesday morning about 5:12 a.m. I was laying in bed, half asleep I heard a roar in the distance, and before I could get up, the house began to shake with that sinking motion peculiar to earthquakes, and then came a twisting lurch, which did the damage, dying away into tremors. The quake passed, the time in all was no more than 20 or 30 seconds. I looked out the window and saw all the chimneys down—went outside and found that the house had shifted 2 inches off the foundation. The plaster was all cracked through the house—it will cost me about $100 to fix up the house. Generally speaking the frame house stood the earthquake well, but when I went downtown, every brick building was wrecked and about all will have to be rebuilt.
>
> When I saw the University buildings, it was there I saw what destruction meant. Those great stone buildings went down in a moment of time undoing the work of fifteen years. About one half of the buildings are destroyed. It will take 15 years to rebuild and they are to commence at once.
>
> In our store the loss was only $25 so I am fortunate. Palo Alto and Stanford will soon rise above this calamity and grow faster than ever.
>
> But we almost forgot the earthquake, in the great fire in San Francisco, the earthquake really did not do so much damage in the city. The old San Francisco is clean gone, and only the newer residence section is left—San Francisco is cleaned up. Chinatown is gone forever, all the old shacks are cleared out, and San Francisco will rise up better, cleaner and more beautiful than ever. About 250,000 are homeless but all are now cared for—a great many are here in Palo Alto...
>
> Ole [a friend] and his wife lived in the city—when the fire started he took her out to the park [probably Golden Gate], got a wheel, came here, hired a team, and went back to get her. They arrived at 3:00 a.m. the next morning.

Christensen's assessment of the damage in Palo Alto was correct—some chimneys, one unfinished building, and a few brick walls crumbled, but most residences, built primarily of wood, remained intact. There were no casualties. Stanford University's stone buildings, however, sustained such severe damage that many of them looked as if they had been bombed. Two people died in the falling debris. Palo Altans immediately began helping to rebuild the university and the damage in Palo Alto, and they aided refugees from San Francisco.

According to Bruce Cumming in "History of the Palo Alto Police Department," Palo Alto Police Marshal Weisshaar first secured the town by deputizing a number of citizens to patrol the streets and prevent looting or other vandalism. Meanwhile, Palo Alto and Stanford formed a relief committee, headed by Professor Arley B. Shaw. According to Cumming, as late as two weeks after the earthquake, 314 San Franciscans who had fled the great fire were still staying as guests in Palo Alto homes.

Anne Hadden, Palo Alto's first librarian, writes about the town's hospitality:

> From our mattresses out on the front lawn, we could see the glare of the fire in the sky, and hear,

Opposite: The ruins of Memorial Church, Stanford, after the Big One. The Stanford campus sustained very heavy damage.
Courtesy Palo Alto Historical Association

all night long, the multitudes going by on foot or in conveyances [very few automobiles then] along the County road, now the Highway. But not all refugees passed Palo Alto by.

We sheltered two refugees in our house on Ramona Street, an elderly brother and sister from the St. Francis Hotel in San Francisco. The man's hobby was cabinet making, and he restored the frame of our tall grandfather clock which had fallen against the corner of the mantelpiece and got damaged.

Palo Altans began to expect that their town might become a permanent haven for the homeless, and for those simply too scared to rebuild in devastated San Francisco. According to a July 9, 1986 article in the *Palo Alto Weekly*, the town's board of trustees tried to promote a real estate boom by printing 200 posters asking, "Why not live in Palo Alto?" and posting them on ruined walls in San Francisco. Unfortunately, when interested buyers stepped off the train in Palo Alto, the first thing they saw was the one building in town that had completely collapsed. Many got right back on the train and went on to San Jose to find new homesites.

So the great earthquake of 1906 came and went without deeply affecting Palo Alto. If anything, it seemed to strengthen the natural optimism of its citizens. Chris Christensen ends his letter with the cheery tone that seemed to characterize the spirit of the townspeople:

> Taking all together in Palo Alto things could be worse and I believe that Palo Alto will go on and grow as well as ever, and the great earthquake of April 18th, 1906, will be a matter of history, and as earthquakes rarely ever come back in the same locality, I do not look for any more at the present.

Chapter Notes

The letters from Chris H. Christensen and Anne Hadden about the 1906 earthquake can be found in the Palo Alto Historical Association files.

The Palo Alto Weekly occasionally runs special "Old News" sections providing exceptionally well-written coverage of past local events. Kathleen Donnelly's July 9, 1986 article, "1906-1920: Prelude to a Modern Era," gives accurate news about the aftermath of the earthquake.

The University Drug Co. at the corner of High Street lost some of its baroque facade, but remained structurally sound; the elegant window casings were replaced, and the building stands remarkably unchanged in 1989. Courtesy Palo Alto Historical Association

The Thiele building on Alma Street, built of cement blocks, collapsed and was demolished. Below: University Avenue after the earthquake. Courtesy Palo Alto Historical Association

NO.16.
FRAZER & Co.
PALO ALTO, CAL.
APR. 18, '06.

Students seemed to enjoy camping out near Encina Hall after the earthquake. Courtesy Palo Alto Historical Association

Opposite top: The handsome arches at the entrance to Palm Drive on campus were flattened, and were never rebuilt. Below: Sightseers marvel at the damage to the Frazer Drygoods store on University. Courtesy Palo Alto Historical Association

The earthquake did little to slow down the work on the new electric streetcar line, shown here on opening day, November 15, 1906, in the 700 block of University Avenue. Courtesy Palo Alto Historical Association

CHAPTER FOURTEEN

Starting the Twentieth Century

As the turn of the century approached, Palo Altans had solved many of the basic problems of survival by installing an efficient water system, paving the roads, establishing schools, developing sewage management, and other municipal functions. Many citizens of the town turned to higher-level concerns, cultural and philanthropic—building a health care system, establishing a library and a theater, and, finally, helping in the nation's World War charity efforts.

Progressive Health Care

The first order of business—health care—was dramatically underscored on December 10, 1902, when Dr. J. C. L. Fish reported the first case of typhoid not brought in by a travelling student. In the town of 2,000 people, few panicked, but those with medical training were hastily mobilized to track the source of the deadly bacterium.

A month later, another case was reported, and by April 1, 1903, 27 cases of the disease had developed. Nurses were rushed from San Francisco to help care for the sick and dying. The nurses stayed at the home of Anna Zschokke, the same spacious building that she had originally built as the town's first high school.

Anna Zschokke herself acted as a nurse, a skill she had learned while assisting her physician husband, and had used during medical emergencies in Palo Alto for years. Irma Zschokke recalls that her mother was often asked by Reverend Charles Gardner, energetic minister of the Episcopalian Church, to help. Writes Irma:

> [Dr. Gardner] came often in the night to tap on our window as a summons for Mother to deliver a baby or nurse the dying, then away they hurried on their bicycles in a cloud of dust. I can still see them peddling out our gate, as I pressed my nose against the window pane. Mother always returned to prepare our breakfast and pack our lunch pails, then usually returned to the sick bed for a few more hours.

During the typhoid epidemic, Anna Zschokke and all available health care specialists were kept busy. By April 15, two cases per day were being reported. Patients too ill to stay home were given care at the Guild Hospital, an institution established in the late 1890s by Dr. William F. Snow. Snow, an instructor at Stanford University, had formed a group that collected small fees every semester from faculty and students. These fees made it possible to provide inexpensive hospital services to students and other Palo Altans, an early form of pre-paid medical insurance. The hospital, located in a converted three-story home at the corner of Lytton and Cowper (a plaque commemorating its existence can still be seen there) became the focus of attention during the frightening time of the typhoid epidemic. Patients agonizingly sick with dysentery-like symptoms were brought in and, sadly, twelve bodies were brought out.

By the time the epidemic peaked, clues were beginning to accumulate as to the cause of the disease. Victims tended to have drunk milk prior to their illness, and most were on the route of one dairy, owned by a man named Parreiro. Members of the ad hoc health department—volunteers among the town trustees—inspected the farm, tested a stream that flowed through the property, and found the water teeming with typhoid germs. Almost as soon as the dairy was boarded up, typhoid cases dropped dramatically, and by June, David Starr Jordan wrote a soothing report to Palo Altans declaring that the crisis was over. In the final medical report, 235 cases of the deadly disease were counted, more than ten percent of the population.

With the crisis past, the townspeople resolved to be better prepared for other medical emergencies.

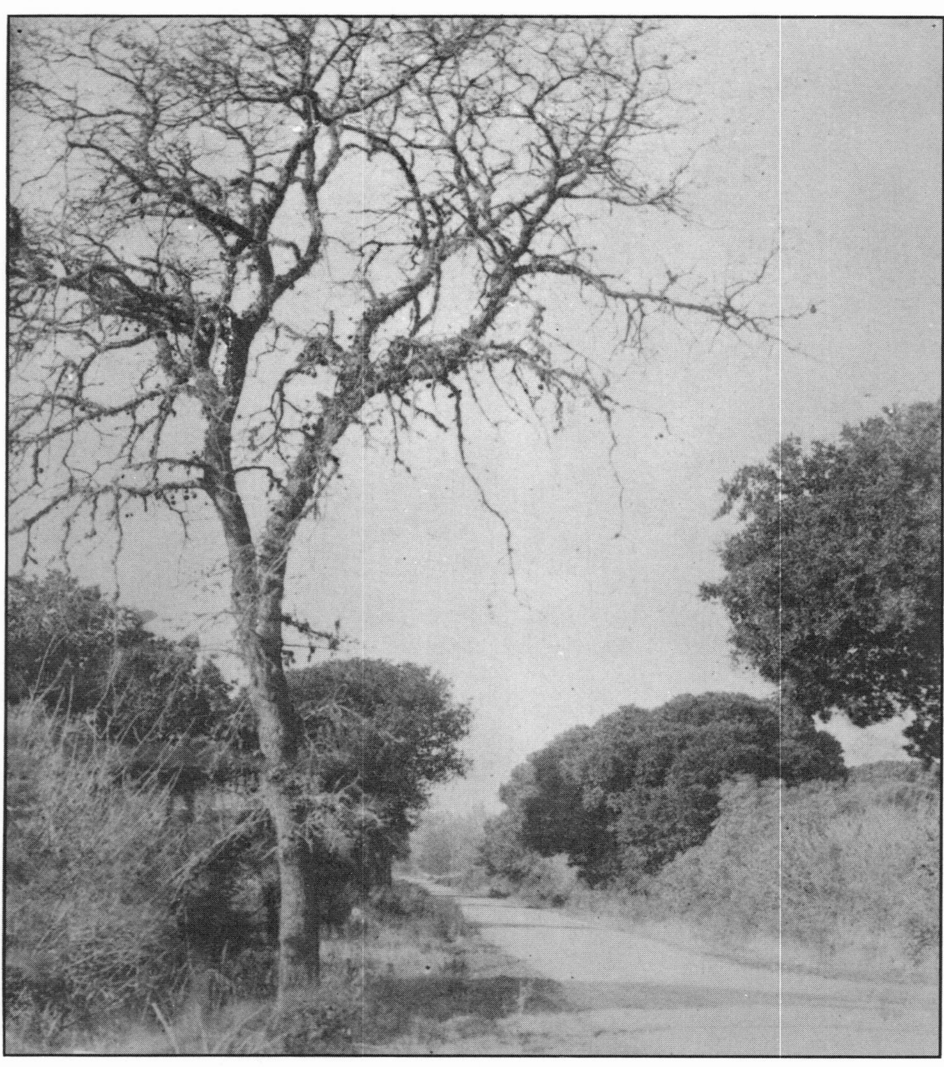

Embarcadero Road near Bryant, circa 1900. Courtesy Palo Alto Historical Association

Opposite: Prices like these could make a grown man cry in 1989. Courtesy Palo Alto Historical Association

One citizen in particular set out to rectify the situation—Elizabeth Hague, superintendent of the Guild Hospital. She and six others, including Dr. Ray Lyman Wilbur (who later became Stanford University president) came up with a plan to build a new hospital for the town, complete with a nurses' training school. This group offered stock certificates at $100 each. Elizabeth Hague personally sold half of the $70,000 worth of stock issued. As townspeople watched happily, the new, three-story frame building was erected late in 1909 at the corner of Embarcadero, Cowper and Churchill.

The Peninsula Hospital became a 48-bed institution. Elizabeth Hague herself founded the adjacent school for nurses, and the good reputation of her school, with the hospital's state-of-the-art medical equipment, attracted top-notch doctors and other staff. In a 1913 *Palo Alto Times* article, Elizabeth Hague declares in her no-nonsense style: "The hospital would have been a failure with a lot of half-baked doctors."

Palo Alto residents were proud of the hospital and of their full-time Health Department, established in 1910, which operated under the supervision of a paid professional health officer. They were also justifiably gratified by the town's health record in the ensuing years. In 1921, public health officer Louis Olsen reported that although there had been nearly 6000 cases of smallpox in California during the year, only one had occurred in Palo Alto. He also remarked that Palo Alto successfully used a quarantine procedure for dyphtheria and other communicable diseases, and so was able to keep its schools open. The next year, the California State Board of Health reported that "Palo Alto has a record of health achievement unparallelled in the country."

$1950 buys this very attractive six room home

On the sunny side of Kipling street, near Lytton avenue. A very attractive home as may be seen from the cut; at a very little money as may be seen from the price : : : : :

Another Bargain

We also have another good bargain in a low priced house, consisting of a very pretty cottage, new; large lot; centrally located. Price $1900.

Any one thinking of buying low priced homes should call on us at once and examine our list.

Co-operative Land & Trust Co.

LEDYARD BUILDING, OPP. FIRST NATIONAL BANK

World War I, however, again over-burdened Palo Alto's health care professional services. Doctors and nurses went off to war, and the Peninsula Hospital was unable to maintain an economical caseload and so began operating at a loss.

Seeing this dilemma, officials from Stanford University suggested that the town of Palo Alto buy Peninsula Hospital and offer its services to citizens at sharply reduced fees—a scheme similar to that of the old Guild Hospital. Stanford, which already managed Lane Hospital in San Francisco, agreed to operate the facility for the town for the next twenty-five years.

The people of Palo Alto, ever forward-looking, responded enthusiastically to this unique proposal for the marriage of town and gown, and in June, 1921, the hospital bond of $80,000 passed by a vote of 779-137. In a *Palo Alto Times* editorial the next day, a staff writer exulted, "The acquisition of the hospital by the city adds one more important enterprise to the number already municipally-owned in Palo Alto. The others are electricity, gas, and water. In each of these lines the city has made a signal success."

For the next ten years, Palo Altans enjoyed excellent medical care and rates provided through the novel Peninsula Hospital plan. As current medical costs soar, the fees posted in 1921 in the outer lobby of Palo Alto's hospital seem minuscule:

Ward	$ 5.00
Deluxe Private Baths and phone	$14.00
Two-bed room	$ 6.50
Infants	$ 1.00
Single Room	$ 8.00

Peninsula Hospital thrived under the arrangement between Stanford and Palo Alto. The relationship was so felicitous that when a larger hospital was needed in 1931, the city and university agreed to operate the new facility under terms similar to those for the old one. Bonds were again enthusiastically approved and in May, Stanford leased campus land to Palo Alto for the building. By the end of 1931, the old building was demolished and all that was left was a weedy vacant lot.

The continuing excellence of Palo Alto's medical care was due not only to municipal participation, but also to private practice. Two of the city's most notable medical pioneers were Drs. Thomas Williams and Russel Lee.

Dorothy Heilmann, a medical receptionist, notes in a 1980 *Palo Alto Weekly* article: "I knew really the first country doctor in Palo Alto. That was Tom Williams." His practice was established in 1913 in a house on the corner of Bryant and Hamilton Streets. Living quarters for nurses were on the upper floor, with his medical office on the ground floor.

Eventually, his practice grew large enough that he needed a partner and was joined by Dr. Russel Lee. According to local editor Don Kazak, 1982 *Palo Alto Weekly* article, Lee, who died January 27, 1982, was a man known throughout his life for his wit and outspokenness. In 1977, *San Francisco Chronicle* columnist Herb Caen described his friend Lee as an older man: "Dr. Lee, elegant, sporting a white van dyke, is a legend himself, with all his marbles, a pace-maker, artificial hip and unquenchable spirit. 'Have another drink,' he suggested, 'it will make us all look younger.'"

The electric tram, the bicycle, the horses and buggies, and plenty of room at the curb all mark the end of one era; the next is about to begin. Courtesy Palo Alto Historical Association

Dr. Russel Lee. Courtesy Palo Alto Historical Association

Dr. Esther Clark, a pediatrician (and sister of architect Birge Clark) told reporter Don Kazak upon Lee's death: "[He was] a brilliant man who always had a great flow of creative, imaginative, important ideas coming into his mind. He was so full of energy that many were put into effect." Some of Lee's more controversial stands included his attitude in the 1950s toward drug addiction as a medical rather than a legal problem, suggesting that addicts should be given narcotics at no charge to eliminate the underworld connection, and his early advocacy of group practice.

In the early days, he and Williams tried to keep their burgeoning practice within bounds. Patients flocked to the little clinic, particularly those in need of obstetric care. Lee said with a characteristic twinkle, "I didn't particularly enjoy obstetrical practice so I upped my delivery fee from $35 to as high as $100. This immediately quadrupled my practice. My patients said, 'If he charges that much, he must be pretty good.'"

The back-firing of this rate schedule led to one of the first group practices in the West. Williams and Lee invited Dr. Clark and surgeon-obstetrician Dr. E. B. Roth to join them. By 1929 the group had grown to seven partners, and incorporated as the Palo Alto Medical Clinic.

By the 1980s, the clinic had expanded to a group of more than 130 physicians treating more than 150,000 regular patients at its current location on Homer Avenue. Moreover, Dr. Lee's advocacy of group practice, which was at first vigorously opposed by many private practice members of the American Medical Association, is now considered a standard aspect of modern medicine.

Lee left another legacy specifically to residents of Palo Alto: Foothills Park. Through a partial gift/partial sale, the Lee family deeded 1400 acres of oak-studded land to the city. This recreational area of hiking trails surrounding peaceful Boronda Lake, has been enjoyed by most families who have settled in the city.

Library

As J.S Holliday mentions in his fascinating book, *The World Rushed In*, the Yankee California pioneers were an unusually literate group, hungry for any reading materials they could get their hands on. Dated newspapers from the East were passed from household to household, and new residents of Palo Alto proudly lent books from their private collections to friends.

Almost before University Avenue was graded, citizens began agitating for a public library. The drive to get one was spearheaded by the Palo Alto Women's Club, a major force in the town's development almost from the beginning. As Judge Egerton Lakin remarked: "The Palo Alto Women's Club ... has typified the true Palo Alto spirit. Our early founders did in fact build a city, which has become the pride of the peninsula. Out of the golden sea of mustard sprang homes that are a delight ..." The women who ran those homes first banded together in June, 1894, to see what they could do for the new city. They met at the old Presbyterian Church at Waverley and University Avenues, and elected Mary Campbell as president.

Anna Zschokke, A.T. Murray and L. M. Hoskins were among the original officers. They and the twenty-five other charter members planted and cared for shade trees; Mrs. Lakin later recalled touring University Avenue in a horse and buggy with watering cans to keep the saplings alive. The club also supplied cans to collect street rubbish, improved school grounds, encouraged school garden-making, established and furnished a lunchroom and restroom for girls at the high school, and, above all, began organizing the public library.

The idea for the library arose in 1896, two years after the founding of the club. The members unanimously endorsed the plan for creating a public library even before a building to house the books was found. Book socials, whereby each participant brought a book, or money to buy one, began in March, 1896. The first such event was a rousing success, with 200 books donated from private collections. Bookseller H. W. Simkins gave space on the shelves of his store for the makeshift library. As reported in the *Palo Alto Times*, "Members of the club thereafter took turns

Palo Alto's first theater featured a curtain with advertisements for local businesses, a precursor of TV commercials. Courtesy Palo Alto Historical Association

serving a day at a time as librarians, bringing their babies and their sewing with them."

By 1899, a total of 1115 volumes had been bought or collected, and these included many classics, such as complete editions of Edwin Arnold, Matthew Arnold, Campbell, Keats, Riley, Rossetti, Tennyson and Wordsworth. Temporary headquarters for the library were set up in the YMCA reading room at Nortree Hall on High Street and University Avenue, but the women were not fully satisfied with operating the library on such an *ad hoc* basis. In 1903, they decided to seek a grant from the Carnegie foundation to establish a permanent library at a new site. As a start toward the required matching funds, $700—quite a sum in those days—was quickly raised among the club members. City of Palo Alto town trustees agreed to appropriate annually an additional 10% of the grant. The full amount of the matching funds was secured, and the new library opened on November 1, 1904, on Hamilton Avenue, where City Hall stands now. Thus, Palo Alto could indulge its citizens' voracious reading habits.

Theater

The people of Palo Alto were interested in live theater almost from the time of the city's founding. At first, productions were given by local amateurs or by traveling groups that drew audiences to Muilens' Hall on High Street. As pioneers describe these early shows, it is clear that few people in the town had pretentions about their cultural offerings.

Marguerite Weichselfelder reports on a local production in 1909 given by the Lytton Avenue School:

> Dozens of good fairies were dressed in white tarleton ballet dresses trimmed with silver tinsel, and approximately the same number of bad fairies wore similar black dresses trimmed with gold tinsel. As part of the performance, two older girls sang a duet sitting in the lap of the man in the moon ... though the bad fairies caused lots of trouble, the good fairies triumphed in the end.

An even more hilarious performance was credited to the Palo Alto audience, not the cast, of "Uncle Tom's Cabin," which played in the first decade of the new century. According to Paul Gibson:

> The [Stanford] students came in mass and when it came time for little Eva to die and go to heaven, the boys took over the stage, danced with the actresses, and made poor Eva ascend and descend like a slow yo-yo, to the amusement of some and the consternation of others. Naturally, our one-man police force was practically helpless. One theatre group was so upset they returned the admission money, but on another occasion, a different group took charge and cleared the stage of students and frightened many patrons when they brought out their blood hounds.

More serious dramatic efforts came to Palo Alto in December 1921 when the Palo Alto Community Players were organized by a civic group. According to the *Palo Alto Times*, "Mrs. Harry J. Moule sent a letter inviting the 8,000 residents to join, for the grand price of $1.00, and received over $200 almost immediately, some by return mail. Everyone in Palo Alto wanted to be a star!"

The first play, "Billeted," was given at the Stanford Assembly Hall of the Community House on January 6, 1922. Admission was 75¢. The newly-appointed drama critic of the *Palo Alto Times* reported that Christine Donahue, production director, had "transformed the Community House into a comfortable, model theatre ... from a rather poor setting for amateur theatricals into a little theatre with 'atmosphere' ..."

The Palo Alto Community Players became so popular that in July, 1933, with a private donation of $44,000 made by local philanthropist Lucie Stern, the town built a new, much larger Palo Alto Community Theater, designed by Birge Clark. The *Stanford Daily* boasted that this theater housed a stage larger than most commercial stages in San Francisco. The theater continues to thrive today, staging classics and a few plays by new authors for the delight of many longtime season ticket-holders.

Women's Suffrage

In 1869, the National Woman Suffrage Association was formed by Susan B. Anthony and Elizabeth Cady Stanton to gain enfranchisement for women in the United States. Their campaign for the Nineteenth Amendment to the United States Constitution was especially vigorous in California.

In the reports of the Palo Alto Women's Club, we can see that local women were listening to the suffragettes and examining their own role in society. They knew their importance in the private sphere, nurturing healthy families, but were also proud of their public contribution to the town of Palo Alto. Several of their meetings in the mid-1890s show a stirring of new feeling about how they should balance the two roles.

As reported in the *Palo Alto Times*, the Women's Club met in January, 1895 "to listen to the exceedingly able lecture of Mrs. Severance on 'Why Should Women Vote?'" A week later, the club's president, Mary Campbell, described the life work of Susan B. Anthony, "noting the difference between the reception given to her when she appears now and

Newfangled inventions arrived often in the early years of the century, and not many people realized what sweeping change they would bring. Here H.C. Schmidt proudly poses in his Novelty Theatre, at 185 University, circa 1909. Behind him, at the head of the aisle, is the piano on which the accompanist played music to match the action on the silver screen. Courtesy Palo Alto Historical Association

By 1915 Palo Altans had clear evidence that culture had truly arrived: the Palo Alto Symphony Orchestra, John Kimber, conductor. Courtesy Palo Alto Historical Association

that of forty years ago." Mary Campbell and other women leaders in town were becoming sympathetic to the movement.

Anna Zschokke herself seems to have spoken for a majority of Palo Alto women when she organized a club meeting on drudgery. After reading extracts from a contemporary article on the subject, she led a group discussion, "the general tenor [of which] proved that the ladies have no greater liking for any form of drudgery than the sterner sex." Though this may seem like a foregone conclusion to modern women (and men), at the turn of the century, many believed that women were somehow more suited than men to boring chores.

One of the most heated debates on suffrage at the Women's Club took place September 18, 1896. Professor H. H. Powers (who had made a speech at the Woman's Congress earlier in the year) came to the regular Wednesday afternoon meeting and declared that little would be gained from giving women the right to vote. He took his view, according to the *Palo Alto Times*, from the "study of biology":

> A storm of questions and objections came upon the speaker from the audience which was evidently hostile to his ideas, but Professor Powers is never so much at home as when engaged in debate ... Miss Shaw [a club member] did her best to combat his arguments, but by far the cleverest reply was made by the President of the Club [Mary] Campbell. She admitted the truth of the Professor's statement, but claimed that after the period of child bearing was past, a woman would have leisure and inclination to devote to public life or a profession."

According to the newspaper, "The whole discussion was brilliant and was attentively listened to by an audience that crowded the [Presbyterian] church."

Through the ensuing years, the Women's Club actively supported such issues as the Women's Parliament's 1901 advocacy of the amendment to the California Civil Code giving women a greater say in the disposition of spousal community property.

Such views were not always admired. On April 21, 1909, Pope Pius X came to Oakland and met with a delegation of the Union of Italian Catholic Ladies. He spoke for the large conservative element in California—and Palo Alto—when, as reported in the *Oakland Tribune*, he said:

> After creating man, God created woman and determined her mission, namely that of being man's companion, helpmeet and consolation. It is a mistake, therefore, to maintain that women's rights are the same as man's ... How mistaken, therefore, is that misguided feminism which seeks to correct God's work.'"

Palo Alto women read the newspapers and worked out their own thoughtful interpretations of the movement. Opinions in Palo Alto ranged from that of the irate editorial letter writer who complained in the *Palo Alto Times* that the Women's Club was decidedly not a suffrage organization, to the delightful militancy of Laura Deforce Gordon, a pioneer feminist.

Cora Bagley Older recounts her feminist struggle:

> In 1860 bobbed, hatless, young Laura Deforce Gordon began the women's suffrage battle with all the valiance of her ancestor, Ethan Allen, declaring, 'Only idiots, Chinese, paupers and women are excluded from office.' She began her long fight to be admitted to the bar after being refused admission to Hastings Law School. Demanding a hearing before the Supreme Court, she was finally admitted to practice in November, 1879.

Throughout California, such women as Laura Gordon helped the state become one of the nation's first twelve to enfranchise women within its borders in 1911. This bloc of voting power was then used by the National Woman's Party to bring about the Nineteenth Amendment to the constitution, passed on August 18, 1920, giving all women in the United States the right to vote.

Native Daughters' float for Admission Day parade in San Francisco, 1915, tells the world where Palo Alto is.
Courtesy Palo Alto Historical Association

"A Glimpse on Forest Avenue in Palo Alto Town" (above) circa 1900, shows how important trees were to early residents, who left oak trees in the middle of several streets. After all, no horse would be stupid enough to run into a tree, so there was nothing unsafe about a tree in the middle of a street. But around the turn of the century a new kind of conveyance spun along the streets (below): the first automobile, a Knox three-wheeler, driven by Fred and Grace Smith and son. Did anyone guess that a new age had arrived? Courtesy Palo Alto Historical Association

Above: The Columbia Cyclery on the Circle, already well-established, has added two new products to its window sign: Automobiles and Eastman Kodaks. The jaunty mudguards on the four-seater parked in front must have drawn admiring stares. Right: The Elite Market outdistanced the competition with a snappy convertible delivery van and an enviable telephone number. Courtesy Palo Alto Historical Association

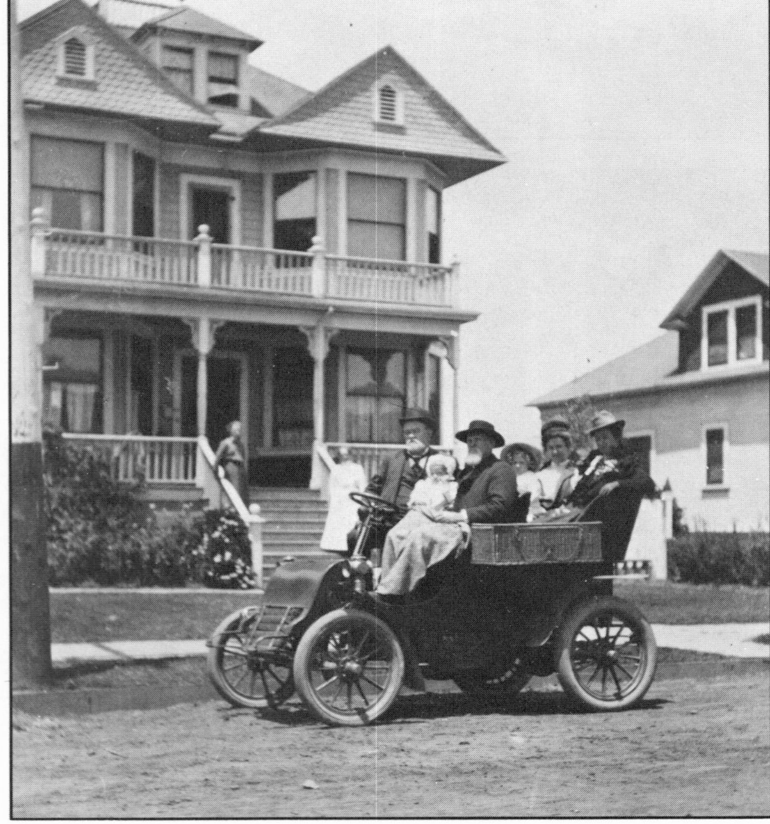

Above: This handy runabout featured pneumatic tires, the latest thing. Left: The Bodley and Tripp families take Capt. John Wood (front seat) for a spin, 1904. Courtesy Palo Alto Historical Association

Opposite, top: A line of taxis waits at the circle in 1914. The one at far left is starting a price war with the others. Below: By 1920 there wasn't a horse in sight at the circle; even draying had been taken over by trucks with solid tires. Did anyone dream that this would mean the end of railroads as well as horses and wagons? Courtesy Palo Alto Historical Association

FOR HIRE
PHONE
15
ANDRUS TAXI
ANDRUS
TAXI
25¢
PHONE 15
67815
TAXI

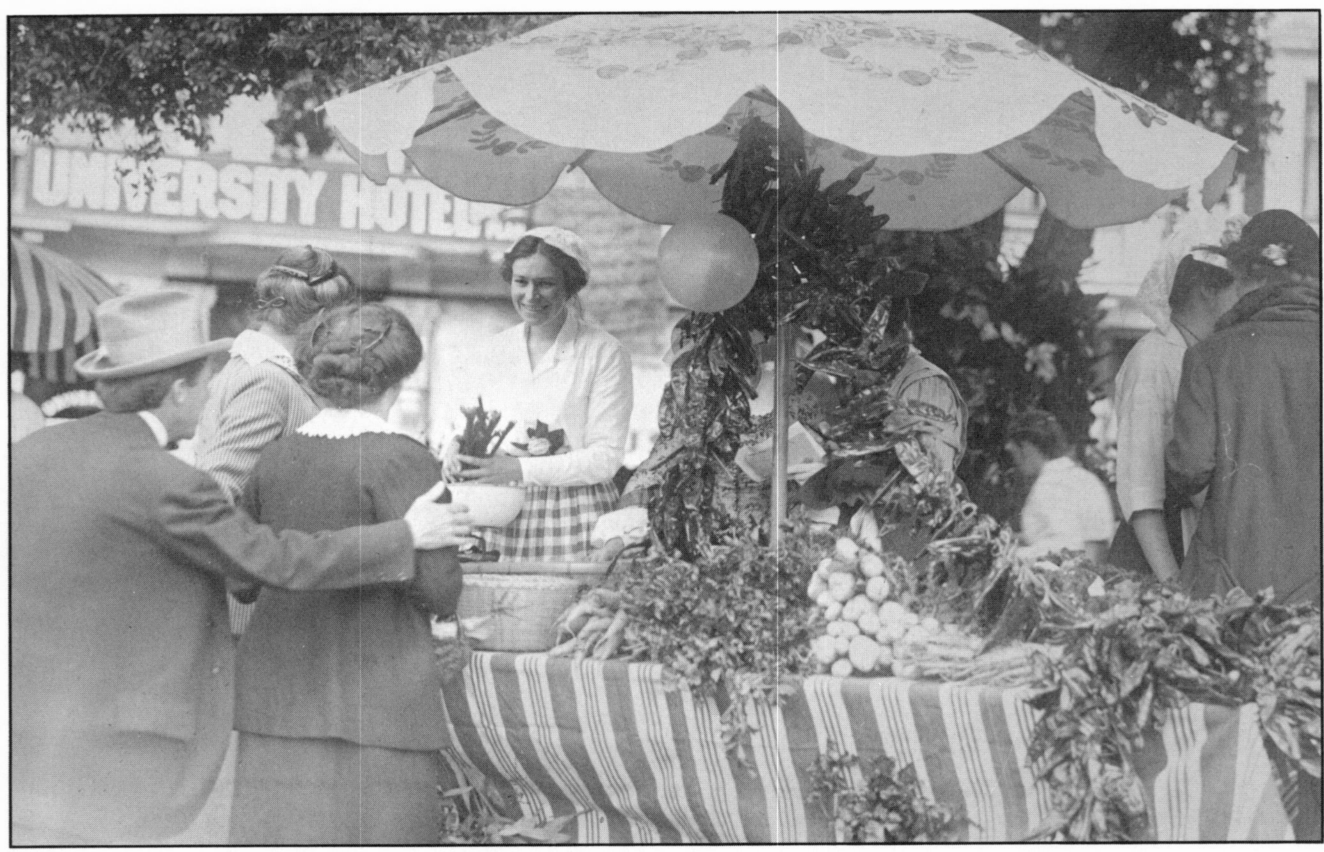

Mrs. F.H. Fowler sells vegetables at the March 1915 Belgian Fair on University Avenue, where customers as well as volunteer workers wore costumes to raise money for Belgian war relief during World War I.
Courtesy Palo Alto Historical Association

Belgian Relief

At the start of the first World War in 1914, the German strategy was to attack France by way of Belgium, and the Germans quickly occupied most of that country. Soon, some of the bloodiest battles of human history were being fought on Belgian soil. The last of the three infamous battles at Ypres, in southwest Belgium, alone resulted in the loss of over 300,000 soldiers of the British army. Belgium was devastated by the war—thousands of civilians were killed and many children faced starvation.

Almost from the beginning, Herbert Hoover, who had graduated with Stanford University's first class, had directed American efforts to provide relief to Belgium. Hoover's wife, Lou Henry, coordinated the massive program to send clothing, blankets and food to the orphans and refugees.

Ellen Coit Elliott spearheaded the movement locally. She sent letters to Palo Alto residents urging them to read Mrs. Hoover's pamphlet, "Belgium's Need," and appealed for donations. From a list of Stanford graduates, many of them Palo Altans, $2540 arrived during the first six weeks of the campaign. By the end of the war, according to Eleanor Cogswell, editor of the *Palo Alto Times* and a local historian, the Stanford-Palo Alto community had raised over $50,000 to help the war's innocent victims.

One of the most colorful and successful fund-raisers was the so-called Belgian markets. Proceeds from the sale of food and handmade gifts at these street fairs were donated to the cause.

Eleanor Cogswell described the festive events:

> Among the lawn-circled oaks of the pre-subway Circle, the townspeople held a series of fairs during World War I ... Great and small, young and old, rich and poor, famous folk and little John Z. milled together among the flowers and vegetables and whatnot, wearing quaint costumes. Some of these were authentic Belgian folkdress and some were just pseudo-peasant, but they all blended into a captivating picture.

Many people contributed their talents to the Belgian Relief Fund. Women's Club members sewed small-sized clothing for European children by cutting

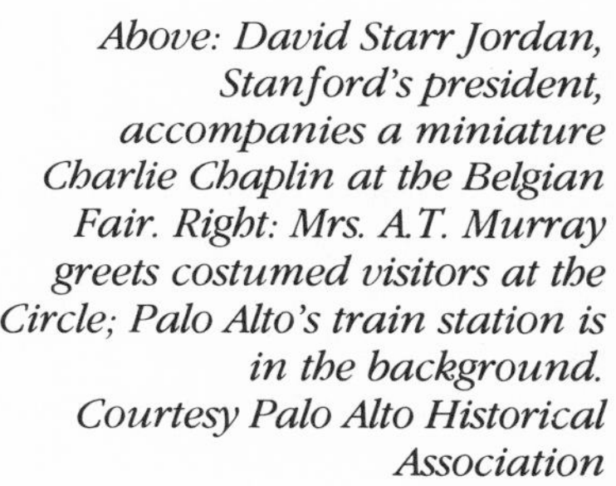

Above: David Starr Jordan, Stanford's president, accompanies a miniature Charlie Chaplin at the Belgian Fair. Right: Mrs. A.T. Murray greets costumed visitors at the Circle; Palo Alto's train station is in the background. Courtesy Palo Alto Historical Association

By 1916 a Red Cross chapter had been organized in Palo Alto. The volunteers pose in front of the old Presbyterian Church at Waverley and University. Courtesy Palo Alto Historical Association

down donated adult shirts and pants. And other benefits were held, such as that of May 4, 1918, which—according to its advertisements—featured dancing by Miss Alice Diaz, an orchestra of thirty pieces by representative musicians of the community, and an oriental playlet by the children of Palo Alto called, "The Ring of Baba Omar."

Besides offering money, Palo Altans contributed to the war effort through their hospitality to the American soldiers stationed at the hastily-erected Camp Fremont, just over the border in Menlo Park. According to ***A Tradition of New Horizons: The Story of Menlo Park***, published by the City of Menlo Park and the Menlo Park Historical Association, this war-time cantonment eventually served 43,000 soldiers:

> Infantry units and calvary regiments, raw recruits and seasoned veterans. Soldiers who had fought in Flanders and France taught recruits and West Point graduates how to make bayonet charges. Trenches were dug for hand grenade and small bomb practice. Every day throughout the south end of the county the large cannons could be heard booming at hillside targets.

The sometimes scared and lonely soldiers were welcomed into the homes of local families, and public entertainment was provided at the hostess house near the railroad tracks at 27 University Avenue, near El Camino Real (it now serves as a restaurant). This building was designed by the renowned California architect Julia Morgan, who also created San Simeon for William Randolph Hearst. After the war, the structure became the first municipally-supported community center in the United States.

As the first quarter century came to a close, the more than 7,000 Palo Alto residents were able to take advantage of the many cultural opportunities available in their small city and the nearby university. About 70 percent of the streets of the city were well-paved, according to the *History of Santa Clara County California* by Eugene T. Sawyer. Sidewalks had finally been installed. About 200 people commuted to San Francisco to do business, a trend that would expand as the years went by. Palo Alto, originally touted as an agricultural haven, was quickly becoming a bedroom community.

Left: Armistice Day parade on University, November 11, 1918. The Great War was over, and there would never be another one. The soldiers all wear flu masks against the epidemic that swept the country in 1918. Below: The Andrus Black & White Taxi Co. provides the comfort of a closed car, a driver with a snappy cap, and a two-digit telephone number. Courtesy Palo Alto Historical Association

The new age of communications created whole new careers: a young lady who worked as a telephone operator was addressed as "Central" by callers requesting a number. Above: Operators had to sit on barrels in this undated picture, probably taken in 1908 after the new telephone building had been built on Ramona Street. Right: Another undated picture, probably around 1920; proper bentwood stools have replaced barrels. Supervisors stand behind the operators to oversee their work. One young lady wears a surprisingly elaborate beaded dress. Courtesy Peninsula Times Tribune.

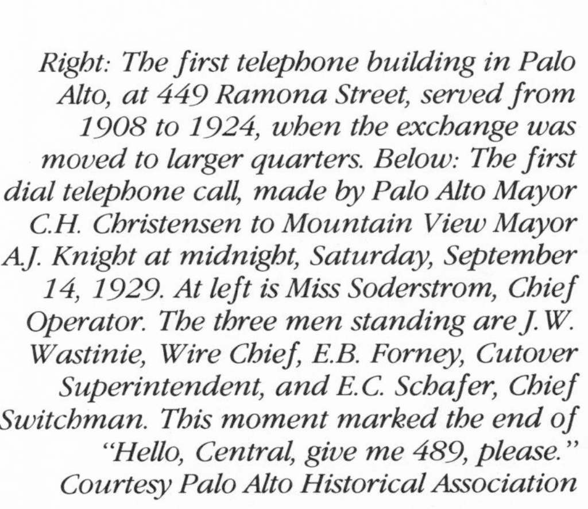

Right: The first telephone building in Palo Alto, at 449 Ramona Street, served from 1908 to 1924, when the exchange was moved to larger quarters. Below: The first dial telephone call, made by Palo Alto Mayor C.H. Christensen to Mountain View Mayor A.J. Knight at midnight, Saturday, September 14, 1929. At left is Miss Soderstrom, Chief Operator. The three men standing are J.W. Wastinie, Wire Chief, E.B. Forney, Cutover Superintendent, and E.C. Schafer, Chief Switchman. This moment marked the end of "Hello, Central, give me 489, please." Courtesy Palo Alto Historical Association

John Montgomery, daredevil inventor, stands beside his glider, built in his shop at Santa Clara, in 1905, just two years after the Wright Brothers' first flight. Montgomery attached his glider to a hot-air balloon, then cut it loose and guided it to earth. He was killed doing this five years later. Courtesy University of Santa Clara Archives.

World News

In the middle of the Roaring Twenties, Palo Alto annexed Mayfield, thereby essentially establishing Palo Alto's modern borders. Outside the quiet, efficiently-run town, the modern world was taking shape in more dramatic ways. The flapper era brought with it gangland bootleggers capitalizing on Prohibition, freer lifestyles, new modes in the arts, and the rise of new and frightening governments in Germany, Russia, and Italy.

The evening of January 15, 1920, the staff of New York's Park Avenue Hotel draped the diningroom tables in black in preparation for a grand farewell-to-alcohol party. At the stroke of midnight, bars closed at the hotel and throughout the United States as Prohibition went into effect, thereby bringing the rest of the country in line with Palo Alto, which had been officially "dry" since Leland Stanford first bought the land in 1887.

In Chicago, prohibition opened the door for organized crime as Al Capone and Johnny Torrio battled with Hymie Weiss in Chicago for the lucrative sale of liquor to secret clubs, called speakeasies. At age twenty-six, Capone gained control not only of bootlegging, but also of gambling, prostitution and the Chicago dance hall business.

Palo Alto did not exactly participate in the wave of terror. The quiet town had yet to experience a single murder since incorporation; most arrests were for such heinous crimes as riding a bicycle too fast on city sidewalks.

Ordinary citizens heard about the day's news on the newfangled radio. The foundation for the electronic age had been laid by Palo Alto area resident Lee De Forest in 1906. Frequently called "the father of radio," he had invented a three-electrode vacuum tube amplifier called an Audion. California Historical Landmark #836 at Channing and Emerson marks the site of his work.

By 1925, people could tune into radio musical programs that included such immortal songs as "Yes, Sir! That's my Baby" by Walter Donaldson and Gus Kahn. Flappers danced the Charleston to these pop

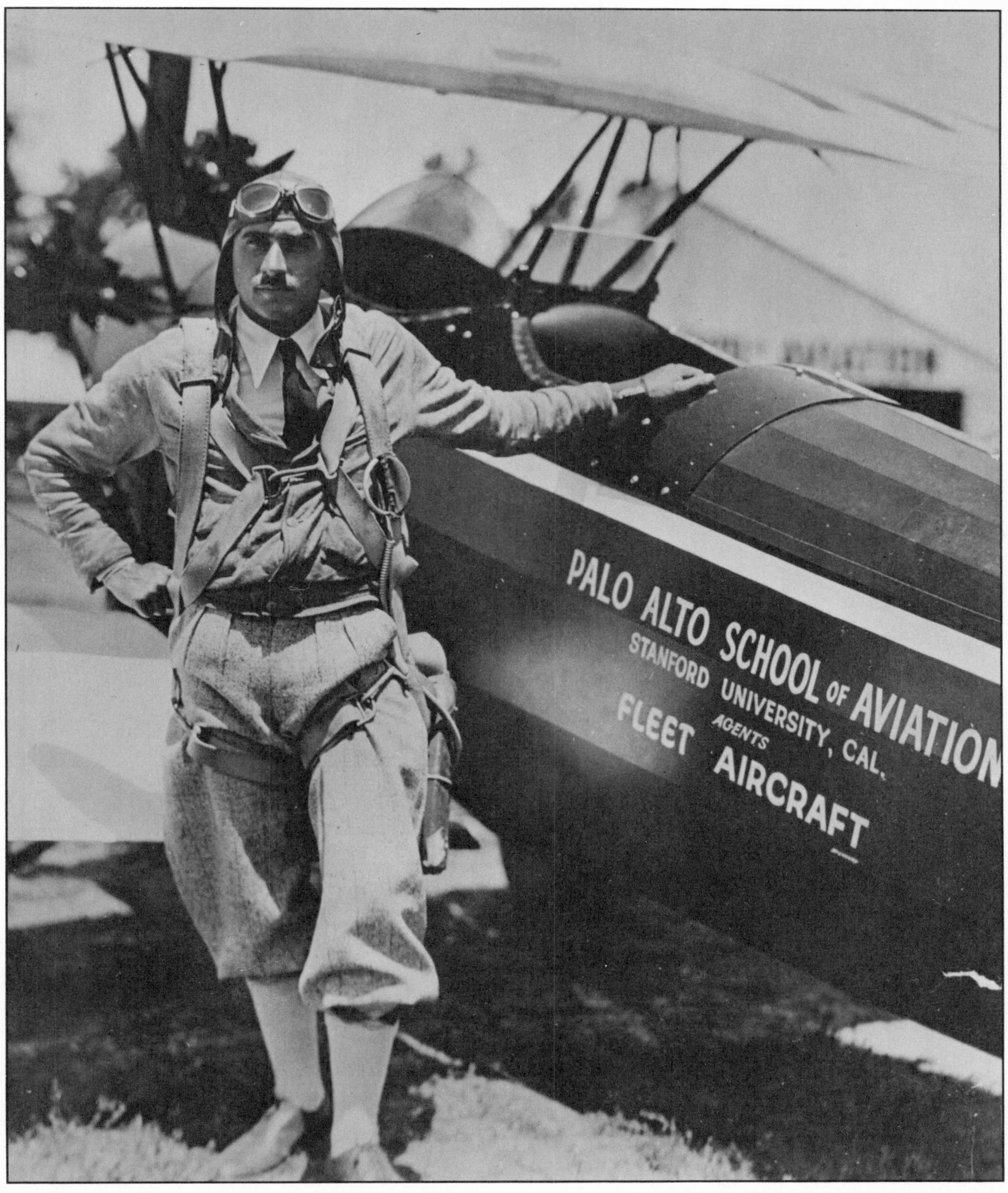

By 1925, only 22 years after Kitty Hawk, airplanes had been used to fight in World War I; stunt fliers were thrilling audiences (and sometimes killing themselves) at air shows, and a new word, "barnstorming," had joined the American vernacular. This young pilot, dressed to the nines, is ready to take a passenger up in his two-seater.
Courtesy Palo Alto Historical Association

Radio brought the latest news and the music of Rudy Vallee and Paul Whiteman into almost every home in the 1920s. The world's first radio broadcast station was set up by Charles Herrold and Frank Schmidt in San Jose in 1909. It was licensed as KQW in 1921, and became KCBS in 1949. "Dr. Herrold's Station," above, reached Palo Alto listeners who had crystal sets.

tunes. In Palo Alto, residents flocked to the Varsity Theatre to see the era's movie idol, Rudolph Valentino, in such immortal movies as *Blood and Sand.* Sports fans began filling the seats of the new Stanford stadium, which opened November 19, 1921.

Female flappers around the world wore their hair in the short, mannish "bob" that had been introduced by stylist Antoine de Paris in 1920. In Palo Alto, popular whipcord suits for men sold at Roos Brothers on University Avenue for $47.

Other trends across the country presaged contemporary lifestyles. The first Miss America was crowned in Atlantic City, New Jersey in 1920; the first shopping center, Kansas City's Country Club Plaza, was designed by developer Jesse Clyde Nichols in 1922; the first motel opened in 1925 at San Luis Obispo. Super highways crossed the U.S., and on the San Francisco peninsula, citizens lauded the proposal for Bayshore Freeway. A July 6, 1922 *Palo Alto Times* article declared, "Never has a highway project met with such hearty endorsement."

In the 1920s, vitamins were discovered and named by British biochemist J.C. Drummond; a method for making corn syrup was patented in 1923; and Wheaties ("breakfast of champions") was introduced in 1924 by Washburn, Crosby Company of Minneapolis. In Palo Alto, the University Creamery advertised its butter with ads declaring, "There's no substitute for nature's own."

It is difficult to pinpoint the *most* significant development of the time, but Palo Alto business people of today may point to the enormous impact of the first coast-to-coast flight in a single day, made by U.S. Army Air Corps Lieutenant James Harold Doolittle in September 1921.

The Jazz Age not only brought changes in living,

but also changes in art, most significantly in fiction. A group of Americans living in Paris in the 1920s—notably F. Scott Fitzgerald and Ernest Hemingway—produced masterpiece after masterpiece during this short period. Their fiction was a frank depiction of the horrors of war and the artifices of society. Fitzgerald's *This Side of Paradise* (1920) and *The Great Gatsby* (1925) gained him celebrity as a writer and as a member of the emerging jet set. Hemingway's haunting collection *In Our Time* (1924) showed his revulsion against World War I, a theme that would run through most of his later works. Publication of *Ulysses* (banned as obscene in U.S. courts) by James Joyce rocked the literary world.

Meanwhile in Palo Alto, author Kathleen Norris, who lived at the corner of Cowper Street and Melville Avenue, wrote over 75 popular, sentimental novels, including the blockbuster *Certain People of Importance* (1922). At Stanford University, John Steinbeck received a "C" in freshman English in 1919. The next year, when tuition was charged for the first time, he moved to a cheap room in a Palo Alto home.

In world class painting, Spanish artist Pablo Picasso (who was born in 1881) had already passed through his blue and rose periods and was developing cubism. Influenced by African sculpture, Picasso produced such works as *The Three Musicians* (1921). His paintings and sculptures advanced the idea that works of art have an imposing reality of their own that is separate from the objects they represent.

The political realities of the early 1920s seemed ominous to many writers and artists. In Italy, Victor Emmanuel III asked Benito Mussolini to restore order to this country wracked by civil war. By 1922, Mussolini had begun setting up his fascist government. In Russia, Nikolai Lenin established the first forced labor camp in the Solovetsky Islands in 1923. The next year, Lenin died and Josef Stalin began a power struggle with Leon Trotsky. In Germany, the mark was falling drastically, setting the stage for a new government. Adolf Hitler, who published *Mein Kampf* in 1925, was slowly emerging as Germany's leader.

Chapter Notes

Coffman provides a comprehensive account of the evolution of the medical care system. Wood's history is especially helpful in understanding the founding of the Guild Hospital.

A complete contemporary record of the typhoid epidemic of 1902-3 can be found in the files of the Palo Alto Historical Association, including Dr. J.C.L. Fish's 1905 report to the Palo Alto Board of Health.

Gary Cavalli's article, "Dr. Lee: A Radical or Simply Ahead of His Time?" in *This World* section of the *San Francisco Chronicle* (May 20, 1973) gives an interesting portrait of that important doctor.

Articles in the *Palo Alto Weekly* that have appeared in recent years provide good background on doctors and their institutions, including Bruce Murray's March 13, 1980 article on the Palo Alto Clinic, and Don Kazak's thoughtful February 3, 1982 obituary of Dr. Russel Lee.

Guy Miller's 1930 pamphlet, *History of the Palo Alto Public Library*, is rich with detail. The yearly development of the library is chronicled in Women's Club Annual Reports published in the *Palo Alto Live Oak*, such as that which appeared September 22, 1899.

The May 23, 1924 *Palo Alto Times* article celebrating the thirtieth anniversary of the Women's Club was useful in understanding the depth of the club's support of the community, as were numerous earlier *Times* reports on Club activities, such as the September 23, 1916 article on the opening of the clubhouse at Homer and Cowper. All these can be found in the Palo Alto Historical Association files.

Critical reviews of local theater events dating back to 1921 are also available in the historical association files. Norris James' historical account of local production in the June 17, 1958 issue of the *Palo Alto Times*, "The Night Aunt Lucie Laughed," shows the community's longtime interest in drama.

By sifting through the minutes of the Women's Club meetings, we were able to discern how local women reacted to and helped lead the suffrage movement.

Ellen Coit Elliott's article, "'Way Back in 1914-18 Stanford-Palo Alto Committee Raised $1,000 Every Month for Relief of Belgians," July 29, 1940, *Palo Alto Times*, is a firsthand account of the local community's generosity. Elinor Cogswell's July 6, 1957 *Palo Alto Times* article, "Ye Olde Days on The Circle," is a fond reminiscence of the Belgian Markets.

University Avenue in 1933: the Age of the Automobile has arrived; "State Fair," with Janet Gaynor and Marie Dressler, is showing at the Fox Stanford, and parking places are at a premium. It's interesting to compare this photograph with those in chapters twelve and fourteen. Courtesy Palo Alto Historical Association

CHAPTER FIFTEEN

Epilogue: Yesterday and Today

"The world keeps beating a path to Palo Alto's door," said the *San Francisco Chronicle* in an article on the best and worst cities in the San Francisco Bay area. The newspaper's January 4, 1988 computer study on the quality of life in 98 cities named Palo Alto number one.

Since its earliest days, the little town built in a wheatfield has thrived. As Palo Alto's Centennial opens in 1989, a glance back over the years reveals enormous growth and change.

In 1925, the era which ends this book, two small business districts existed, University and California Avenues. Only a few classified ads offered employment; available jobs were as servants or fruit workers. A Swedish maid with just the right qualifications was offered a salary of $75 or $80 per month. The unemployed were offered government "ordinary work" at $4.00 per day.

The two shopping streets are still important. California Avenue has become upscale with ethnic luncheon spots, nail salons and stylish condominiums. University Avenue abounds with restaurants and banks, but now competes with the Stanford Shopping Center, opened in 1956, and located in what were strawberry fields in the 1920s.

Business has grown dramatically since 1925. In 1939, in a garage on Addison Street, William Hewlett and David Packard founded the firm which not only changed Palo Alto, but heralded a world-wide revolution in electronics. About 150 of the nation's top high technology firms now have offices and plants in Palo Alto.

The town's population has increased from 10,700 in 1925 to 57,000 in 1989. The average household income in 1988 was $58,000. In 1925, houses were in the $4,000-$8,000 range, with a nine-room house in a "select neighborhood" going for $16,000. In 1988, the price of the average house was $407,016.

Palo Altans continue to indulge their love of reading. From the makeshift library with donated books in H. W. Simkins' back room, the Palo Alto library system has grown to such an extent that in 1988, 984,000 library materials were circulated, more than 17 items per citizen, as compared with a national norm of six. Its computerized card catalog, available to patrons via computer modem, its computers, compact discs, video casettes and 110,000 volumes provide services the members of the Women's Club could never have dreamed of.

Such statistics produce the aura of a Dream Town, according to David Blundy, a British reporter who wryly notes Palo Altans' penchant for contentiousness:

> While the big American cities battle the problems of crime, violence, drugs, the unemployed and the homeless, the town of Palo Alto, a little paradise south of San Francisco, has a different sort of crisis. The town is divided on whether leaves should be blown away by [noisy] mechanical blowers or raked. The controversy has raged through the city council. ... The issue may seem trivial and it is indeed easy to make fun of the good life in Palo Alto. But Palo Alto cares passionately about its quality of life, which is one of the reasons why it is perhaps the nicest place to live in America.

Palo Altans are at times amused by the accolades their town receives. They accept some good-natured teasing about the various honors bestowed. In 1987 and 1988, Palo Alto received more than 24 awards for excellence, ranging from a National Award for Outstanding Wastewater Treatment Facility Operations and Maintenance to the First Annual Hospitable Cycling Cities Award from *Bicycling Magazine* to the Outstanding Planning Award for the Multiple-Family Zoning Ordinance Study.

With progress, however, come high pressures. Local newspapers carry stories about the stressful lives of Palo Alto high school students trying to achieve the success of their parents. New families moving into

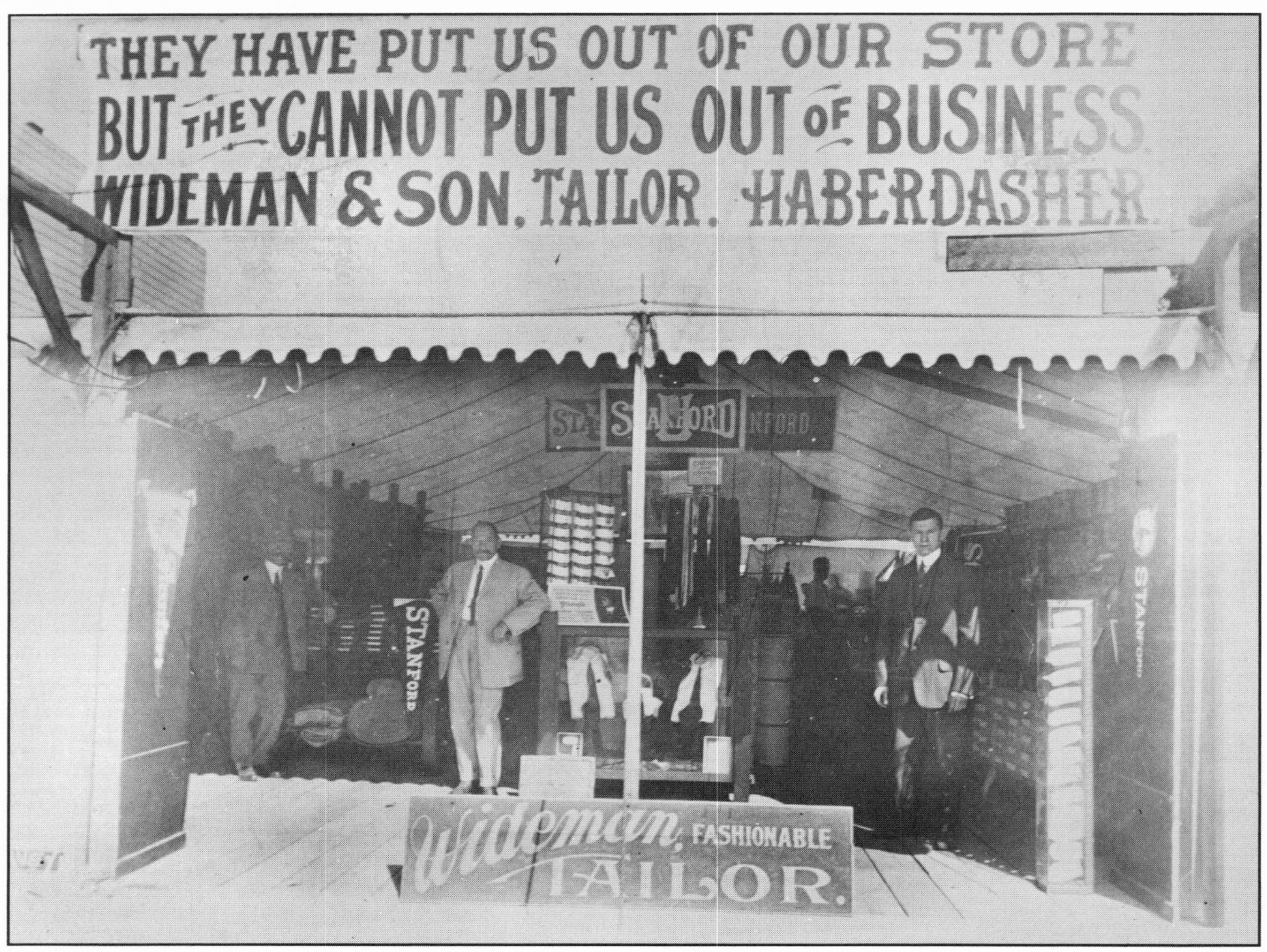

The optimism and tenacity that have always characterized Palo Alto are evident in this picture, taken in 1906, when Wideman's set up shop in a tent after the Thiele Building collapsed in the earthquake.
Courtesy Palo Alto Historical Association

town must take on crushing mortgages. Commuters to high tech jobs find freeways clogged and have little time to enjoy the parks, libraries, and tree-lined streets.

As modern day residents search for balance, they may find it interesting to reflect on the history of their town. Looking beneath Palo Alto's sleek exterior, one can still hear echoes of the town's past.

Ohlone women gathered acorns to be ground for *atole* where today's shoppers at Neiman-Marcus try on expensive blouses and sweaters in the Stanford Shopping Center. Indian men hunted deer near the Co-op at Midtown where Palo Altans buy steaks for their grills.

Leland Stanford, Jr., played with his toys in his parents' elegant country house, located where seriously ill children now listen to the Doobie Brothers Christmas Show Children's Hospital.

Maria Luisa Greer tended her Roses of Castile where the Town and Country Shopping Center's bougainvillea-covered walkways shelter today's shoppers.

On Sunday mornings various Buelnas and Sotos and Juana Briones would gather for Mass at the tiny St. Denis Church, now the site of the Stanford linear accelerator, where atomic particles are studied to reveal the nature of the universe.

The strains of a fiery *tarantella* from a dance at the Robles' rancho may drift through the mind of a commuter listening to traffic reports as he eases his BMW onto the San Antonio overpass.

Where Sarah Wallis' beautiful estate graced the edge of Mayfield, the quaint and charming Barron Park neighborhood has emerged.

The genteel luncheon spots on California Avenue bear scant resemblance to the Occidental Saloon or the Railroad Brewery of the bawdy town of Mayfield that so dismayed Ellen Coit Elliott when she first saw it in 1891. Surely the fashionable small Hotel California, with its white walls and green awnings, offers more comfort and privacy to travelers than did the cloth walls of Uncle Jim's Cabin, which stood just down the street.

At Cowper and Lytton, now the site of a small grocery store, typhoid patients were nursed at the Guild Hospital during the widespread outbreak of 1902. Where Palo Alto senior citizens pass the time lawn bowling at Embarcadero, Cowper and Churchill, Palo Alto's Peninsula Hospital tended victims of the 1918 influenza epidemic.

People sip cappuccino and buy computer supplies at Waverley and University, site of the First Presbyterian Church, where members of the Women's Club held their first meetings and discussed how to save Palo Alto's oak trees.

Instead of horse-drawn wagons carrying fish, meat, or kerosene to their customers at the turn of the century, the vans of Gopher Groceries deliver all the riches of the supermarket to customers who have no time to shop for themselves.

Where today's teenagers get outfitted for mountain trips at Waverley and University, joking Stanford students of the Roaring Twenties hopped onto the Toonerville Trolley for the ride down to Mayfield's saloons.

Where present day residents buy bicycle parts or eat organically-grown health food at University and High, a huge bonfire blazed to celebrate the incorporation of the city in 1894.

And over along San Francisquito Creek, tucked

The well-equipped school band poses with leader Dave Davidson in June 1928. Courtesy Palo Alto Historical Association

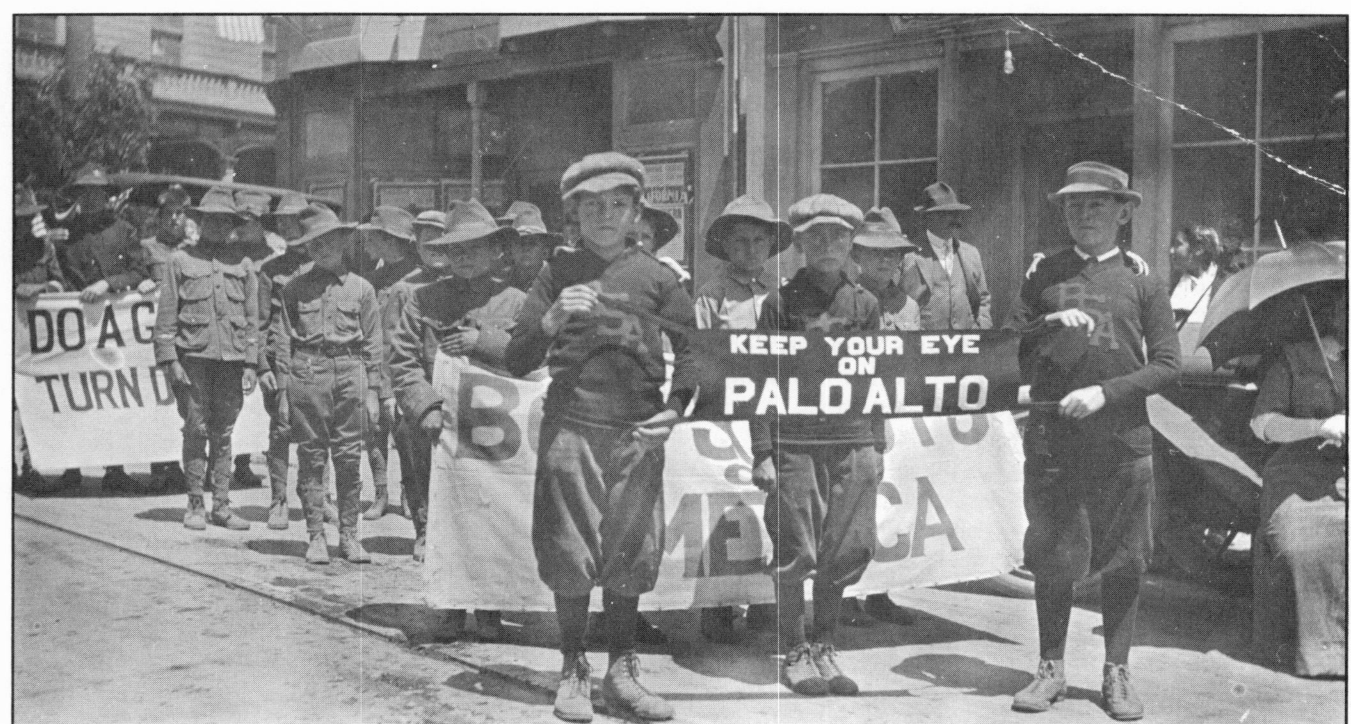

Palo Alto Boy Scouts offer some excellent advice in a parade in Santa Cruz, July 4, 1913.
Courtesy Palo Alto Historical Association

between El Camino Real, the railroad tracks and Alma Street, is El Palo Alto, the 113-foot redwood tree that has survived all the changes for 1063 years. It stood silent witness to 800 years of Ohlone life before the Spanish explorers camped along the creek. It was a landmark for the rancheros and squatters. It gave Senator and Mrs. Stanford a name for their stock farm and a symbol for their great university. It endured as a bustling little town spread out beneath and beyond its branches. The tiny park surrounding this historic tree is a good place to listen for echoes of the past and to meditate on the future of the century-old town named for it.

Chapter Notes

The January 4, 1988 *San Francisco Chronicle* contains a lengthy article explaining how Palo Alto won its number one status among bay area cities. David Blundy's article, "Palo Alto, California, Dream Town," appears in the November 13, 1988 issue of the British magazine *7 Days*.

Statistics about 1925 come from random issues of the *Palo Alto Times* of that year. Current statistics are from several sources. "Working Together, An Annual Report to the Community" from the City of Palo Alto, 1988, provides in twelve pages an excellent summary of the year. A press packet prepared by June Fleming, Assistant City Manager, for Super Bowl XIX was also helpful. David Lawrence, Palo Alto Board of Realtors Executive Officer, supplied the average house price. The *American Library Directory*, 1988-1989, provided the book count. The height of El Palo Alto, which hasn't been measured officially since the mid-1970s, was estimated by city arborist Gary Nauman.

Centennial Time Line

Oct. 28, 1887	Timothy Hopkins buys 700 acres from Henry Seale for $60,000 to establish Stanford's university town.
March, 1888	Palo Alto is laid out and called University Park. Lot sales begin.
May 21, 1888	College Terrace is mapped (platted) as Palo Alto.
Feb. 27, 1889	Plat for University Park (the first name of Palo Alto) is filed.
1889	Professorville is opened for development (Ramona, Bryant and Waverley crossed by Kingsley, Lincoln and Addison).
1890	Palo Alto, population 37, has 6 buildings and two passenger trains per day, which stop when flagged.
1891	Mayfield has 1,000 citizens.
Fall, 1891	Stanford University opens.
Oct. 8, 1891	Subdivision originally called Palo Alto becomes College Terrace.
Dec., 1891	Population is 76.
Jan. 30, 1892	University Park becomes Palo Alto.
May, 1892	A post office opens.
August, 1892	A book store opens.
1893	Population is 400. A twelve room house, the most expensive in town, costs $4,500. There are grocers, a real estate office, a mason, two hotels, a bank, a lumber and hardware store, a stable, a plumber, and a builder.
Jan. 5, 1893	The *Palo Alto Times* begins publishing. Subscriptions are $1.00 per year.
Sept. 9, 1893	The first school, built in 3 days, opens on Bryant near University.
1893	Senator Stanford dies.
1893	Castilleja Hall Preparatory School for Girls opens.
1894	Palo Alto has 165 buildings and a population of 700.
April 9, 1894	Palo Alto has a successful election for incorporation. The vote is: 98 yes, 21 no.
May 2, 1894	Palo Alto becomes an incorporated city.

Palo Alto Time Line

c3000 B. C.	Ohlone Indians arrive.
Nov. 6-10, 1769	Gaspar de Portola's party camp on the banks of San Francisquito Creek near a tall redwood, today celebrated as El Palo Alto.
Nov. 28, 1774	Rivera and Palou place a cross at Portola's earlier campsite, to mark location for a proposed mission.
Mar. 26, 1776	Juan Bautista de Anza and Pedro Font cancel plans for a mission here.
Jan. 12, 1777	Mission Santa Clara is established.
Nov. 29, 1777	San Jose is founded.
1810	There are no Ohlone villages left in their original form.
Apr. 11, 1822	California declares allegiance to Mexico after Mexico gains independence from Spain.
1839	Antonio Buelna is granted Rancho de San Francisquito.
1840	Jose and Ramon Gorgonio are granted Rancho La Purisima Concepcion.
1841	Jose Pena is granted Rancho Rincon de San Francisquito.
1844	Juana Briones de Miranda buys La Purisima Concepcion for $300.
1845	900 people in San Jose area, according to H. H. Bancroft.
1847	Secundino and Teodoro Robles buy Rincon de San Francisquito.
1853	E.O. Crosby buys 250 acres of Rancho Rincon de San Francisquito for $2000 and calls it Mayfield Farm.
1853	James Otterson opens his roadhouse, "Uncle Jim's Cabin," the beginning of the town of Mayfield.
1856	Sarah Wallis buys Mayfield Farm, today's Barron Park, from E. O. Crosby for $10,701.

1863	The San Francisco–San Jose Railroad is completed as far as Mayfield. Governor Stanford attends ceremonies.
1863	George Gordon buys Mayfield Grange.
1867	Mayfield is platted by William Paul.
1874	Peter Coutts arrives.
1876	Gordon's heirs sell Mayfield Grange to Leland Stanford for $170,000.
1878	Edward Barron buys the Wallis estate for $36,500.
1884	Leland Stanford, Junior, dies.
1886	One of El Palo Alto's twin trunks falls; it is 960 years old.
1889	The plat for University Park (Palo Alto's first name) is filed.
1891	Stanford University opens.
1893	Leland Stanford, Senior, dies.
1894	Palo Alto is incorporated. Women's Club is formed.
1896	First municipal water system is constructed. Downtown streets are electrified.
1902–1903	Typhoid fever epidemic.
July 17, 1903	Mayfield is incorporated.
1904	Library is dedicated.
Jan. 1, 1905	Mayfield bans liquor.
1909	Peninsula Hospital is erected at Embarcadero and Cowper.
1909-1910	Population is 4,500.
1916	Mayfield and Palo Alto form a union high school district.
1917	Garden Club started. Gas plant is dedicated.
1919	Barron Estate is sold to developers for small home sites.
1920	Population is 5900.
1921	Art Club is started. Palo Alto Community Players is organized.
1923	Southgate addition is annexed.
1924	Bayshore Freeway construction begins.
1925	Mayfield is annexed to Palo Alto.

Selected Bibliography

Hubert H. Bancroft, *The History of California*, Volumes II, III, IV, V, including Pioneer Register and Index. (San Francisco: The History Company, 1886).

Karen Bartholomew and Roxanne Nilan, *Stanford: A Centennial Chronology* (Stanford: Stanford News and Publications Service, 1985).

Eleanor Pearson Bartlett, "Beginnings in Palo Alto," in *The First Year at Stanford*, edited by the English Club of Stanford, including Alice Windsor Kimball (Stanford: English Club of Stanford, 1905).

Herbert Bolton, *Anza's California Expeditions* (Berkeley: University of California Press, 1930).

Birge Clark, *An Architect Grows Up in Palo Alto*, 1982, unpublished.

Arthur Coffman, *An Illustrated History of Palo Alto* (Palo Alto: Lewis Osborne, 1969).

Bruce Cumming, *History of the Palo Alto Police Department*, 1985, unpublished.

Margo Davis and Roxanne Nilan, *The Family Album: A Photographic History of Stanford* (Stanford: Stanford University Press, 1989).

Ellen Coit Elliott, *It Happened This Way* (Stanford: Stanford University Press, 1940).

John Galvin, Editor, *The First Spanish Entry into San Francisco Bay, 1775* (San Francisco: J. Howell, 1971).

Paul B. Gibson, "Big Doings in a Small Town;" Lester R. Morris, "The Missing Finger and Other Recollections;" and Marguerite Weichselfelder, "Mud Pies and Parties" in *The Way It Was As Told By Those Who Were There* (Palo Alto: Retired Senior Volunteer Program, 1979).

M. E. Hoover, H. E. Rensch and E. G. Rensch, *Historic Spots in California* (Stanford: Stanford University Press, 1966).

A. L. Kroeber, *Handbook of the Indians of California* (Berkeley: California Book Company, 1953; originally published Washington: U.S. Government Office, 1925).

Estelle Latta, *Controversial Mark Hopkins* (New York: Greenberg, 1953).

Oscar Lewis, *The Big Four* (New York: Knopf, 1938).

Timothy J. Lukes and Gary Y. Okihiro, *Japanese Legacy: Farming and Community Life in Santa Clara Valley* (Cupertino: California History Center, De Anza College, 1985).

Menlo Park Historical Association, *A Tradition of New Horizons* (Menlo Park: City of Menlo Park, 1974).

Malcolm Margolin, *The Ohlone Way* (Berkeley: Heyday Books, 1978).

Eliot Grinnell Mears, *Resident Orientals on the American Pacific Coast: Their Legal and Economic Status* (Chicago: University of Chicago Press, 1928).

Guy Miller and Hugh Enochs, *Palo Alto Community Book* (Palo Alto: Arthur H. Cawston, 1952).

J.P. Munro-Fraser, Historian of the Santa Clara Historical Society, *History of Santa Clara County* (San Francisco: Alley Bowen, 1881).

Gunther W. Nagel, *Jane Stanford: Her Life and Letters* (Stanford: Stanford Alumni Association, 1975).

Marie Northrop, *Spanish-Mexican Families of Early California 1769-1850*, Volumes I, II (Burbank: Southern California Genealogical Society, 1984, 1987).

Palo Alto Historical Association, Tall Tree Series, which has been published from June, 1950 to the present.

Francisco Palou, *Founding of the First California Missions*, translated and edited by Douglas S. Watson (San Francisco: Nueva California Press, 1934).

Francisco Palou, *Historical Memoirs of the New California* (Berkeley: University of California Press, 1926).

Dorothy Regnery, *Enduring Heritage: Historic Buildings of the San Francisco Peninsula* (Stanford: Stanford University Press, 1976).

Alfred Robinson, *Life In California* (New York: Wiley and Putnam, 1846).

Betty Rogaway, "Oral History of Fremont Zschokke," 1988, unpublished.

Eugene Sawyer, *History of Santa Clara County* (Los Angeles: Historic Record Co., 1922).

Bayard Taylor, *Eldorado* (Palo Alto: Lewis Osborne, 1968).

James Trager, *The People's Chronology: A Year by Year Record of Human Events from Prehistory to the Present* (New York: Holt, Rinehart, and Winston, 1979).

Norman E. Tutorow, *Leland Stanford: Man of Many Careers* (Menlo Park: Pacific Coast Publishers, 1971).

George Vancouver, *Vancouver in California*, edited by Marguerite Eyer Wilbur [3 volumes] (Los Angeles: Glen Dawson, 1954).

Edith Buckland Webb, *Indian Life at the Old Missions* (Los Angeles: Warren Lewis, 1952).

Dallas Wood, *History of Palo Alto* (Palo Alto: Arthur H. Cawston, 1939).

Irma Zschokke (Crawford), "Our Family Diary: 1886-1968," unpublished, Palo Alto Historical Association Archives.

Index

R

S

T

U

V

W

Y

Z

Sponsors

Following is a list of those who ordered this book in advance of publication, to benefit the Friends of the Palo Alto Library.

Mr. & Mrs. Jan C. Aarts
Mr. & Mrs. Michael A. Aasen
Jacob Abba
Mr. & Mrs. William H. Abbott
Frank and Kaleen Abel
C. Joshua Abend
Ted Aberg
Carol Abrahamian
Billie Achilles
Dr. Carol Achtman
Anne and John Ackerman
Frances and Arthur Adams
Kathryn & Clark Akatiff
Khaver & Muhammad Akhter
Mr. & Mrs. Donald H. Alden
Mr. & Mrs. John G. Alden
Mr. & Mrs. Raymond M. Alden
Mr. & Mrs. Roland H. Alden
Mr. & Mrs. Christopher A. Alders
Meredith and Marshall Alexander
Nancy and Richard Alexander
William G. and Barbara Alhouse
Mr. & Mrs. William P. Allan
Barbara & Judson Allen
Dorothy Mears Allen
Heather E. Allen
Kenneth R. and Susan H. Allen
Samuel Jacob Allen
William H. Allen
Donna J. Allison, Ph. D.
John W. Allured
Ann and Tau Rho Alpha
Jeanne and Mike Althouse
Edward and Dorothy Ames
Thalia Anagnos & Jeffrey Koseff
Marie I. Andersen
Arlan Anderson
Barbara & Dick Anderson
Evelyne & William Anderson
Jean Anderson
Mr. & Mrs. Richard Anderson
Roger and Corrine Anderson
Mr. & Mrs. George Angwin
Don and Sumy Anhorn
Jan and Brad Anker
Antiques Unlimited
Sue and David Apfelberg
Jane and Mike Ardley
Dr. Paul R. Armel
Yvonne B. Armstrong
Christopher and Jodie Arnold
Alvera Nelson Asplund
Mrs. Dan Atell
Damaris Atwater
Jeanne and Larry Aufmuth
Bob Aulgur
Tom and Jean Austin
Lori Lee & Nicole Avila
Ayrin and Atul Ayer
Francis and Shalini Azariah
Bob and Cilia Bach
Beverly and David Backer
Karen and David Backer
Leslie A. Backus
Melinda Day Backus
Richard & Doris Bailey
Georgina and Kim Bailie
Len & Mary Anne Baker
Catherine and James Balboni
Diane & Karl Balcom
William Randolph Baldschun
Alan Baldwin
Davis W. & Patricia O. Baldwin
Joseph L. Baldwin
L. Blake & JoAnn D. Baldwin
Kent and Caroline Barber
Philip Barkan
Peter and Julie Barney
Scott and Barbara Barnum
Amy Barr
Bernadine & Harry Barr
Jim Barr
Lois Barr
Walter M. Barret
Janet and Raymond Barrett
Gwen and Michael Barry
Mr. & Mrs. James Barta
Bob Bartholomew
Betty Elliott Barton
Carol M. Bartz
Susan and Richard Bass
Douglas C. Bassler
Leonie Frances Batkin
Isabelle & Patrick Baudelaire
Alois and Christa Baum
Dick Baumgartner & Liz Salzer
Charles Baxter
Arthur E. Bayce
Alice L. Beach
Captain and Mrs. Edward L. Beach
John Blair Beach
Beverly and Bill Beames
Mr. & Mrs. Paul V. Bearce
Malcolm & Joanne Horsfall Beasley
Louise & Stuart Beattie
Mr. & Mrs. Heston Beaudoin
George & Betsy Bechtel
Anne V. Becker
Mrs. Ernest T. Becker
Mr. & Mrs. Joe Bedell
Leon and Margaret Beeler
Mr. & Mrs. Maurice Beeson
Maggie and Douglas Beetlestone
Michael and Janet L. Bein
David and Jan Belfor
Mr. & Mrs. Elton H. Bell
Darrell Benatar
Lucile G. Benedetti
Don and Deborah Bennett
Barbara E. Bent
Jerome K. and Carol A. Berg
Rhoda & Seymour Bergen family
Florence Wright Berger
Goran & Barbara Berglund
Mickey & Lyn Bernstein
Martin Bernstein & Marian Hirsch
Mr. & Mrs. Robert F. Berry
Tim and Vange Berry
Joan and Richard Bialek
Martin Bicker
Julia H. Bien
Helen Park Bigelow
Mr. & Mrs. Chris Billat
MaryAnn & Richard Bills
Dennis and Lois Bird
Grace & John Bird
Laetitia and Peter Bird
Alex and Julie Bishop
Cordy and Stan Bishop
Mr. & Mrs. Earl Bishop
Mr. & Mrs. Paul Blake
Mr. & Mrs. William Blake
Mr. & Mrs. Frederick Blankenship
George and Pat Bliss
Gene E. Bloch
M. J. Block
Jane and Bill Bloom
Bonnie and Bill Blythe
Phil and Mary Bobel
Kathy and John Bobick
Mary Jane Boettcher
Charles and Barbara Bonini
Elizabeth H. Bonn
Olive and John Borgsteadt
Don and Carolyn Bott
Laureen K. Boulden
Fred and Eleanor Bourquin
David Bower & Sally Glaser
The Boy Family
Abby Boyd
Steven and Deborah Boyd
John and Marion Bracken
Dorothy Bradley
Mary Sarah Bradley
Sam and Susie Brain
Lois and Donald Brand
Sharon and John Brauman
Susan K. Braun
Lucinda Moser Breed
John Thomas & Kathryn Brethauer
Betty MacLachlan Brichta
Mr. & Mrs. Robert Brickley
Thelma & Bob Brinker
Ralph H. Britton
Lorain C. Brookman
Anne Pavlina Brooks
Evelyn M. Brother

Dr. & Mrs. J. Sewall Brown
Elissa Beth Brown
Ellen and Marc Brown
John L. Brown
Loren & Dee Brown
Mr. & Mrs. Robert V. Brown
Pauline Brown
Shannon & Judith Brown
Terry and Mary Brown
Mark Brown & Mary-Claire van Leunen
Andrew Charles Browne
Charles H. Browning
Hallie Warren Bruce
Joan Bruce
John A. Brugge
Robert D. Brummer
Marjorie and James R. Buckley
David and Jamie Buckmaster
Carla and Natale Bujatti
Mary Bulf
Mary Lou and David Bull
Paul Bundy
Mr. and Mrs. Norman R. Burdick
Helen N. Burgess
Doris & George Burke
Shari and Terry Burkoth
Mary Ellen Burnley
Nelson & Helen Burrill
Katy Burt
Pat and Sally Bemus Burt
Laura H. Burtness
Yvonne M. Burtness
Richard R. Burton
Joanne Burton & Wes Sorby
Barbara & Bill Busse
Curt Busse
Matt & Kathy Busse
Peter and Polly Butterfield
Bill and Gina Byxbee
Mr. & Mrs. R. W. Byxbee
Gary and Nancy Caldwell
California State Library
Louis and Geraldine Caligaris
Arthur H. Calvert
Mr. & Mrs. Donald C. Cameron
Dr. & Mrs. K. Gordon Campbell
Meg Campbell
Mr. & Mrs. Donald Campbell
Pamela Campbell
Karen Cardoza
Alvin and Virginia Carlson
Bob Carlson & Judy Kincaid
Carrie Carlstead
Martha A. Carlstead
Mary & Robert Carlstead
William M. Carlstead
Ralph Carmichael
Carol Carnevale
J. Roney Carpenter
Marshall Carrick
Leon & George Carrie
Lois Barry Carroll
Lynn Carroll
Claire Carter
Mrs. Elizabeth Alden Carter
Elsie P. Case
Mr. & Mrs. R. B. Cassidy
Judith and Jacques Castaillac
Ellie and Earl Caustin
James Cesano
Bernadette & William E. Chamberlain
Xan and Cindy Chamberlain
Janet & Clifford Chambers
Elaine B. Chan
Alice Anne and Denny Chandler
Channing House Library
John and Brenda Chaparro
Chat Chatterton
Mary Anne and David Chazan
Mr. & Mrs. Henry Chezar
Mary Chin & Antoine Gaessler
Mr. & Mrs. Ole A. Christensen IV
Larry & Lyn Christenson
Raymond and Lin Chuang
City of Palo Alto
Heather Clancy
Jeannie Clancy
Mr. & Mrs. Charles C. Clark
Mr. & Mrs. Lawrence M. Clark
Richard N. Clark
Robin Clark & Mary Mackiernan
Mr. & Mrs. Charles E. Clark, jr.
Daniel Wood Clarkson
Mr. & Mrs. Bob Clarkson
Peter and Helena Clarkson
Mr. & Mrs. William Clayton
Thomas Hailey Clewe
Mrs. Mary Edith Jones Clifford
Laura and Jack Cline
Mr. & Mrs. Mike Cobb
Natalie Cobby
Andrew Hale Cochran
Marilyn and Jim Coghlin
Margaret and Mel Cohen
Charlotte and Wendell Cole
Rae and Gordon Cole
Mr. & Mrs. Kevin Coleman
Roberta and Larry Colin
Alison and Harry Collin
Marge and Tom Collins
Sylvia & Tony Coluzzi
Mavis and George Conner
Dorothy and Victor Connett
Evelyne Conquaret
Jean Cook
Sheila Cook
Peter and Susan Corning
Coryell-Weinberg family
Cynthia Costell
Steve and Andy Costell
Stan & Mary Cottrell
Alison & George Cox
Mary & Bill Cox
Claire & Harold Cramer
Alison and John Crane
Ellen Elizabeth Crane
Constance Crawford
Mr. Perry Crawford
John B. Crews
Lisa and Scott Crist
Mr. & Mrs. Frank Lee Crist, Sr.
John and Ruth Cross
Chip and Donna Crossman
Bob Crothers
Richard J. Cuevas
Michael and Patricia Cullen
Mr. & Mrs. John Cumberpatch
Frances L. Cummins
Tom and Suellen Cunningham
Mr. & Mrs. Steve Curtiss
Patricia A. Dalton
Joan E. Dammann
Dr. & Mrs. David Daniels
Elaine Darrah
Hal W. Daseking
Gary and Brenda Dau
William B. Daul
Irene Davidson
Richard S. and Marian L. Davies
Vaughn & Lennie Davis
Harriet Allen Davis & Roland C. Davis
Barbara A. Dawson
Emily Anna Dawson
Betty and Tom Dayharsh
Devra De Angelis
Peter A. De Meo
Mr. & Mrs. E. De Moor
Alan and Miriam de Schweinitz
Bruce E. and Rachel B. Deal
William J. DeBord
Jan & Gita Dedek
Marty and Judy Deggeller
Carl F. Dehrer
Lilia Del Cioppo, M. D.
Anita and Bill Delaney
Pat Dentinger
Sheila Kelley Dentoni
Mr. & Mrs. Howard Dernehl
Betsy & Gary DeSeelhorst
Bruce and Monica Devens
Mary and Warren Deverel
Donna and Bob Devries
Dorothy and Bill Dewing
Steve Diaz
Susan & Roy Diederichsen
Jeff Dielle & Kelly Brown
G. Jerahian Diers
Neva and Fred Diestel
Mr. & Mrs. Fred Dietrich
Digital Pathways, Inc.
Scott K. Dinwiddie
Robert L. Doerschuk
Kenneth and Carolyn Dole
Hilary and James Donahue
Joan & John Donegan
Sara Doniach
Adriano Geusippi Donnaloia
Linda Levine Donnaloia
Eleanor and Andy Doty
Marlene and Richard Douglas
Mr. & Mrs. Chesley Douglas, Jr.
Cathleen and Wayne Douglass
Michael & Sharon-Joyce Dowler
Mr. & Mrs. L. C. Downer
John Kenneth and Babette B. Doyle
Ed and Lisa Dreessen
Charles & Margot Drekmeier
Mr. & Mrs. Thomas J. Drewek
Donna Lorraine Driscoll
Danta & Larry Drummond
Irene & Michael Duffy
John and Glenda Duggan
Erik David Duisenberg
Jeanne Duisenberg

Deborah Duncan & William E. Stone
Alan and Elizabeth Dunckel
Mary C. Dunham
Mr. & Mrs. Jeff Dunker
Margo Dutton
Pat and Ron Eadie
Sandra & Gilbert Eakins
Mr. and Mrs. Benjamin M. Eaton
Mrs. Monroe Davis Eaton
Virginia G. Eaton
Shirley and James R. Eaton, Jr.
Mr. & Mrs. Jackson Eaves
Mary G. Eberle
Dr. & Mrs. Jack P. Edelstein
Carol Edmiston
K. H. Edwards
Marilyn Edwardson
John H. Eft & Darlene F. Russ-Eft
Julie Anne Eggert
Jack E. Eisen
Sarah J. Elder
Dr. & Mrs. Franklin R. Elevitch
Sharon and Grant Elliot
Nancy and Rich Elliott
Frank and Bernice Ellis
Robert and Margery Ellis
The A. Ellis Family
Donald Duane Ellison
Gary & Dee Ellmann
Elmwood Inn
Shannon Elvitsky & Nick Elvitsky
Leonard W. Ely III
Susan K. Emanuelson
Pamela and Greg Emery
Ruth and Burton Endsley
Christina Engelbart
Timothy Enos
Connie Enzminger
Nancy R. Enzminger
Maureen & Tony Eppstein
Mr. & Mrs. Victor H. Erickson
Mrs. Leif Erickson
Mr. & Mrs. Theodore G. Erler
Jack Creighton Erwin
Stephen and Ruth Escher
Marion and Jack Euphrat
Dr. & Mrs. A. McChesney Evans
John and Katie Evans
Marie Evans
Mr. & Mrs. Carroll C. Evatt
Michael & Linda Ewing
Henry C. Faber
Madeleine and Stephen Fackler
Helen L. Fairborn
Chester R. Fairclough
Dr. Luis and Lorela Fajardo
Betsy and Glynn Falcon
Charles & Judy Faltz
Clyde Farmer
Pat & Louis Fasani
Carolyn Marie Faul
Bill and Ernestine Faxon
Kate and Marvin Feinstein
Peter Fenerin
Bette Jane and John Ferandin
Michael and Margaret R. Feuer
Patricia & Richard Feundeling
Thomas and Nancy Fiene
Wendy and Cruz Fierro
Margaret and Walter Fink
Solon and Diane Finkelstein
George A. Finnan
Paul Fitzpatrick
Sue and Adrian Flakoll
William and Mary Flanagan
Lee A. and Ranette C. Fletcher
Mrs. Wm. Ben Floyd
Roy H. Fogelqvist
Mary and Tim Foley
Diane and Jim Foote
Mr. Thomas A. Forbes
Delbert & Verna Ford
Zev Foreman
Elizabeth and John Forrest
Cathleen and Michael Foster
Col. & Mrs. Herbert R. Foster
Robert Ray Foster
Katharine M. Frank
Diane Frank and John Clifford Mitchell
Doug and Maria Franke
Barbara and Dick Franklin
Franz Termite Control
Dr. & Mrs. Joseph Franzini
Ruth and Elvis Frapwell
Rita and Marc-David Freed
Andrew L. Freedman
Robert & Sarah Freedman
Betty and Bob French
Gerald & Miriam Friedland
Bonita & Steven Friedman
Eileen & Len Friedman
Martin E. Frost
Mr. & Mrs. Charles P. Frost
Carroll and Catharine Fruth
Robert Fruth & Cynthia Finnell-Fruth
William & Elizabeth Frye
Fred and Alice Fujikawa
Allen & Linda Fujimoto
Mr. & Mrs. Russell Fuller
Marilyn Fulsaas
Alys & Forrest Futtere
Marilyn and Paul Galli
Sandra M. Gardner
Mr. & Mrs. John L. Garibaldi
Barbara Garlitz
Mr. & Mrs. John B. Garmany
Mark and Elke Garner
Jean and Paul Garrett
Sherm Garsha
Shirley M. Gehman
Philip Geller & Dr. Diane Morrissette
Loi & Ivan Gendzel
Leslie Gentle & Kathryn Kelly-Gentle
Carolyn and Brian George
Eloise George
Emmett and Lorraine Gerrity
Howard and Melva Gerrity
Lynn and Jim Gibbons
Dr. & Mrs. Weldon B. "Hoot" Gibson
Mr. & Mrs. Jonathan Berry Gifford
Dr. and Mrs. Jack M. Gill
Melissa and Jeremy Gillan
Marilyn & Robert Gillespie
Roy & Nancy Ginsburg
Mr. & Mrs. Rene A. Girerd
Dexter G. Girton
Barbara Marx Givan
Edward & Frances Glaeser
James & Erna Glanville
Dr. Robert J. Glaser
Valerie and Peter Glassford
John P. Glathe, M. D.
Amy Elizabeth Glaze
Harry J. Glaze, Jr.
Katherine and Bill Glazier
David Glen & Katharine Esslinger
Charlene Gliniecki & Stephan Crothers
Nancy and Michael Goddard
Ruth and Robert Goldbeck
Phyllis and Daniel Goldberg
Friends of James Golden
Avram & Dora B. Goldstein
Elizabeth Esther Thompson Goldstein
Jane Goldstein
Paul Goldstein & Dena Mossar
Mike Golick
Jeanine & Richard Goodale
Dores Goodenough
Gail Goodenough
Nancy and Gary Goodenough
Alfred L. Goodman
Thomas and Rachel Goodrich
Dr. & Mrs. Rufus Goodwin
Ruth & Jack Goodwin
Colin F. Gorman
Boots and Chuck Gould
Douglas and Verna Graham
Josephine A. Graham
Sylvia Grainger & Brian Burns
Pat & Vince Grande
Pria A. Graves
Jean C. Greeley
Margaret and Paul Green
Richard D. Green
Harry B. & Diane S. Greenberg
Nancy and Allan Greenland
Paul & Martha Gregory
Thomas G. Gregory
Barbara and Robert Greider
William and Mary Rena Gretz
Mr. & Mrs. Philip S. Grimes
Judith and Milton Grinberg
Tim and Karen Grippi
Mr. & Mrs. Ford Griswold
Mr. & Mrs. Robert Y. Griswold
Bill and Sue Groechel
Mr. Melvin B. Gross
Kenneth R. Grover
Mr. & Mrs. Lindo C. Guerra
Anita L. Guidoux
Jane and Edouard Guidoux
Dorothy Erickson Gullixson
John and Genevieve Gusman
Norman S. Gussin
Rosalind and Seth L. Haber
James V. Hacker
Maral M. Haddeiand
Hooman Hafezi
V. Kay Hafner
Patricia A. Hagan
Brian and Rhonda Hall
Doris and Joseph L. Hall
John W. T. & Kevin D. (Jr.) Hall
Kevin & Cindy Hall

Michael W. Hall
Ronald Hall
Duane and Mary Hallesy
Laura & Kiyoshi Hamai
J. Scott Hamilton
Marjorie Fagan Hamilton
Mr. & Mrs. Hugh M. Hamilton
Mike & Sara Hammond
Mr. & Mrs. Philip Hanawalt
Mr. & Mrs. George F. Hand
Helen Handa-Fujimoto
Gina & William Handel
Nancy Jean & Christopher Handel
Tom and Peg Hanks
Stuart and Carol Hansen
Carolyn & Gary Hanson
Linda & Gary Hanson
Dennis D. Harman
Margie and Bob Harrington
Joyce and James S. Harris, Jr.
Dorothea S. Hart
Jeannine and Barry Hart
Mr. Edmund Shea Harvey
Mrs. Katherine Wrapp Harvey
Roberta Harvey
Sue and Gerald Harwell
Mary and Bob Haslam
Anne Wheeler Haughton
Deborah Hawkins
Anne Kathryn Haynes
John and Reo Haynes
Megan Elizabeth Haynes
Mr. & Mrs. Bill Haynes
Marguerite T. Hays
Mr. & Mrs. Richard M. Hays
Mr. & Mrs. Dan Heath
Bill and Mickey Hebard
Erin McGauley Hebard
Mr. & Mrs. Walter K. Heitzmann
Diana L. Hellman
Erik C. Hellman
Kristina J. Hellman
Sherill and Carl G. Hellman
Robert and Martha Helseth
Sherman L. & Dorothy K. Hemstreet
Alan and Myrene Henderson
Larry & Amber Henninger
Clive A. Henrick
Arnold and June Henrikson
Janice Hepper
Millicent M. Herbst
Doris and Bob Herdman
Konrad F. Herman
Mr. & Mrs. Robert W. Hermsen
John and Cliff Herndon
Steven and Irene Herring
Pat and Bob Herriot
Margaret and Larry Herte
Robert D. Hess
Sylvia J. Heurlin
Neil E. Heyden
Kathe & Edward Hickey
Mr. & Mrs. Tom K. Hickey
Bethel Neel Hill
Commander & Mrs. Ronald S. Hill
Mr. & Mrs. A. Alan Hill
Mr. & Mrs. Albert A. Hill
Mr. & Mrs. Bryson Hills
Ned and Sheila Himmel
Mr. & Mrs. Carl J. Hipp
Sarah S. Hoffman
Mr. & Mrs. Richard R. Hogan
David B. Holland
Joan and Roger Holland
Janice and Roger Holliday
Myron and Linda Hollister
Bayard and Ida Holmes
Cheryl and Jim Holt
Hazel M. Hood
Randal B. Hopwood
Charles and Joan Horngren
Dave & Geri Horsma
Emile H. and Linda Catlin Houle
Bob and Bev House
Robert & Christy Hubbard
Joseph H. & Nancy A. Huber
Karyle & Peter Hughes
Laddie and Donald Hughes
Richard & Penelope Hughes
Mr. & Mrs. Harold E. Hughes, Jr.
Connie and Mike Humphries
Minnie and George Hurley
Mr. & Mrs. Ralph A. Hurvitz
Ki and Kent Hutchinson
Mr. & Mrs. I. B. Hutchinson
Mrs. Charles W. Huttmann
John L. Hyde
Mark and Victoria Hyde
James N. and Marianne Ida
Charles & Jeannie Ingham
Drs. Robert and Maxine Ingham
Law Offices of Irvine & Cooper
Perry Irvine & Linda Romley-Irvine
Paul Irwin
Violet Irwin
Mr. and Mrs. Matthew Ives
Gail and Tom Jack
Dr. & Mrs. R. J. Jackman
Esther Levin Jacobson
Mr. & Mrs. Ray Jacobson
Ray and Eleanora Jadwin
The Jaggard Family
Anna & Rudolf Jaklitsch
David and Ellen James
George and Beverly James
The Michael R. James Family
John and June Jenke
Dr. Jobe Jenkins & Jean F. Jenkins
Diane and John Jennings
Mr. & Mrs. William C. Jensen
Virginia L. Jensen
Gertrude John Jepson
Ann C. Jerahian
Julie and Jonathan Jerome
Gregory & Lori Jirak
Elina Johari
Clara and Wilton Johnson
James and Annie Johnson
Jessica Ruth Johnson
Margaret Ann & Bruce Johnson
Mark and Sue Johnson
Mitchel B. Johnson
Mr. & Mrs. Enard K. Johnson
Mr. & Mrs. Oliver W. Johnson
Mr. Mrs. Reynold B. Johnson
Norma & Denis Johnson
Peggy and Fred Johnson
Trish Johnson
Winnie & Robert W. Johnston
Robert S. Johnstone
Dick & April Jones
Mrs. Mirriam Johnson Jones
Patricia Pearce Jones
Randolph B. & Vicki L. Jones
Alvin E. Jong
R. Emmett Jordan
Anthea and Timothy Josling
Erin and David Jost
Joseph Jurow Family
Zelda Jury
Joan Fugazzi Kagel
Patricia and Warren Kallenbach
Dorothy and Joel Kaplan
Rebecca and Douglas Karlson
Ruth and Arnie Kaufman
Anne and Louis Kavanau
Dr. & Mrs. Ronald L. Kaye
David H. Keefer
Michael & Barbara Keen
Carmen and Mac Keiser
Dr. Arthur M. Keller
Jacob Keller
Meredyth Manning Keller
Merijean and R. Colin Kelley
Alice and Beecher Kellogg
Dr. & Mrs. Francis J. Kelly
George and Barbara Kelly
Kathleen Kelly
Michael J. Kelly
Mr. & Mrs. Robert G. Kelly
Mel and Zoe Kelm
Star St. John Kemper
Carolyn and Keith Kennedy
Carol and Don Kenyon
Leo and Marlys Keoshian
Mr. & Mrs. Geoffrey J. Kerber
Mr. & Mrs. George H. Kerber
Keys School
Eithel (Brister) Kidder
Jack & Barbara Kidder
Dee Dee Kim
Dennis & Marsha Kimber
Marsha Lee Kimber
Dr. Philip R. King
Lurine and John King
Mr. & Mrs. John W. King
Mrs. Mary D. King
Steward A. Kiritz
John M. Kirk
Nadine B. Kirk
William T. Kirk, Jr.
Lillian Ledoyen Kirkbride
Bernice R. Kiser
J. Kenneth Kiser
Albert B. Klay
Abe & Helene F. Klein
Denise Hogan Klein
Larry Klein
Michael and June Klein
Rolf and Pamela Klibo
John and Nancy Klimp
Barbara and Robert Knapp
Robert & Helen Knapp

Tom and Judy Knight
Setsuko and Shigueru Kobayashi
Kathryn Wehrend Koch
George H. Koerner
Debbie and Roger Kohler
Roger and Debbie Kohler
Martin D. Koob
Eileen B. Kosby
Ann and Jefferey Kot
Valerie and John Kot
Marjorie Harsh Koukouras
Sherri Lea Laundis Kranzler
Bradley and Terri Kravitz
Virginia Krebs
Ken Krechmer
Eileen & Don Kreps
Ruth H. Krow
Mabel Kruse
Mr. & Mrs. William Kruse
Jean and Yosh Kumagai
Richard E. Kurovsky
Mr. & Mrs. Richard J. Lamb, Jr.
Caroline H. Landes
Joseph and Martha Lane
Leora R. Langs
Mr. & Mrs. Dennis R. Langs
Mr. & Mrs. Kirk R. Langs
Mr. & Mrs. Marc R. Langs
Mary Lanigar
Ellen Lapham
Melvin & Larkin Lapides
Ethel L. Lapuyade
Dave and Elayne Larimer
Eric Larouse
Mrs. Ruth Silliman Larsen
Ted and Peggy Larsen
Wade Larsen
Bill and Jane Larson
Bob Larson
Brett Larson
Henry and Doris Larson
Nicole Larson
William R. Larson
Richelle Larson-Andre
Dave and Debbie Larson-Ladd
Bill and Linda Larson-Overton
Kathryn Larson-Presti
Las Lomitas School District
Gilles and Christine Lasfargues
Michael T. Lash
Latin American Studies/Stanford
Kelley Kathleen Lauer
Bea & Bill Laundis
Guy Laundis
Bill Laundis, Jr.
Eugene and Barbara Lawrence
Mr. John Michael Lawrence
Mary Ellen and Dan Lazare
Jacynth Lara Le Maistre
Jo Ann Levine Le Maistre
Mike and Julie Leach
Frank Leahy
Alma Leamey
Sherry and Lou Leardini
Elizabeth F. LeCount
Dr. and Mrs. J. S. Ledgerwood
Jeanette & Gene P. Lee
Ning Lee
Peter S. Y. Lee
Yee Lee
Jane and Bernard Leitner
Mr. & Mrs. Ross Lemcke
Jeanne and T. R. Leonard
Mr. & Mrs. Robert Leonard
Elizabeth Leone
Samuel & Suzanne Leong
Robert & Eileen Lerch
James and Vera Leung
Susan Levenberg & Paul Podrid
Barbara Hoyt Levernier
David & Winnie Levin
Irving Levin
Richard & Emmy Lou Levin
Stanley & Donna Levin
Sydney & Virginia Larsen Levin
Mary Snaidman Levine
Adele Levy
Arlene and Leland Levy
Mary Jo & Len Levy
Mrs. Donald M. Levy
Jack, Nancee and Betty Lewis
John and Alicia Lewis
Julien B. Lewis (Mrs.)
Jeanette Levin Lewon
Ron and Michelle Lewton
Galina & Lev Leytes
Ralph and Jean Libby
Mary Jo & George Liddicoat
Mr. & Mrs. Walter Liddicoat
Andrew F. Light
Jiang-nan and Susan Lin
Gary Lindgren
Michael D. Litfin
Elizabeth Stella Little
Frank Livermore
Ellen and Raymond Lloyd
Marian C. Lockwood
Barbara and Russell Long
Ray and Sarita Longanecker
Georgia Longsdon
Linda and Steve Longstreth
John and Brenda Lovas
Mr. & Mrs. Ward Low
Harold and Marion Lowe
Mary and Brian Lowe
Manuel and Emily Lozano
Bob and Kathy Luchini
Betty and Henry Lum, Jr.
Alice and Walter Lundin
F. G. Luscher
Sue Luttner & Jerome Coonen
William C. Lynch
Lytton Properties, Inc.
Adrian and Margot Maarleveld
Joan and John Scott MacDaniels
Marion MacGillivray & Peter Milward
Anne and Fred MacKenzie
Anthony & Alice Makjavich
Irene R. Malaspina
Elizabeth C. Mallory
Mr. Kelly H. Mandel
Louise Levin Henriques Mann
Robert March & Lisa Lawrence
Alan G. Marer
Gerald Z. Marer
Anne and Jack Margolis
Michael & Arlene Markakis
James and Patricia Markevitch
Marilyn Markkanen & Craig Steinman
Margaret & Michael Markowitsch
Edward M. Marks
Heather M. Marlow
Michael and Elaine Marlow
Sean P. Marlow
Drs. Jane & Michael Marmor
Marnie & Cathy
Ernest & Sue Marshall
William W. Marshall II
Norman & Elayne Weissler Martello
Marion E. Martin
Mr. & Mrs. Richard Maruhashi
Ellen & Jean-Louis Maserati
Maria W. Mather
Jim and Janet Mathiott
MaryAnna & Franklin Matsumoto
Barbara and Ted May
Marjorie O. Mays
Bob and Silvia Mazawa
Mr. & Mrs. Martin Mazner
Janine Mazur
Dr. & Mrs. S. V. Mazzara
Bruce and Caroline McAllister
John and Leona McCabe
Barbara & the late Francis J. McCarthy
Lauren McCarthy
Tim and Karen McCarthy
Kevin & Elayna McCarty
Leo & Alice McCarty
Bud & Dawn McClelland
Kevin and Anne McCluskey
Charles, Susan & Chelsea McCollum
Mr. & Mrs. Robert McCollum
Michael F. McCord
Bruce and Corinne McCourt
Randall & Helen McDermott
David McDonald
Joan Stuart McDonnell
Leah and Joe McDonough
Edgar McDowell
Kate McDowell
Cyanne & Bill McElhinney
Dana McElhinney
Glenne McElhinney
Gregg McElhinney
Mr. and Mrs. C. R. McEwen
Marinita H. McFadden
P. Michael McFadden
Mr. and Mrs. James McFall
Merre Jayne & Earl McFate
Mrs. Albert F. McGillivray
Anne Caroline McGilvray
Stepheny McGraw
Mr. & Mrs. John McGuire
Robert W. McIntyre
Robert W. McIntyre
Skip and Luci McIntyre
Mrs. William H. McKaig (Jerry)
Virginia and Bob McKim
Terri and Dennis McKinsey
Marianne Mckissock
Robert and Mary Pat McLean
Karen and Rick McMichael
Marjorie Nattras McNay
Bryant & Susan McOmber

Jane B. Meiggs
Gladys and Torben Meisling
Lynnie & Joe Melena
Miriam and Miles Mellberg
Robert and Susan Gray Mellberg
Major General & Mrs. Thomas W. Mellen
Betty and Bob Meltzer
Laura J. Melvin
Alice and John Menches
Menlo Park Historical Association
Menlo Park Library
Menlo School & College Library
Al and Montel Menting
Sam and Joann Meredith
Lewis Mermelstein & Jane Marcus
Mrs. Wilson Merriam
Mr. & Mrs. John Merritt
Nancy L. Merritt
Tony and Peggy Merz
Marlene and Ski Meshinski
Victor and Mary Mezzapelle
Eugene and Lisette Micek
Mid-Peninsula Bank
Robert H. Millavec
Christopher Lorin Miller
Kay and Tom Miller
Kristine D. Miller
Christine Miller & Gary Glaser
Mr. & Mrs. Robin Milligan
Mitchell and Pedy Millman
Mary C. Mills
William R. Mills
Mary L. Minto
Meg & Rafael Miranda
Carol C. & John Wright Mitchell
Charles Mitchell
Dr. and Mrs. Steven P. Mitchell
Fred and Barb Mitchell
Jean & Sidney P. Mitchell
Mr. & Mrs. R. Wayne Mitchell
Ruth and Allen Mitchell
Trisha and Dennis Mitchell
Ikuko and Atsushi Miyajima
David Scott Moberly
Lina L. Moffitt
Shantha & Joseph Mohan
Mr. & Mrs. Ordway Monette
George and Dorothy Monica
Stefan and Martha Monica
Jessie W. Montrouil
Mary and Stephen Moore
Mr. and Mrs. Robert C. Moore
Mr. and Mrs. Terrence N. Moore
Patrick R. Moran
Hal and Charmien Moreno
Mr. & Mrs. Robert E. Morgan
Martha Morrell
Patricia Custer Morris
Mr. & Mrs. John J. Morris III
David W. Morrison
Mr. & Mrs. John J. Morrissey
Jack and Jackie Morrow
Barbara Morton
Dr. & Mrs. Peter S. Moskowitz
The David Moss Family
Mr. & Mrs. Kamron Motamedi
Mr. & Mrs. William W. Moulden
Mountain View Public Library
Carol and Edward Mrizek
Kathleen Much & Stanley Peters
Mr. & Mrs. Glenn M. Mueller
Richard L. Mueller
Betty B. Mulcahy
Alfred and Sharon Mullen
Trish and Jim Mulvey
Mr. & Mrs. Michael Munro
Phyllis Munsey
John and Carol Murden
Barbara and Bob Murray
William & Olga Myers
Gayle and Don Nathe
Judith E. Naughton
Carr B. Neel
Robert K. Neel
Janet H. Neikirk
J'anny and Ed Nelson
John S. Nelson
Nelson Capital Management
Dr. & Mrs. Rudi Neumarker
Mary and Eugene Nickell
Mr. Robert Niederman
Otto V. & Lois M. Niehues
Dr. Russell A. Nielsen
Eric A. Nielsen
Mr. & Mrs. Glen Nielsen
Roland W. Nielsen
Ron and Avy Nielsen
Penny Nii & Edward Feigenbaum
Kjell A. Nilsson
Dena Nishihara (aka Kondo)
Christopher J. Noerdinger
Susan and Tom Nolan
Sandra Elizabeth Nolen
Mrs. Eunice M. Norberg
Sally and Craig Nordlund
Bessie Mae Wade Norman
Mr. & Mrs. H. L. North
Joan and Robert Northcott
Linda L. Northway
Adam and Mary Ann Norton
Stan Norton
June Moore Novotny
James M. O'Donohue
Mark O'Leary
Fran and Jack O'Rourke
Mrs. Joan W. Oakley
Robert and Doloris Oakley
E. R. & N. M. Oblander
Katy Obringer
Dorothy M. & Julius F. Oehlschlager
Mr. & Mrs. Julius F. Oehlschlager
Carl Joseph Oeschger
Christoph Emil Oeschger
Eldora Miller Oeschger
Joseph Emil Oeschger
Marc C. Oeschger
Nancy & Daniel Okimoto
Norman and Dolores Okner
Adrienne and Jay Oliff
Franklin and Jean Olmsted
Sharon Olson
Kay Strasser Oravets
Mr. & Mrs. Greg Osborn
Steve & Jacci Osborn
Lolly & Tom Osborne
Richard A. & Patricia Osiecki
Mr. & Mrs. A. Thomas Ovenshine
Mr. & Mrs. John T. Ovenshine
Pamela Page
Stephen and Louise Pahl
Charles and Miriam Palm
Palo Alto Bayshore Rotary
Palo Alto Buddhist Temple Library
Palo Alto City Libraries
Palo Alto Elks Lodge #1471
Palo Alto Unified School District
Palo Municipal Library, Philippines
Roy and Linda Parfitt
Brett R. Parker
Jason T. Parker
Nan and Bruce Parker
Tom & Kathy Parker
Cynthia A. Parkinson
Ivo and Doris Parra
Kay M. Partelow
Joan Manning Paulin
Karen Paulsen
Mary and David Pauly
Christopher Sabin Payne
Janet Peacock
Fabian and Caroline Pease
Douglas and Sally Peck
Maren Pedersen & James Herriot
Mr. & Mrs. Al Pellizzari
Dr. & Mrs. Robert D. Pepper
Sylvia and Joaquin Perez
Katherine and Richard Pering
Martin L. Perl
David Perlmutter & Kathleen Murren
Susan O'Connell Perrigo
Jeannine and Michel Perrin
Robert and Armella Perry
Howard and Sally Peters
Joel and Audrey Peters
Warren and Renette Peters
Alan B. Petersen
Bill and Bea Peterson
Bill and Yvonne Peterson
Judy Peterson
Kitty Petty
Kathryn McDonnell Peuvrelle
Joan Phelan
Mr. & Mrs. Howard Phillips
Susan Phillips-Moskowitz
William and Mary Pickthorn
William J. & LedaBeth G. Pickthorn
Helene and Gene Pier
Edward R. & Rhonda A. Pierce
Hiram and Arden Pierce
Steve and Carolyn Pierce
Carol and Peter Piercy
Edna and Robert Pike
Lee Pimental
Melissa Pinney
Cathryn Pinter
Mr. & Mrs. Dominique Pitteloud
Martha and Jeremy Platt
Judy and Joe Podolsky
Relda A. & Elmer J. Poffenroth
Ruth L. Polansky
Jim & Guila Pollock
Polly & Jake
Mr. & Mrs. William D. Pomeroy III
Louis Ponte

Annette Portello
Karen Ann Porter
Mr. & Mrs. M. Crawford Pratt
Shirley and Frank Prausa
Elsa and Ralph Preminger
Nicci Prentice
Dana & Lynn Prescott
Sylvia Anne Prestage
Evelyn and Oliver Preston
Jeff Preston
Mr. & Mrs. Clifford Preston
Mr. & Mrs. William A. Preston
Marilyn D. Price
Mr. & Mrs. Lee Price
Mr. & Mrs. Michael J. Price
Julia Price-Madison
Margaret Ely Pringle
Billy Prior
Patricia & Daniel Pritchard
Suzie Provo
QED Research, Inc.
Carter & Shirley Quinby
Calvin and Shirley Radl
Robert A. & Jane B. Radosevic
K. Woodford Ralph
Martha W. Ralph
A. J. and Ruth Ramberg
Irene J. Ramos
Jeanne and Andy Ramos
Hazel and Roy Rand
Mr. & Mrs. Howard Raphael
Tom and Lisbeth Rau
Kathy and Grant Rauzi
Larry J. and Pat K. Raynak
Blythe and Charles Read
Anne and Chris Ream
David Millar Rector
Katherine Elaine Rector
Robert Hart Rector
Russell Mark Rector
Carmen Redmond-Brown & David Brown
Jeffrey and Irene Reichenthal
Lorinda and Tim Reichert
Mr. and Mrs. Scot S. Reid
Jon and Leah Reider
Paul and Jinny Reinhardt
Marty and Laura Reininger
Mr. & Mrs. Robert Reklis
Jeannette and Ray Remmel
Ken Renworth
Jenifer A. Renzel
Jim and Diane Resneck
Francis Charles Reynolds
Olivia Kathleen Reynolds
Charles and Nancy Rhea
Margaret and Michael Rice
Paul and Joyce Rice
Jean and Carter Rich
Gil and Sally Richards
Jan and Will Richmond
Wayne and Louise Richter
R. Bruce Ricks
Dale Riddle
Dan & Laura Rider
Israel & Shoshana Rind
Mr. & Mrs. Lars V. Ringheden
George & Inez Ritchie
Karl and Tani Robe
Mr. & Mrs. Kevin D. Robe
Burton and Sherri Roberts
The John Roberts Family
Mr. & Mrs. W. James Robertson
Aggie Robinson
H. Ed Robison
Joseph Robles
Karla and David Robson
Mr. & Mrs. Richard T. Roche
Mr. and Mrs. Emery H. Rogers
Joseph and Diane H. Rolfe
James Kenneth Rolin
Kenneth F. Rolin
Mr. & Mrs. Thomas J. Roll
Mrs. Wally Roo
Heinrich and Barbara Rose
Janet M. Roseland
Maureen and Paul Roskoph
James H. Ross
Karen and Steve Ross
Adam B. Rossi
Franco and Carol Rossi
Jason M. Rossi
Scott H. Rossi
Ann and Don Rothblatt
Helen Glynn Rovegno
Elizabeth Rovetto
Michael and Elizabeth Rowan
Christopher and Joshua Rubin
Jacob Rubin
Shulamith & David Rubinfien
Vicci M. Rudin
Johns F. and Janet Rulifson
Mrs. Ruth B. Running
Lucio and Marcia Ruotolo
Enrique and Susana Ruspini
Anne E. Russell
Jessica L. D. Russell
Shannon K. C. Russell
Hollis and Jack Russo
Bruce and Helen Rutledge
Michael J. Rymer
Nadine J. Sady
Dottie and Dave Sager
Diane & Daniel Sagolowicz
Susan T. Sailow
Carmen and Bob Saint
Alan Saldich
Anne Rawley Saldich
Cindy Salisbury & Claude Leglise
Mr. & Mrs. E. Wm. Salsbery
Ron & Sharon Sampson
San Francisco Public Library
San Jose Public Library
Jean and Chet Sandberg
Santa Clara Co. Off. of Education
Santa Clara County Free Library
Daniela and Marco Sarti
Mr. & Mrs. Frank Sasagawa
Eleanor and Hugh Satterlee
Mark Satterlee
Mark Jonathan Satterlee
Martha Alice Satterlee
Ruth & Ed Satterthwaite
Bill and Pomona Sawyer
Loren and Shelley Saxe
Barbara Grimes Scandalis
Virginia Scardigli
John and Ruby Schanzenbacher
William and Karen Scharfenberg
Annette & Leif Schaumann
Arthur Schawlow
Richard J. Scheible
In memory of Bert & Jessie Scherf
Wright & Laura Mitchell Schickli
Jonathan D. Schink
John and Maria Schipper
Joyce and Gregory Schmid
Friedrich W. Schmidt
Jo & Jack Schmidt
Beth Johnson Schmoller
George and Mildred Schneider
Karl O. Schnell
The John C. Schniedwind, Jr. Family
Carol R. Schroeder
Rudy & Jean Schroeter
Linda and Mark Schuman
Sally Schuman
Mr. & Mrs. Irving Schump
Robert and Georgia Schwaar
Dr. Aristotle & Varvara Scoledes
Catherine & Reid Scott
Mary & John Scouffas
Aidan Sara Seale-Feldman
Deborah & Henry Seaman
Eric & Katie Seedman
Kemp and Chris Segerhammar
The Richard Seiter family
Joyce and Rob Selig
John and Elizabeth Selover
Hubert H. Semans Library
Prof. & Mrs. George F. Sensabaugh
Denise and Andrea Severino
Max E. Shaffer
Peter and Christine Shambora
Tirzah and Stanley Sharp
Stan Shaver
Janet S. Shaw
Mary and Bob Shaw
Joyce and Jerry Shefren
Mr. & Mrs. B. C. Shen
Robert & Margaret C. Shepard
Mary Thygeson Shepardson
Brian and Alexandra Sheridan
David M. Sherwood
John G. Sherwood
Patricia Sherwood
David & Jean Shier
Mr. and Mrs. Terrell Doe Shores
Drs. Edward H. & Linda D. Shortliffe
George B. Shott
Marilyn A. Shurtz
Leonard J. Shustek
Jean Pierre Sicard
Jane Sideris
Alberta E. Siegel
Brenda and Jay Siegel
Lois and Milt Siegel
David & Sandra Siegmund
Robert and Gloria Sikora
Mr. & Mrs. John C. Silliman
David L. Silverman
Peter and Noele Silverman
Joan Silvers
Lewis J. Silvers, Jr.
David and Rhona Simmons

Margaret A. Simmons & Robert Lyhne
Bob and Diana Simoni
Mr. & Mrs. Laurence Simonini
Jane and Bill Simons
Alan and Peggy Simpson
Raymond and Amy Sims
Mr. & Mrs. Buttery Singleton
John and Lynette Skelton
Howard Sklar
Mr. & Mrs. D. A. Skoog
Michael Slater & Irene Stratton
Meg & Phil Sloan
Joyce Pace Small
Celeste L. Smith
Dan & Roger Smith
Drs. Marion and Kendric Smith
Florence and Robert Smith
George and Myrna Smith
Kristina P. Smith
Leland and Edith Smith
Lydia Leah Smith
Margaret and Derry Smith
Mary F. Smith
Mr. & Mrs. Earle F. Smith
Mr. & Mrs. Thor E. Smith
Phil and Helene Smith
Robert L. & Nancy W. Smith
Rutherford and Joyce Smith
Stan and Lois Smith
Stephen L. Smith
Stevo Smith
Dorie Levin Smolen
Dr. and Mrs. Allen E. Smoll
Renee Sicard Smrkousky
The Albert Snell family
Mr. & Mrs. Donald D. Snider
Dr. & Mrs. William R. Snow
Mr. & Mrs. William D. Snow
Mrs. William B. Snow
Gretchen and Rodney Snyder
Mr. & Mrs. Jeffrey Soltis
Edith and Simon Sommer
Mrs. Warren B. Sorensen
Mr. & Mrs. Jackson L. Sothern
Shelly Spaeth
Merrill Thomas Spalding
Dr. & Mrs. Arthur Spar
Pete & Elvezia Speciale
Mr. & Mrs. Merritt C. Speidel
Marty and Bart Spence
Doris and Douglas Spotten
Edward A. Sprague
Gerardus & Mary Staal
Jonas & Christine Stafford
Alma & Adrian Stahl
Cathy Stahl
Ross and Jane Staley
Paul and Penny Stanaford
Stanford Barn Enterprises
Stanford Property & Finance
Green Library, Stanford University
Suanne P. Starner
Drs. Pamela & James Starr
The Stauffers
John and Kim Stautner
The Stehle Family
Josephine M. Steine
Ida M. Stelling
Robert M. Stelzer
Susan L. Stephens
Alison Stern
Hong Ja and Rick Stern
Jim & Cheryl Stern
John & Betty Stern
Tom Stern
Nancy Stern & David Ross
David Steuer & Barbara Shufro
Jenna Lee Stevens
John E. Stevens
Janis Stevens & Alan Peterson
Joan and David Stevenson
Dr. John P. Steward
Shirley and Sam Stewart
Claire Still
Rebecca Stillwell
Hartman & Shirley Stime
Jim and Valerie Stinger
Paul L. Stock
Dr. & Mrs. William Stocker
Drs. K. & C. Stocker
Richard and Eileen Stolee
Ben and Rebecca Stolpa
Lynne & Sumner Stone
Margaret and James Stone
Ruth T. Storey
Lisa and Richard Stovel
Donald & Margaret Straka
Calvin W. Street
Myra H. Strober
Bob & Jan Strohecker
Roger and Jane Strom
John and June Strong
Jane and Jack Strubbe
Mr. & Mrs. Albert P. Stura
Arline and Archie Sturdevant
Steve and Nancy Suddjian
Janell Y. Sumida
Mr. & Mrs. Steve Summers
Don and Marlo Surath
Deborah Suslovic
Gwen and Norman Sutherland
Jack and Mary Ella Sutton
Ron & Cathy Swan
Mr. & Mrs. Robert E. Swank
George S. Swarth
David & Elaine Swartz
Susan and James Sweeney
Paul and Gail Switzer
Odon and Nona Sy
Peter Sylvester
Minchun and Keh Yeh Szutu
Rev. Mr. and Mrs. Martin R. Taddey
Yukiko and Takuji Takada
Kurt and Marilyn Talbot
Caroline Orris Tanner
Fielding and Mary Jane Tapp
Alex & Virginia Brink Tarn
Kumiko and Masakazu Tateno
Bette E. and Harry M. Taylor
Craig and Anne Taylor
Helen P. Taylor
Katharine and Glen Taylor
Mr. & Mrs. Garth B. Taylor
Pat and Budd Taylor
Richard G. and Jana S. Taylor
Nancy Teater & Richard Johnsson
Laura J. Testa
Rod and Maureen Thoits
Craig and Susie Thom
Linda and Garry Thomas
Anita and George Thompson
Chuck and Jean Thompson
Gail & Ed Thompson
Helen & Homer Thompson
Carl and Susan Thomsen
Blair and Lindsay Thomson-Levin
Karin H. & Roderick E. Thorne
Eileen H. Thurman
Ticor Title Insurance Co. of CA
Robert S. & Rita Connolly Tilton
John H. Tilton III
E. Jo Tims
Mr. Jan Tjernberg
Joanne and Robert Tobin
Jane & Leonard Todd
Timothy and Sally Tomlinson
Ellie Tone & Jim Stevenson
Lynn and Dave Torin
Bob Tousey
Town of Los Altos Hills
Ann Classen Treadwell
Elwynne Orris Trepel
Francisca Trevino
Richard C. Trimble
Chet and Ramona Trossman
Benny M C Tsang
Lillian & Masatsugu Tsuji
Dr. & Mrs. Charles R. Tucker
Gerald & Jacqueline Tucker
Paula-Marie & Julie-Anne Tucker
Jan and Dan Tuerk
William P. Turnell
Thelma and Ron Tuttle
Angela Uomini
Mr. & Mrs. Michael B. Upton
Lenore Urbani
Pat and Paul Vadopalas
Margaret and Andrew Vais
Julie Valentine
Mr. & Mrs. Fred G. van den Haak
Dirk and Ginger van der Linden
Harry Van Horne
John Van Horne
Mr. & Mrs. H. Van Valkenburgh
Jean & Edwin Van Wyk
Dr. & Mrs. David Vander Wilt
Letty and Frits VanderLinden
Karen L. Vanderpan
Mr. & Mrs. John VanDoren
Sandra & James Vannice
Mitra and Jim Varza
Rachel R. Vasiliev
Renee & Bob Veatch
Mario and Susan Veloro
Dr. and Mrs. Fernando G. Vescia
Dr. and Mrs. Francis T. Villemain
Jennifer and Eric Vlasic
Tom and Linda Vlasic
Carolyn D. Vogt
A. T. Volonakis
Paul and Margaret S. von Kempf
Paula Von Simson, M. D.
Dr. & Mrs. Henry von Witzleben
Peter S. Vroom

Tom and Janice Wacha
Christine and Robert Wachs
Alan Wachtel
Ron and Priscilla Wagner
Waldorf School of the Peninsula
Caitlin & Justin Walker
Cummings G. Walker
Jackie and Jerry Walker
Tom & Jeanne Walker
The Willard Walker Family
Peter W. Waller
Kelly L. Walrod
Richard R. Walrod
Mr. & Mrs. Joseph E. Walsmith
Richard & Deanna Walston
Erick Phillip Michael Walter
Walter Hays Elementary School
Drew Wanderman & Steve Milne
Ming and Amy Wang
Paul & Tricia Ward-Dolkas
John & Meredith Warren
Lois D. Warren
Mr. & Mrs. Robert S. Washburn
Ben and Melinda Wassam
Ted and Jane Wassam
Isabel and William Waters
Bradley & Monique Watkins
Watkins-Johnson Company
James and Beverly Weager
James and Cheryl Weaver
Mr & Mrs. Robert Benjamin Weaver, Sr.
Sally & Roland Webb
Carol L. Weber
Richard M. Wedge
Nancy and Bob Weeks
Florence and Edward Wegner
Stephen Wehrend
William R. Wehrend III
Frederick & Simone Weigert
Hilda & Len Weisberg
Mr. & Mrs. Bruno Weiser
David R. Wells
Bruce Wentler
Alfred E. Werry
Laurence Charles Wertman
Floyd and Alice Weseman
Nancy Weston & William Euphrat
Susan and Lewis Wexler
Garratt R. Whaley
Joan and Richard Whaley
Bobbie & Rod Wheeler
Nelson O. & Mary Louise Wheeler
Harriet & Curtis Wherry
David A. Whitaker
Meredith and Ralph Whitaker
Jon and Jody White
Kenneth & Priscilla White
Roberta Handy White
Dr. Keith White-Hunt
Sally Margaret Whittemore
Wallace & Gwen Whittier
Wes & Susan Wickham
Leland and Diane Wieder
Beatrice M. Wiegman
John & Diane Wielt
Mr. & Mrs. Ralph Clay Wiesjohn
Dr. & Mrs. Dwight L. Wilbur
Ray L. Wilbur
Alice, Molly, & Brendan Wilder
Mr. & Mrs. Rene Willdorff
Steve Wille
Frank and Marilyn Williams
Gertrude S. Williams
Glen Williams
James and Sandra Williams
Mr. & Mrs. R. H. Williams
Bruce and Elinor Wilner
Catherine Wilson
Edith Wilson
Scott & Shirley Wilson
Jack Winet
Jan David Winitz
Mark M. Winitz
Alan & Schatzie Winkleman
Winkie & Juanita Winkleman
Phyllis Winkler
Susan Bright Winn
Mr. & Mrs. Alan Winterbotham
Clem "Bud" Wiser
John Mark Wiser
Mark Steven Wiser
Yvette Marie Wiser-Custer
B. M. Withers
Bill & Gerry Wolfinbarger
Mrs. Shalah S. Wolfsohn
Dr. and Mrs. Laurence S. Wong
Laurence and Linell Wong
Linda S. Wong
Randolph and Doris Wong
Sharon and Bradley Wong
James and Arlene Wong-Mathewson
Eleanor & Bill Wood
Richard & Betty Wood
Annabelle and Vernon Woodard
Gladys and Clifton Woodhams
John and Valerie Wookey
Mr. & Mrs. W. U. Wookey
Gil and Gail Woolley
John & Beverly Working
Fred and Nancy Worrell
Mr. and Mrs. J. Nelson Wright
Tony and Sheila Wu
Hen-Shin Wu, M. D.
Brian and Rebecca Wunder
Charles and Ellen Wunder
Irene L. Wunderlich
Ernest and Nancy Wuthmann
Mr. & Mrs. Ernest F. Wuthmann
Thomas and Tracey Wyatt
Tom and Ellen Wyman
Yumiko and Hideho Yamamura
Harold & Georgia Yang
Shaunee and Leon Yang
Don R. Yarkin
Nick and Darlene Yee
Monica L. Yoon
Marjie and Charlie York
Bud and Lora Youngren
Neal and Pat Yowell
Camille & Christopher Zawojski
Bob & Toni Zeiss
Sandy and Al Zeller
Jay and Kay Zerfoss
Mary-Bell Meredith Zetterquist
David & Virginia Ziegler
Dr. & Mrs. Jerome F. Zobel
Mr. & Mrs. Fremont Older Zschokke
Phillip & Jo'Anne Zschokke

Other Books by Scottwall Associates

The San Francisco Fair
Treasure Island, 1939-1940,
Patricia Carpenter and Paul Totah, Editors
168 pages • 8½ X 11 inches • 70 full-color photographs

History of Petaluma, A California River Town
by Adair Heig
166 pages • 8½ X 10 inches • 90 illustrations

Pictorial History of Tiburon
A California Railroad Town
by James Heig
184 pages • 9 X 12 inches • 240 illustrations

Both Sides of the Track
A Collection of Oral Histories
from Belvedere and Tiburon
James Heig and Shirley Mitchell, Editors
232 pages • 8½ X 10 inches • 132 illustrations

Place Names of Marin
by Louise Teather
112 pages • 6 X 9 inches • 32 illustrations

Mount Tamalpais, A History
by Lincoln Fairley
200 pages • 8½ X 10 inches • 150 illustrations

Scottwall Associates
95 Scott Street
San Francisco, California 94117
Telephone (415) 861-1956

Photo by Carolyn Clebsch, Palo Alto Weekly

About the Authors

Pamela Gullard's fiction has been published in *The Iowa Review, Writers' Forum, Primavera, Iris,* and other literary and national magazines. In 1987 she won a PEN Syndicated Fiction Project Award. She has taught creative writing at Mission College, and teaches a seminar on Book reviewing for Writers' Connection. She graduated with honors in philosophy from Stanford University, and has lived in the Palo Alto area for twenty years.

Nancy Lund is a Phi Beta Kappa graduate of the University of Iowa, and holds a Master's degree from Harvard University. She has lived in the Palo Alto area since 1967, and is a founding member of the Los Altos History House Association Auxiliary and of the Portola Valley Archives Committee. Her interest in California history developed from her experience as a teacher. She is co-author, with Hallis Friend Ayres, of *Ladera Lore*, published in 1974.